WHO ARE THE EUROPEANS NOW?

Who are the Europeans Now?

EDWARD MOXON-BROWNE
Jean Monnet Chair of European Integration and Director,
Centre for European Studies, University of Limerick, Ireland

ASHGATE

Published by
Ashgate Publishing Limited
Gower House
Croft Road
Aldershot
Hants GU11 3HR
England

Suite 420
101 Cherry Street
Burlington, VT 05401–4405
USA

Ashgate website: http://www.ashgate.com

British Library Cataloguing in Publication Data
Who are the Europeans now?
    1.European Union 2.National characteristics, European
    3.Citizenship - Europe 4.Europe - Ethnic relations -
    Political aspects 5.Europe - Economic integration -
    Political aspects 6.Europe - Economic integration - Social
    aspects 7.Europe - Politics and government - 1989-
    I.Moxon-Browne, Edward
    320.9'4

Library of Congress Control Number: 99-073634

ISBN 1 84014 429 7

Printed and bound by MPG Books Ltd, Bodmin, Cornwall

Contents

List of Figures and Tables

Acknowledgements

The Carlingford seminar, from which this book is derived, was generously funded by the Jean Monnet Project (Complementary Initiatives) File no. 96/367. Supplementary funding to assist the attendance of participants from Northern Ireland was provided by the British Council in Dublin. Needless to say, the seminar would not have taken place without the support of these organisations. The seminar discussions were guided, inspired and enriched by the presence of three of my Jean Monnet colleagues: historian Mike Smith (Director of the Institute for European Studies at Queens University Belfast); political scientist Elizabeth Meehan (Jean Monnet Chair of Social Policy at Queens University); economist Bernadette Andreosso (Jean Monnet Chair of European Economic Integration at the University of Limerick); as well as anthropologist Tom Wilson (Lecturer in the Institute for European Studies at Queens). As well as representing four distinct disciplines, my colleagues reflected a variety of national origins: English, Scottish, French and American, respectively. We all appreciated, and benefited from, the diversity of their expertise.

In the production of this book, I must express my thanks to Rachel Hedges at Ashgate who patiently and helpfully guided us during the preparation of the manuscript for printing. The preparation of the manuscript was carried out in the Centre for European Studies at the University of Limerick by Kathleen Warfield and Tracey Cooney to whom I owe an enormous debt of gratitude.

Finally, as the cognoscenti are aware, Carlingford is the 'oyster capital' of Ireland; and it is possible, therefore, that the quality of our deliberations may have been enhanced by the consumption of the local delicacy.

The Editor

Chapter 1

Identity and Culture at Europe's Frontiers[1]

Thomas M. Wilson and Hastings Donnan

To many social scientists and other scholars the 'new Europe' of which we hear more and more is that of the metamorphosing European Union (EU), but this particular manifestation of an altered Europe cannot and should not be isolated from other sometimes complementary, sometimes competing, 'new Europes'. These include the democratising states of post-Soviet Eurasia, the globalizing Europe of youth, consumer and popular cultures, the Europe of transnational corporations, communications and services; and the Europe of transformations in ethnic, regional and national identities, in which national minorities, migrants and refugees must adapt to a variety of new institutions and cultures in order to survive. One thing all of these new Europes have in common is their attention to new and old borders and frontiers. To some critics international borders in Europe are declining in importance and strength, while to others they persist in their roles as markers of state power and national identity. It is our belief that there is no better place to approach and understand the pressing problems of sovereignty, citizenship, cultural adaptation and changing identities in Europe than at international borders.

In 1987, the geographer J.R.V. Prescott, in his excellent analysis of *Political Frontiers and Boundaries*, concluded that (1987: 8):

> The factors that encourage co-operation or conflict along international boundaries and the consequences that follow from policies connected with these two activities involve many aspects of national life. These aspects include strategy, administration, economics, politics, and culture. No single discipline deals exclusively with this field of scholarship.

In this chapter we wish to examine some of the issues and concerns which constitute the political anthropology of borders and frontiers, for it is anthropology, of all the social sciences, which has been most concerned with culture, which, in turn, has been the area of scholarship which is increasingly tying all of the social sciences closer together. We further suggest that it is the study of border cultures which may bring us closer to the type of 'discipline' which could serve to present more holistic and integrated views of institutions, policies and peoples at Europe's borders.

It is not our goal in this chapter to examine specific European frontiers (except in our brief review of the Irish border), nor is it our intention to present a typology of frontiers in the new Europes we have outlined. Rather, we intend to review ways in which the concepts of identity and culture may aid anthropologists and other social scientists to better understand the role of borderlands in the past and present of European nations and states, and to explore some of the problems anthropologists face in their attempts to contribute to the comparative study of international frontiers, in Europe and beyond (subjects we and others have dealt with in more detail elsewhere (see, for example, Donnan and Wilson, 1994a; Wilson and Donnan, 1998a). We begin with some definitions.

We regard international borders as the visible, literal political manifestations of state power. They have three components: the legal borderline between states, the institutions of the state which exist to demarcate and protect the borderline, composed of people and structures which often extend far into the territory of the state, and frontiers, zones of varying width which stretch away from borders, within which people negotiate a variety of behaviours and meanings associated with their membership in nations and states. All borders are thus composed of physical structures which are surrounded by frontiers of political and cultural negotiation. Some of these frontiers may very well reach as far as state capitals and other core areas of the state, though the greater the distance from the territorial limits of state power, the more potent is the metaphorical use of the idea of frontiers (see also Wilson and Donnan, 1998b: 9).

In this chapter we suggest that a focus on international borders in Europe, which hitherto have seldom been the subject of systematic and sustained study in anthropology, may not only tell us much about identity and the politics of difference in the late twentieth century, but may also lead us to rethink some of anthropology's most basic concepts. In the modernist and late modernist world orders, state borders have been perceived as markers of the limits of 'national', i.e., nation state, sovereignty. As such, borders could be closed, open, ignored, taken-for-granted, defended, and violated, but in the main they were not considered by their states to be negotiable or flexible. Today, however, forces of internationalization and globalization, as found in a redefined NATO and an expanding European Union, are putting pressure on states to weaken their borders voluntarily without dismantling them. Ironically, the integration of states at supranational levels, and intergovernmental cooperation of world agencies, may be forcing some states to redefine their notions ᴏ. sovereignty at the very same time as nationalist movements are emerging in the Soviet successor states and in Central and Eastern Europe whose aims are self-determination and the creation of sovereign states with strong borders.

International borders today are not only the locus of contests which threaten the sovereignty of states, but they are also the focus of forces of universal social, economic, political and cultural transformations, which threaten the future of the 'nation state' as it has come to be known in the modern era. The movement of capital, migrant labour, media images, and consumer products across international frontiers now depends more than ever on the realities of a global political economy (see, for example, Ahmed and Donnan, 1994), and increasingly challenges the traditional symbolic paraphernalia of the nation state. Transnational industry and media compel states to keep their borders open and in the process begin to take on some of the meaning-making roles previously the preserve of the state itself (Appadurai, 1990: 305). In short, there is a growing tension between nationalism and globalization, which affects all areas, in the core and peripheries, of European states. It is this tension which border studies in general can throw into sharp relief. We will return to this point in the conclusion, where we briefly consider its implications for anthropological notions of culture.

Borderlands and Nation States

The examination of the demise of old borders and the redefinition of new ones is still largely seen in terms of the nation states which borders simultaneously separate and join together. Yet the processes taking place at those borders involve people and institutions who are in extremely fluid dialectical relationships with people and institutions of other ethnic groups and nations, both within and outside of their states. These local border communities are not simply the passive beneficiaries or victims of world statecraft. They are often agents of change in socio-political processes of significance to many people beyond their locality and even beyond their state. Although the successful processes of nation and state building may seem to be, in retrospect, a matter of top-down decision making, or the product of the demands and desires of national elites, in most cases, both historically and in the contemporary world, they are a matter of the dialectics between 'bottom' and 'top', as well as among diverse groups 'at the bottom'. The socio-political ideologies and movements which are at a nation's core depend on diverse local and national communities for their support and the successful achievement of their aims. In this respect, at least to the extent that they are attempting to create a new supranational Europe on the model of the nation state, the leaders of the European Union would be wise to mark the importance of locality and local culture to the peoples of this new Europe.

Eurocrats may be forgiven their past omissions of locality in their decision making, however, because their notions of building nations, states, and the European Union from the top down has been shared by many in Europe, including many social scientists. Simply put, much of the research and writing on borders and national sovereignty seems to ignore people in favour of theories, causes, and events. Given the emphasis in social and cultural anthropology on small groups at local levels of society, it is surprising that more ethnographers have not examined communities at international borders (for a review of anthropological perspectives on borders, see Donnan and Wilson, 1994b).

Ethnographers of borderland communities can provide distinct profiles of social, cultural, and political identities at the interfaces of nation states. These identities reflect the contradictory nature of representing nations at the limits of state sovereignty, in particular the ways in which identities reflect a cultural landscape which often transcends the borderline between divergent state political terrains. Marriage, smuggling, theft, shopping, commerce, tourism, sports, and religion are some of the ways that borderland peoples are tied to each other both across state borders and with peoples further afield in each of the states they inhabit. We do not wish to suggest, however, that all people at European borders experience cross-border *communitas* and/or *societas*. All borders are structured as barriers of exclusion and protection, and many continue effectively in this role. But it is in the understanding of how border people live with, or without, their cross-border neighbours that anthropologists may make their most valuable contributions to the study of nations, states, and national sovereignty, as these concepts are experienced in the lives of those who inhabit such frontiers (Wilson, 1996).

Borders in the Ethnography of Europe

There have been few ethnographic studies of national borders in Europe. Most anthropological studies worldwide of the political and social borders of large social and political formations have been studies of ethnic groups, or other groups deemed to be state minorities whose ties to each other, for primordial or other reasons, seem to depend more on culture than the ties provided by the organs of political and civil society. With few exceptions (most notably Cole and Wolf, 1974), anthropologists have not investigated nationalism and the state at European borders, favouring instead studies of the cultural and symbolic boundaries between groups in and across state societies. Two anthropologists in particular have generated research into the symbolic construction of boundaries between local-level communities, and have thus been important influences on ethnographers who theorise the connections between local communities and the nation and state. Fredrik Barth's *Ethnic Groups and Boundaries* (1969) focused on cultural boundary maintenance and boundary-crossing. Anthony Cohen (see, for example, 1985; 1986; 1987) has addressed the many ways in which small communities culturally construct and reproduce a distinctive sense of self, even when to an outsider they might seem no different from others. The research of these two scholars has stimulated a great deal of anthropological investigation of cultural boundaries between small and in some cases large communities, but few of these have been at international borders, and some have led to uncritical views of ethnic homogeneity when groups are viewed from across state borderlines (see Driessen, 1992).

A number of anthropological case studies have been done on culture and politics at national and state borders in Europe. Among these are Ronald Frankenberg's study of a village on the Welsh-English border (1989 [1957]), John Cole and Eric Wolf's analysis of two villages with different national backgrounds in the Tyrol of northern Italy (1974), Peter Sahlins' anthropologically informed historical analysis of national policies and identities along the French and Spanish border in the Cerdagne region (1989), Douglass' examination (1977) of border influences on Basque village life, and Henk Driessen's exploration (1992) of the rituals of ethnic and national boundaries in Spain's last enclave in Morocco. These ethnographic studies of national borders are milestones in the worldwide anthropology of frontiers, but they also highlight the relative dearth of such analyses in Europe. This is surprising for a number of reasons. The old and new (i.e., twentieth century) borders between European states have figured prominently in a wide range of scholarly treatises on politics and nationalism, which have certainly influenced the intellectual pioneers in Anglophone anthropology. Many of the leading anthropologists in Europe and North America before the Second World War were refugees, while others had done studies at and across state borders in regions of the world, such as Sub-Saharan Africa, which were and had been in conditions of great flux and where borders were not as fixed, at least in the everyday lives of local populations, as their state and colonial governments would have had the world believe. Borders are political realities which all anthropologists must negotiate in their field research, and their relative absence in the anthropology of Europe seems to deny borders roles as significant symbols of statecraft and conflict, in Europe and beyond, as well as important legal barriers to any anthropologist seeking his or her faraway research locale.

Furthermore, anthropologists outside of Europe have shown deep and lasting interest in international borders. In American anthropology there has long been a theoretical interest in frontiers, especially in their role in state building (see, for example, Aronoff, 1974 and the range of cases in Bohannan and Plog, 1967). Recent anthropological scholarship at the USA-Mexican border has turned to studies of power and the state, thus situating the border within its wider political and economic contexts (see, for example, Alvarez and Collier, 1994; Heyman, 1991). Kopytoff's analysis of African frontiers (1987) builds on some of the American perspectives on borders and frontiers, while other anthropologists in Africa, Asia and America have had to go beyond them in order to deal with the importance of national borders as barriers or hurdles to the successful movements of refugees, migrants, transhumants, and nomads (see, for example, Hann and Hann, 1992; Hansen, 1994; Kearney, 1991; Malkki, 1992).

Thus, although there have been many border studies in anthropology world-wide, there have been few in Europe, either in comparison to anthropological works in Europe in general or to studies of European borders in other disciplines. It is also apparent to us that overall the anthropological literature on borders has been relatively uninfluential in the discipline as a whole, and is relatively unknown among the other social sciences in Europe. This is lamentable and surprising, since anthropologists are perhaps better placed than other researchers to provide insights into how people experience nationalism in their everyday lives at borders. Anthropologists have a great deal of experience at and across state borders (Donnan and Wilson, 1994: 6–7), Europe's borders, borderlands and border peoples. The general social scientific attention paid by scholars, legislators and cultural critics of all persuasions to the symbolic boundaries to all manifestations of society and culture, especially in terms of the real and metaphorical frontiers which figure so prominently in the many new Europes. These developments have led more and more anthropologists to question the role of local communities within the larger political, legal and administrative institutions of which they are a part, such as regions, provinces, states and supranations (as in the European Union (Wilson, 1993a)).

Because other social scientists have analysed the formal arrangements between states, without taking into account the needs, desires, and other

cultural realities of the people who live at borders, anthropologis
to define a new role for themselves in border studies (Wilson
1998b). They recognise that the factors that encourage cooperat
along international borders not only involve many aspects of 'national life,
including state administration, economics, politics, and culture, but they
involve just as much of a commitment from regions and localities, because
all communities and the larger cultural and political entities of which they are
a part have cultural frontiers which they continually renegotiate. Nations and
states have political frontiers which entail all of these negotiations, as well
as mark the limits of their sovereignty. To many people who actually live in
borderlands, however, cultural and political frontiers diverge.

Consumer Culture and the Irish Border

The Irish border, near which both authors live, informs our perceptions of
borders elsewhere. There is often a striking if perhaps superficial resemblance
between border towns everywhere; thus small towns on the Irish border, for
example, recall some of the characteristics of towns in Pakistan's Northwest
Frontier: the money changers, the lorries lined up for customs (ended not so
long ago in Ireland as a result of the European Union's single market), the rush
to buy consumer durables (some of which are smuggled), even the sporadic
and deadly violence. But if our personal experience of the Irish border plays
a part in our understanding of borders elsewhere, our knowledge of it from
anthropological accounts probably has less to offer. It has been left largely
to scholars in other disciplines, notably geography and political science, to
address issues in which anthropologists might be interested, such as the extent
to which the border is a socioeconomic, a political, and/or a cultural divide.
It is disappointing to us that in the tradition of anthropology outlined above
few anthropologists working in Ireland have mentioned issues of borders and
culture, never mind explored them systematically. There are a few passing
comments here and there (see, for example, Harris, 1972; see also, Shanks,
1994), but these generally conceal a multitude of questions about, for instance,
issues of cross-border security and about what happens when existing county,
provincial, or federal borders are transformed into national ones, as in Ireland
70 years ago (Vincent, 1989), or today in what was once the Soviet Union and
Yugoslavia. This, in turn, might stimulate questions about the opposite process
of transforming national borders into local ones as in German reunification
(see Borneman, 1992).

It is clearly impossible to elaborate on all of these examples, or indeed on developments elsewhere in the world, so we take here as an illustration of certain border processes which could well repay further study, the example of that border with which we are both most familiar: the Irish border. In some respects border culture has had a very short history in Ireland, dating from the creation of a partitioned 'state' in 1921. In other respects Irish people consider border culture to have a much longer history, tracing it back to mythic times when the tribes of the north raided south and west into what is now the Republic of Ireland. Nevertheless, the last 40 years have been the most formative, as economic transformation and cultural modernisation in both parts of Ireland have created and strengthened a common commercial economy, a growing middle class, and the harmonisation of both popular and consumer culture, in large part through the media of radio and television.

It is upon consumer culture that we wish to concentrate here, as one of the key factors which draws ethnic groups and nations together – consumer culture defined as those aspects of modern culture which involve buying, selling, marketing, bartering and smuggling. We want to suggest that the process of EU integration, which includes the harmonisation of taxes and the removal of customs barriers, will alter cross-border consumer relations to such a degree that it will result in less cross-border shopping and may cause the disintegration of aspects of local border culture (this process is treated at length in Wilson, 1993b).

A number of ties unite people across the Irish border: family, sport, church. One area largely overlooked is that of cross-border shopping, and the attraction for many of those in the Republic to travel north to buy consumer goods. By the mid-1980s the government in the Republic was experiencing such a severe loss of revenue that it began to plan measures to limit cross-border shopping. These measures contravened many aspects of traditional border culture, including relatively free access to the shopping and commercial centres at the northern side of the border which, for many people in the south, had been their market towns before partition of Ireland.

At a number of border towns, shoppers from the south had been a key feature in the commercial development of the towns themselves, and of the relationships between towns across the divide. This tradition intensified after both countries joined the EU. However, tradition could not sustain those southern shopkeepers who were losing their customers to the north, nor was tradition a match for the Republic's loss of revenue through the loss of Value Added Tax and excise duties on goods purchased in Northern Ireland. In fact, the issue of cross-border shopping was considered so critical for the

Republic's finances that they were prepared to challenge EU law because of it.

In 1987, the Irish Minister for Finance made virtually all items taxable on one-day shopping trips to the north. Anyone leaving the Republic of Ireland for less than 48 hours would no longer be able to claim tax-free allowances for goods bought duty-free or in shops. Many shopkeepers just across the border with the north had depended on lower prices in order to maintain cross-border consumer interest. In 1986, for example, there was a 30 per cent difference in the price of alcohol. In Newry, the first town one enters in the north on the main road from Dublin to Belfast, cross-border culture had come to be defined in terms of frequent and regular visits from people in the Dundalk area, twelve miles south across the border. Both towns have populations of over 20,000 and are used to being in a 'twin-like' relationship with each other. Throughout the 1980s and into the 1990s, however, most visitors went north rather than the reverse. Most people from the south who visited Newry shopped for alcohol, beer, wine, tobacco, petrol and household appliances (such as TVs, VCRs, washing machines). Electrical appliances were always over the import tax free limit, so that the 1987 restriction did not modify the illegal nature of their importation into the south, usually on one of many unapproved roads. But the savings might be worth the risk: in 1986, a large television set cost IR356 in Northern Ireland, and IR540 in the Republic (Fitzgerald et al., 1988: 80). Throughout the early 1980s it was not uncommon for coach loads of shoppers to arrive in Newry from large urban areas at the other end of Ireland, some five hours or more away. A few frenzied hours would be spent shopping – mainly for alcohol and cigarettes – before the five-hour journey home.

In Newry the effects of the Republic's 48 hour rule were almost devastating. As the Republic enforced its ruling, stopping cars and coaches at border checkpoints, large-scale cross-border shopping dwindled rapidly. Southerners still came north for petrol, alcohol and tobacco, but their visits were less frequent and more focused. In fact, continuing demand for 'petrol at Northern prices', as the hoardings had it, led to the growth of a small 'village' five miles from Dundalk and just north of the border: boasting two large filling stations, two shops and a fast food restaurant the site catered for the demand for petrol, which was almost one-third cheaper than in the Republic. Spirits, beer, and wine sales dropped dramatically in Newry, as they became the targets of customs officers once the cross-border trade in electrical appliances all but ceased by 1989.

Eventually the EU forced the Republic to modify its 48 hour rule, but the Irish rules remained much more stringent than anywhere else in the EU. The cross-border shopping trade became much more modest than before. Many of the changes to Newry which had come about as a result of cross-border shopping suffered: the pedestrian zones, the large warehouses selling electrical appliances, the off-licences and the supermarkets on the edge of the city. The impact all of this has had on Newry life is both significant and difficult to detect. In the heyday of the shopping expeditions many Newry people complained of the crowds, noise and litter which these generated. But garage men, restaurateurs, newsagents, and shopkeepers certainly miss the trade and they, after all, are the economic core of what is now primarily a service town. Certainly the wider economy is suffering. Very few people in Newry admit to regular face-to-face contact with their neighbours in the south. And whether border people desire the connection of shopping or not, its decline has resulted in another rift in the fabric of cross-border culture. Although the IRA and Loyalist paramilitary cease-fires encouraged the return of some southerners as tourists, it is too early to predict the effect which an uncertain peace may have on cross-border face-to-face contacts.

Without the lure of shopping, especially at a time (1998) when the Irish punt is weak against sterling, fewer southerners visit Newry. Like the rest of Ireland, Newry may become increasingly isolated from both the UK and the Republic of Ireland, which is certainly not the goal of either government. Nor is it the goal of the EU, which is hoping to better integrate its member states through the Single Internal Market and the harmonisation of taxes. If this process continues, then the comparability of prices between nations, one goal in the free market goals of the EU, may lead to sociocultural breakage across borders. One relationship which has maintained person-to-person communication over the last decade in the Irish case has been the consumer relationship between customer and merchant. Shared histories, common political allegiances and philosophies, and the wishes of their governments were all important incentives for neighbours to explore actively their shared culture. But the most important incentive to continued contact between people from both sides of the border seemed to be a material one, a fact which many social scientists have chosen to minimise or ignore. In the British and Irish economies, which are largely influenced by EU regulations, cross-border price differentials have begun to disappear: a result may be less cross-border contact. If this is so, this in turn is likely to result in changes in how communities on each side of the border culturally construct their symbolic boundaries. The process of EU integration may, in fact, strengthen the symbolic boundaries between border towns, creating less of a common culture and more of an international divide.

An Anthropology of Frontiers

It is the ethnographic focus on the local communities which live and work at international borders which makes an anthropology of frontiers distinctive. In the other social sciences, the cultural constructions which symbolise the boundaries between communities and between nations are too often lost in the midst of the macroperspectives of national and international relations. So, in one sense, we are reminding scholars in and beyond the field of anthropology that nations and states are composed of people, not just institutions, and that people cannot or should not be reduced to their voting behaviour, their rhetoric, or their image as constructed by the state, the media, or people of other groups who wish to represent them as 'others'. Thus, an anthropology of frontiers is an anthropology of nations and states, as these are experienced at local levels, which are often, in the case of border zones, highly contentious areas. Borderlands are symbolic of the histories of nation state building, and all national education systems privilege the times and places where the nation was victorious and its territorial limits reached. These limits are not only historically constructed but are continuously negotiated and reinterpreted through the dialectics of everyday life among all people who live in the borderlands.

Anthropology brings certain theories and methods to bear, in its study of local communities, which focus on both the material and symbolic foundations and processes of culture. Although culture as an operational concept in social scientific research is often an amorphous entity, it is extremely useful as a methodological strategy, as a metaphor for the interconnections of the economic, the political, and the social in community life, and as a way of describing the totality of a group's perceptions of their past, themselves, and their daily experiences. When ethnographers approach border cultures, they do so with the intention of narrating the lived experience of a group of people who, in most cases, have no difficulty with the notion that they are tied culturally to many other people, in a number of polities of which they are members. However, definitions of polity are often more problematic at state borders than they are elsewhere. An anthropological approach attempts to construct notions of 'nation' and 'state' from the bottom up, in political, administrative, and social senses, and from the outside in, that is, from the limits of a state back to its centre. At the same time, such an approach also attempts to show the flexibility both of borders and of the sociocultural groups that construct borders in political and ideological ways. Anthropologists do this by chronicling the means whereby frontiers are both created and crossed in everyday experience. Thus, an anthropology of frontiers must incorporate the analysis of the inheritance, negotiation, and invention of cultural boundaries between and among groups of people who identify themselves as members of one nation as distinct from others. These nations need not be, and in fact rarely are, coterminous with one state. In most cases, many nations live within one state's borders, while many nations also live astride state borders.

An anthropology of nations and states in the modern world must entail the comparative study of identities. Cultural identity to anthropologists is shorthand for the multiplicity of social, economic, and political identities and identifications which people carry and share with others. In a world where the nation state's role as the arbiter of civic culture is under threat, if not being transformed, the issues of cultural identity are no longer simply matters of internal 'national' concern. The anthropology of frontiers is part of the wider social science of class, ethnic, religious, and national identity, but it is an anthropology specifically concerned with the negotiation of identity in places where everyone expects that identity to be problematic. The conclusions we reach at the frontiers of nations and states may help convince others that the presumption of negotiations of identity at international borders should also be a presumption about all people and places within the modern nation state, and that the processes of integration and disintegration at Europe's borders may very well reflect parallel processes of European culture and identification elsewhere.

But an anthropology of frontiers does not just concern local communities at the margins of the nation state. The deterritorialization of culture allegedly characteristic of the contemporary world (see, for example, Hannerz, 1992) ensures that all of us, wherever we live, dwell in an interstitial borderland between different cultures. Only in the modern age could culture, society and territory be considered coterminous, to be marked out and associated with particular nation states in the atlases of the geographers and broken up into the ethnographic patchwork of the anthropologist. In this new age the cultural distinctiveness of locality has been steadily transformed, at times enriched by cultural imports from elsewhere, at other times dismantled by being packaged for export. It is in this sense that we might speak of a multi-locality (see Rodman, 1992), and it is against this background that Clifford (1988: 275; see also Gupta and Ferguson, 1992: 9) asks: 'What does it mean, at the end of the twentieth century, to speak ... of a "native land"? What processes rather than essences are involved in present experiences of cultural identity?'.

For those at the frontiers these questions have a particular resonance, since for them 'the fiction of cultures as discrete, object-like phenomena occupying discrete spaces' is especially implausible (Gupta and Ferguson,

1992: 7) as too for those whose lives depend on border crossings such as migrants and refugees. Contemporary processes – of diaspora, globalization, deterritorialization – have destabilized the self-evidentness of a distinction between 'ourselves' and 'others'. And by destabilizing that distinction, the critical sense of 'difference' which perhaps above all else has characterised the anthropological enterprise, is itself called into question, just as it so often is among those whose daily existence straddles borders. In short, an anthropology of frontiers may force us to re-evaluate the very idea of 'culture' itself, where this is taken to mark 'difference'.

This is not to say that an anthropology of borders is primarily or chiefly an arena in which one might focus on the postmodern processes of the globalization of culture, the internationalisation of economies, and the creation of transnational regimes and communities. It is much more than this, because it accords us the opportunity to reconsider the importance of culture, space, and time in ways which call into question many of the bases of postmodernist analyses. Cultural boundaries and borderlands may exist everywhere in this postmodern age, but the characteristics of postmodern life have been evident at international borders since the demise of the traditional and the birth of the modern ages. Because the boundaries to national identities have always been contested at the frontiers between empires and states, in ways which threaten notions of the union of space, time, place, and culture, and yet at the same time have been zones of cultural production and integration, such borders provide a testing ground for empirical approaches to the study of culture and identity in relation to the future of nations and states in the postmodernist era.

National identity is by definition ambiguous and ambivalent at international frontiers, where since the creation of such frontiers there has been a continuous process of transnationalism, deterritorialization, and the cultural ebb and flow which results from local communities adapting to the forces of wider world systems. We do not suggest that the issues raised by scholars of post-industrialism, globalization, and postmodernism are irrelevant to the understanding of national identity at frontiers. On the contrary, many of the processes of cultural construction and deconstruction newly heralded as a focus of study have been evident at international borders for some time. But we hope that an emerging anthropology of frontiers will shed light on processes of cultural production which indicate that at international frontiers culture continues to have spatial and territorial contexts, in the midst of, and perhaps as a direct result of, the destabilizing pressures of postmodern life.

Conclusion

There is much of great value in recent efforts to theorise ways in which to liberate culture from notions of continuous or fractured place. Those who study diasporas and the emergence of so-called 'third cultures' have had to develop new ways to understand culture. Similarly, those who study media, public culture, popular culture, and the globalization of culture have also had to grope their ways towards new ideas of hybrid cultures. These views of culture also make all social scientists rethink their definitions of the nation and the state (in ways reminiscent of the many calls by Walker Connor to be clear about the distinctions between nation and state; see, for example, Connor, 1978; 1990).

But in our efforts to free notions of culture from the problematic constraints of time and place, we must also recognise that ethnic groups, nations, classes, and other groups of people may themselves believe in the fixity of time and place in their constructions of self. The vast majority of borders in the world today are not being renegotiated by their states. As a consequence, all negotiations of culture which take place at borderlands, either by border communities or by those who travel greater distances to cross frontiers, must take into account the fixity of place in the political economies of these states. In other words, national culture is continuously negotiated but state citizenship and residence, which are subject to a wide range of legal, constitutional, and political forces (and sometimes military and/or police enforcement), are less malleable. In short, in rethinking the notion of culture, we should be careful not to lose sight of the significance of locale. We must remember that many people, perhaps especially those at frontiers, do associate culture and nation with a place, defined in part by its association with a polity, and the sovereignty of the state. Moreover, people clearly enter into relations of differential power and wealth which are temporal, spatial, and real to both winners and losers. In this regard, a cultural analysis of frontiers must complement but not replace political and economic perspectives. As Eric Wolf (1990: 587) reminds us, we must attempt to 'delineate how the forces of the world impinge upon the people we study, without falling back into an anthropological nativism that postulates supposedly isolated societies and uncontaminated cultures, either in the present or in the past'.

We began this chapter with one of J.R.V. Prescott's conclusions regarding the multidisciplinarity of the scholarly study of political borders and frontiers. We conclude with another of his insightful assessments from the same book (1987: 8):

Attempts to produce a set of reliable theories about international boundaries have failed. Attempts to devise a set of procedures by which boundaries can be studied have been successful.

We have put forward a variety of ways in which an anthropological approach to the study of identity and culture at international borders and frontiers might be useful to social scientists, in the new Europes and beyond. We have not done so to help formulate a theory of borders, but to add to the comparative scholarship of nation, state and identity in Europe today.

Note

1   An earlier version of this chapter appeared as H. Donnan and T.M. Wilson, 'Identità Cultura sulle Frontiere Internazionali', 1995, *Ossimori*, Vol. 6, No. 1, pp. 49–57.

References

Ahmed, A.S. and Donnan, H. (1994), 'Islam in the Age of Postmodernity', in A.S. Ahmed and H. Donnan (eds), *Islam, Globalization and Postmodernity*, Routledge, London, pp. 1–24.

Alvarez, R.R. and Collier, G.A. (1994), 'The Long Haul in Mexican Trucking: Traversing the Borderlands of the North and the South', *American Ethnologist*, Vol. 21, No. 3, pp. 606–27.

Appadurai, A. (1990), 'Disjuncture and Difference in the Global Cultural Economy', in M. Featherstone (ed.), *Global Culture: Nationalism, Globalization and Modernity*, Sage, London, pp. 295–310.

Aronoff, M. (1974), *Frontiertown: The Politics of Community Building in Israel*, Manchester University Press, Manchester.

Barth, F. (1969), 'Introduction', in F. Barth (ed.), *Ethnic Groups and Boundaries: The Social Organization of Cultural Difference*, Little Brown, Boston.

Bohannan, P. and Plog, F. (eds) (1967), *Beyond the Frontier: Social Process and Cultural Change*, The Natural History Press, Garden City, NY.

Borneman, J. (1992), *Belonging to the Two Berlins: Kin, State, Nation*, Cambridge University Press, Cambridge.

Clifford, J. (1988), *The Predicament of Culture*, Harvard University Press, Cambridge, MA.

Cohen, A. (1965), *Arab Border Villages in Israel: A Study of Continuity and Change in Social Organization*, Manchester University Press.

Cohen, A.P. (1985), *The Symbolic Construction of Community*, Ellis Horwood and Tavistock, London.

Cohen, A.P. (ed.) (1986), *Symbolising Boundaries: Identity and Diversity in British Cultures*, Manchester University Press, Manchester.

Cohen, A.P. (1987), *Whalsay: Symbol, Segment and Boundary in a Shetland Island Community*, Manchester University Press, Manchester.

Cole, J.W. and Wolf, E.R. (1974), *The Hidden Frontier: Ecology and Ethnicity in an Alpine Valley*, Academic Press, New York.

Connor, W. (1978), 'A Nation Is a Nation, Is a State, Is an Ethnic Group, Is a …', *Ethnic and Racial Studies*, Vol. 1, No. 4, pp. 379–88.

Connor, W. (1990), 'When Is a Nation?', *Ethnic and Racial Studies*, Vol. 13, No. 1, pp. 92–100.

Donnan, H. and Wilson, T.M. (eds) (1994a), *Border Approaches: Anthropological Perspectives on Frontiers*, University Press of America, Lanham, MD.

Donnan, H. and Wilson, T.M. (1994b), 'An Anthropology of Frontiers', in H. Donnan and T.M. Wilson (eds), *Border Approaches: Anthropological Perspectives on Frontiers*, University Press of America, Lanham, MD, pp. 1–14.

Douglass, W.A. (1977), 'Borderland Influences in a Navarrese Village', in W.A. Douglass, R.W. Etulain and W.H. Jacobsen Jr (eds), *Anglo-American Contributions to Basque Studies: Essays in Honor of Jon Bilbao*, Desert Research Institute, Reno.

Driessen, H. (1992), *On the Spanish-Moroccan Frontier: A Study in Ritual, Power and Ethnicity*, Berg, Oxford.

Fitzgerald, J.D., Quinn, T.P., Whelan, B.J. and Williams, J.A. (1988), *An Analysis of Cross-border Shopping*, Economic and Social Research Institute, Dublin.

Frankenberg, R. (1989 [1957]), *Village on the Border*, Waveland Press, Prospect Heights, IL.

Gupta, A. and Ferguson, J. (1992), 'Beyond "Culture": Space, Identity, and the Politics of Difference', *Cultural Anthropology*, Vol. 7, No. 1, pp. 6–23.

Hann, C. and Hann, I. (1992), 'Samovars and Sex on Turkey's Russian Markets', *Anthropology Today*, Vol. 8, No. 4, pp. 3–6.

Hannerz, U. (1992), *Cultural Complexity: Studies in the Social Organization of Meaning*, Columbia University Press, New York.

Hansen, A. (1994), 'The Illusion of Local Sustainability and Self-sufficiency: Famine in a Border Area of Northwestern Zambia', *Human Organization*, Vol. 53, No. 1, pp. 11–20.

Harris, R. (1972), *Prejudice and Tolerance in Ulster: A Study of Neighbours and 'Strangers' in a Border Community*, Manchester University Press, Manchester.

Heyman, J. (1991), *Land, Labor, and Capital at the Mexican Border*, University of Arizona Press, Flagstaff.

Kearney, M. (1991), 'Borders and Boundaries of State and Self at the End of Empire', *Journal of Historical Sociology*, Vol. 4, No. 1, pp. 52–74.

Kopytoff, I. (1987), 'The Internal African Frontier: the Making of African Political Culture', in I. Kopytoff (ed) *The African Frontier*, Indiana University Press, Bloomington, pp. 3–84.

Malkki, L. (1992), 'National Geographic: The Rooting of Peoples and the Territorialization of National Identity among Scholars and Refugees', *Cultural Anthropology*, Vol. 7, No. 1, pp. 24–44.

Prescott, J.R.V. (1987), *Political Frontiers and Boundaries*, HarperCollins, London.

Rodman, M.C. (1992), 'Empowering Place: Multilocality and Multivocality,' *American Anthropologist*, Vol. 94, pp. 640–56.

Sahlins, P. (1989), *Boundaries: The Making of France and Spain in the Pyrenees*, University of California Press, Berkeley.

Shanks, A. (1994), 'Cultural Divergence and Durability: The Border, Symbolic Boundaries and the Irish Gentry', in H. Donnan and T.M. Wilson (eds), *Border Approaches: Anthropological Perspectives on Frontiers*, University Press of America, Lanham, MD, pp. 89–100.

Vincent, J. (1989), 'Local Knowledge and Political Violence in County Fermanagh', in C. Curtin and T.M. Wilson (eds), *Ireland from Below: Social Change and Local Communities*, Galway University Press, pp. 92–108.

Wilson, T.M. (1993a), 'An Anthropology of the European Community', in T.M. Wilson and M.E. Smith (eds), *Cultural Change and the New Europe: Perspectives on the European Community*, Westview Press, Boulder, CO and Oxford, pp. 1–23.

Wilson, T.M. (1993b), 'Consumer Culture and European Integration at the Northern Irish Border', in G.J. Bamossy and W.F. van Raaij (eds), *European Advances in Consumer Research*, Vol. 1, Association for Consumer Research, Provo, UT, pp. 293–9.

Wilson, T.M. (1996), 'Sovereignty, Identity and Borders: Political Anthropology and European Integration', in L. O'Dowd and T.M. Wilson (eds), *Borders, Nations and States: Frontiers of Sovereignty in the New Europe*, Ashgate, Aldershot, pp. 199–219.

Wilson, T.M. and Donnan, H. (1998a), *Border Identities: Nation and State at International Frontiers*, Cambridge University Press, Cambridge.

Wilson, T.M. and Donnan, H. (1998b), 'Nation, State and Identity at Interational Borders', in T.M. Wilson and H. Donnan (eds), *Border Identities*, Cambridge University Press, pp. 1–30.

Wolf, E.R. (1990), 'Facing Power – Old Insights, New Questions', *American Anthropologist*, Vol. 92, pp. 586–96.

Chapter 2

European Citizenship and European Identity: From Treaty Provisions to Public Opinion Attitudes

Stefania Panebianco

Introduction

In order to answer the question whether the establishment of European citizenship helped to develop a European identity, both treaty provisions concerning the European citizenship and public opinion attitudes towards European identity have to be taken into account. The distinction between the formal meaning of citizenship as established in the Treaty of Maastricht on the European Union (TEU) and recalled by the Treaty of Amsterdam, and the attitudes of the Europeans is useful as it results from the *Eurobarometer* (EB) data on whether European public opinion is aware of the attempts to bring the European Union (EU) closer to the citizens.

To understand the current debate on the meaning of European identity, issues such as the relationship between European identity and national identity, and the necessity of strengthening the *Europeanness* in order to indirectly increase the public support to the EU, are addressed.

The process of European integration is today faced with contradictory trends. On the one hand, there are global constraints such as increasing economic interdependence, the advantages of a large scale economy, the necessity of co-operation to cope with environmental disasters, epidemics, drug-trafficking or terrorism. On the other, there are different national interests, rising unemployment and local movements claiming for independence in the name of a particular local identity.

In an era of globalization and fragmentation, the only way to cope with the clash between identities is to develop and spread a broader concept of European identity. The TEU established a 'multiple citizenship'; in a similar way, we can refer to a 'multiple identity' by considering local, regional, national and European identities as compatible without excluding the one from the other.

Recent empirical results indicate that the majority of Europeans declare having both a national and a European identity, demonstrating that they consider them compatible. But when asked to make a choice, the national attachment prevails. In reality, in the treaty provisions the citizens are not asked to choose to have *either* a national identity *or* a European one. Identity cannot be analysed in terms of zero-sum games, instead it is better understood through sociological lenses.

The Origins of European Citizenship

The process leading to the establishment of European citizenship was rather long and linked since the beginning to the concept of European identity. At the Copenhagen summit in 1973, a paper on European identity was issued and at the Paris summit in 1974, the question of a 'citizens' Europe' arose officially. Then, the heads of state and government agreed on the establishment of special rights, in order to bring political and civil rights acknowledged by the European Community (EC) closer to rights traditionally acknowledged to the national citizens.

In 1984, at the European Council of Fontainebleau an *ad hoc* Committee was set up to address issues relating to a 'people's Europe'. Then the Adonnino Committee published two reports concerning the enlargement of economic rights and the establishment of new rights to bring Europe closer to the citizens. The Committee put forward proposals on rights of citizens, culture, youth exchange, health, social security, free movement of people, town twinning and symbols of EC identity. So the European passport, the European flag, the European anthem, which are elements of citizenship traditionally linked to nation-states, were adopted in order to increase the awareness of the EC as a new political actor and foster the feeling of belonging to the Community among the European citizens. Moreover, exchange programs for students and professors were created to favour an open-minded European culture through mobility.

In 1986, the Single European Act (Art. 8A) clearly referred to the right of free circulation of people by granting European citizens some substantial rights. But a big step forward was made with the inclusion in the TEU (1992) of a chapter on 'Citizenship of the Union', adding political rights to economic and social rights, then shifting from EC workers to EU citizens.

If in the 1980s European citizenship had developed mainly in the economic field creating a 'welfare citizenship', in the early 1990s the TEU focused on political rights, constitutionalizing some rights which were already part of the *acquis communautaire* and establishing some new rights. By formalizing the European citizenship, the TEU gave clear visibility to a step-by-step process that had already started two decades earlier.

At the end of the millennium, due to increasing unemployment in most European countries, common socioeconomic strategies are the main focus at EU level. The Treaty of Amsterdam reflects these concerns by adopting the new employment policy and granting the social policy a treaty status.

European Citizenship as Established in the Treaty of Maastricht

In the TEU, European citizenship appears among the main objectives of the Union listed at the beginning of the treaty: 'The Union shall set itself the following objectives: ... to strengthen the protection of the rights and interests of the nationals of its Member States through the introduction of a citizenship of the Union' (Title I, Art. B).

Title II Part Two of TEU establishes the 'Citizenship of the Union' stating that: 'Every person holding the nationality of a Member State shall be a citizen of the Union' (Art. 8, 1). Then the citizenship of the Union does not replace the national citizenship, because it acts at a different level – the European level – entitling Union citizens to specific EU rights. A supranational citizenship is established offering EU citizens the possibility of exerting Union's rights along with national rights. The Union citizenship as established in the TEU is not supposed to compete with national citizenship, rather the former is additional to the latter and the nationality of a member state is the *conditio sine qua non* for European citizenship. The citizenship of the Union has been established in addition to national citizenship and has a different status.

European citizenship as established in the TEU entitles the EU citizens to some rights which have important implications for their everyday lives. These are namely the right to move and reside freely within the territory of the member states (Art. 8a); the right to vote and to stand as a candidate at municipal elections and in elections to the European Parliament in the member state in which one resides under the same conditions as nationals of that state[1] (Art. 8b); the diplomatic protection of any member state in a third country[2] (Art. 8c); the right to petition to the European Parliament[3] and the right to access to the Ombudsman (Art. 8d).[4]

In order to stress this complementarity between the Union and the national citizenship, the Treaty of Amsterdam states that 'Citizenship of the Union shall complement and not replace national citizenship'. As far as political rights are concerned, there are no substantial changes in the Treaty of Amsterdam, which is focused mainly upon social issues.

Some other treaty provisions are worth being mentioned because, even though not directly linked to the European citizenship, they have been adopted in order to redress the democratic deficit and develop a higher degree of social consensus towards the European integration process. For instance, the TEU introduced the subsidiarity principle, aimed at taking decisions as closely as possible to the citizens. Then, the Treaty of Amsterdam stresses the EU goal to create 'an ever closer union among the peoples of Europe, in which decisions are taken as openly as possible and as closely as possible to the citizen' and fosters the openness and transparency policy, stating the necessity of guaranteeing a broad access to documents of EU institutions and intensifying the dialogue with interest groups.

The aim of the establishment of European citizenship was clearly to reduce the gap between the EU institutions and its nationals, and it has been welcomed by many scholars both for its high symbolic value and concrete effects. For example, in his analysis of the new electoral rights of the European citizens, De Guttry (1995) positively greets the political rights established by the TEU underlying the great number of citizens directly affected by these new rights.[5]

Telò (1995: 49) underlines a peculiar aspect of the European citizenship as *dual* citizenship: a dual citizenship is usually destined to transform into a federal citizenship. However, the European citizenship is a special case, because the evolution towards a unique supranational citizenship is clearly excluded in the declaration on the nationality of a member state annexed to the TEU. European citizenship is not comprehensive of national and local citizenship, but it goes along with them. Then, instead of envisaging the European citizenship as having a *dual* character, it is more fruitful to define it as a *multiple* citizenship which takes into due account also the local and regional levels (Meehan, 1993).

The Visibility of European Citizenship: Some Empirical Evidence

Besides the provisions of the TEU, the positive analysis of scholars and the warm welcome of European practitioners, I shall concentrate here upon the empirical findings in order to verify whether this favourable attitude is shared by European public opinion.

EB has systematically conducted surveys on several aspects of European citizenship to investigate Europeans' real knowledge and interest in EU citizens' rights, their feeling of being informed about these rights, and their preferred sources providing information about EU citizenship.

As far as electoral rights are concerned, namely the right to vote and to stand as a candidate at local and European elections, what emerges from these surveys is a dichotomy between local and European elections.

In general, there is strong and increasing support for the right to vote and to stand as a candidate in one's country of residence at European elections (two Europeans out of three are for the extension of both passive and active electoral rights at European elections). When referring to the right to vote and to stand as a candidate in one's country of residence at local elections, a slight increasing trend is also registered, but at a much lower level. Without taking into account those respondents who did not answer, in 1997 six out of ten respondents were in favour of voting at local elections and five out of ten were in favour of the right to stand as candidate at local elections.[6] As one might expect, the lowest levels are registered in those countries where support for EU membership is less strong (in Denmark, Sweden, Finland and Austria) and in Belgium, where local tensions and separatist feelings are rather high.

Europeans then seem to be rather jealous of their local affairs, and in particular, they are not enthusiastic about letting non-nationals represent their local interests. One of the main reasons of this reluctance may be that Europeans do not fully trust people of different countries.[7]

EB surveys regularly inquire about some specific policy issues such as teaching in schools the functioning of the EU, a common defence and a common foreign policy, the creation of the European Central Bank, the adoption of the Euro and local electoral rights. It might appear surprising, but respondents are much more in favour of technical proposals such as a common defence or a common foreign policy rather than local electoral rights.[8] In reality, when dealing with the right to stand as a candidate or vote at local elections, issues are addressed with a more concrete appeal for Europeans, who are personally entitled to exercise these rights. Therefore, the influence of political elites and media in forming an opinion is much slighter, and personal interests much stronger.

Variables such as age and education level of respondents very much affect support for non-nationals' electoral rights. As a survey I conducted in early 1997 on a group of graduate and postgraduate Italian students confirms, young people with high level of education are more willing to grant EU nationals electoral rights in their country of residence. Having studied the functioning of the EU – European studies being part of their courses – they do not express much reserve, not even as far as local elections are concerned (more than 70 per cent were in favour). Half of them would not mind allowing community citizens the right to vote even at national elections, and one third would grant them the right to stand as a candidate at national elections. On the one hand, these data are consistent with the high level of Europeanism usually registered in Italy; but on the other hand, they give evidence for the positive impact of knowledge and education on a 'Europe-minded' mentality, offering some positive indications for constructivist initiatives.

However, in general this support or opposition does not reflect a precise knowledge of rights actually granted to EU citizens. As a matter of fact, EB surveys show that if faced with the statement 'You are allowed to vote in local elections in another EU country', only four out of ten Europeans do know it is true.[9] And it is in those countries where the opposition to the EU (Finland, Sweden and United Kingdom, but also Belgium) is the strongest that percentages of correct answers are under the average.

Many factors such as an insufficient information about EU citizens' electoral rights, little media coverage, a certain degree of political disaffection spread all over Europe, may explain why electoral rights seem to be of a lower salience than freedoms of movement, in particular the right to study in any EU country and the look for work in other EU countries (in these cases on average above 80 per cent of the respondents give correct answers). But certainly the utilitarian interest of citizens plays a major role, because in judging the rights granted by EU citizenship, Europeans focus much more on practical gains and concrete benefits such as medical coverage, buying goods or work conditions in other member states than on electoral rights.

Even though the establishment of the European citizenship has set political rights to promote the feeling of belonging to the EU as a political entity, EU citizens are still more sensible to and more aware of rights from which they think they can benefit more, namely the right to work or study in other EU countries.

The Public Support of European Integration: An Historical Overview

The creation of the European Communities is often considered as the result of the project of a strict group of pro-European politicians who did not take into account European public opinion. Integration was at first realized in a functional sector (coal and steel) by Schuman, Adenauer, De Gasperi, following

Jean Monnet's idea to *spill over* later into other areas. Although integration has often been seen as the bulwark of liberal-democracy, integration has been almost totally a creature of this elite (Shepherd, 1975: 1).

Lindberg and Scheingold's (1970) analysis of the process of European integration indicates that public opinion had not played a decisive role; nevertheless public support for 'Europe' was quite high and increased from the late 1940s to the late 1960s. Data indicated distinct and reasonably steady increases in favourable attitudes towards Europe between 1950 and 1962 in each of the member states; the rise was from just over 50 per cent evidencing favourable attitudes to over 70 per cent. But these data give no clues at all as to what it is about the system that was attractive or why (ibid.: 38). There was an element of utilitarian sentiment in the Europeans' expectations:

> The support for supranational institutions or policies [was] more marked than feelings of shared needs and interests. Publics [did] not yet conceive ... common interests or needs, they [were] attached to the Common Market only in so far as it provide[d] clearly perceived benefits and accord[ed] with an underlying affective-identitive sentiment (ibid.: 156).

In general there was *permissive consensus*, because the Community enterprise was seemingly taken for granted as an accepted part of the political landscape, making it relatively easy to mobilize support for projects to advance or protect the economic programmes of the Community. There was a favourably prevailing attitude towards the subject, but it was generally of low salience as a political issue, leaving national decision-makers free to take steps favourable to integration if they wished, but also leaving them a wide liberty of choice (Inglehart, 1970: 773).

Public opinion was in favour of European integration, but without any knowledge of the connected implications (Slater, 1982). Consequently, when it was clear that the process of European integration could also imply personal sacrifices, the support of certain sectors decreased. This means that nationals were in favour of the integration in the same way they favoured peace: both were desirable goals, but when the costs of attaining a goal such as European integration were considered, some doubts arose.

In the 1970s support for European integration suddenly decreased both due to the international economic crisis and to the internal impact of the first enlargement of the EC (Handley, 1981). Thanks to the first European elections this public support crisis was overcome. According to Handley the European Parliament (EP), with its periodical elections, could stimulate the European identity. But the great optimism which had welcomed the first European elections decreased as a consequence of the low participation rate and of the *second-order* status of the European elections which was soon revealed (Reif, 1985).

European Integration and Public Opinion in the 1980s and 1990s

In order to measure public support for the EC/EU, specific EB surveys have been systematically conducted since the early 1980s. What emerges over the past twenty years is, on average within the member countries, a general pattern of public support for Europe. It was characterized by a continuous rise of basic approval of EC/EU membership until early 1991 (when average public support stood at 72 per cent compared to about 50 per cent in 1980s), and a downturn thereafter, followed by a consolidation at lower levels of support.[10]

To better understand this trend, it is now necessary to recall some concepts which are often used in public opinion analysis and which give account for the European attitude towards the European integration process. *Utilitarian support* for supranational institutions is a support for integration that stems from recognition of common interests and positive, mutual benefits that will result (Lindberg and Scheingold, 1970). *Affective support is* emotional support which may exist between peoples, and which may also comprise a sense of common identity (Deutsch, quoted in ibid.). When defining *permissive consensus*, Reif (1993) refers more to a declaredly negative attitude towards European integration rather than supportive, as it 'allows for integration by political, economic, military and cultural elites, as long as those segments of these elites that are opposed to integration (or to more integration) do not succeed in mobilizing significant support. If and when they do, they slow down the speed of integration, stop it or even reverse its direction'. As the trend of the last two decades demonstrates, public support of Europe is more permissive, acceptive and benevolent, than demanding, challenging, pressing or pushing.

The erosion of a 'permissive consensus' had started long before the December 1991 Maastricht meeting of the European Council and the February 1992 signing of the TEU. It seems that in the late 1980s and early 1990s the Europeans had very high expectations from the new European system which was being based upon the common market and unified Germany. But then the EU countries were faced with economic crisis and increasing unemployment which, together with the difficulties linked to the reunification of the East and West German parts, particularly reduced the support for EU membership.

Moreover, since the 1995 enlargement of the EU the sceptical public of the new Scandinavian member countries and Austria tempers the EU data.

Public opinion surveys clearly reflect that the early 1990s were characterized by a certain degree of optimism. The collapse of communist regimes in Eastern Europe was accompanied by a strong confidence in democratic institutions and, therefore, in closer European integration. So, in spring 1991 the rates referring to 'support for unification' (81 per cent), 'EC membership' (72 per cent), 'benefits from the EC' (59 per cent) and 'regret of dissolution' (50 per cent) were all at their highest levels.[11] Then enthusiasm and hope suddenly decreased for events which slowed down the coming into force of the Maastricht Treaty: the Danish referendum saying no to the Treaty, the slight 52 per cent at the French referendum, the British hostilities leading to the opting out in the social field. But apart from these EU internal events, there were also external causes to the decreasing of public support. At the end of 1992, the level of insecurity among Europeans had risen, as Western Europe entered an economic recession accompanied by high levels of unemployment.

Utilitarian support, constitutional support and *general support* reflect events both internal and external to EU.[12] The Maastricht summit and the controversial discussion which accompanied the ratification of the TEU, the Danish and the French referenda, the withdrawal of the pound sterling and the Italian lira from the exchange rate mechanism of the EMS, the recession hitting many member state economies, the official start of the Single Market, but also the Gulf War, news from Eastern Europe turning sour, all have resulted in the decline of public support since spring 1991. As a consequence of the recovery from the economic recession in many member states and the appeased Maastricht debate, the most recent public opinion polls register a new consolidation, even though at considerably more modest levels than four, five or six years before.

Yet, support for European integration tends to be *utilitarian.* Public attitudes towards integration reflect the perceived costs and benefits of EC membership: 'support for the EC does not translate into a willingness to make sacrifices for other member states in economic difficulties' (Laffan, 1992: 123). Empirical evidence to the *utilitarian support* is given by an EB survey inquiring about the worries of European public opinion. When asked 'In your opinion, which of the following should be the most important objective of the European Union policies towards less favoured regions?', the great majority of the respondents indicates the creation of jobs as the most important.[13]

As Franklin, Marsh and McLaren (1994: 458) argue 'Maastricht pushed the "permissive consensus" regarding Europe beyond its limits'. In fact, the live debate on the ratification of the TEU revealed that European public opinion is now more attentive to what happens in Brussels. Recent political events demonstrate that the public is neither supportive of European integration nor deferential to elites on EC issues as previously assumed. European integration is not merely a process run by political elites, but depends also on fluctuations in public sentiments as well (Gabel and Palmer, 1995: 3). Today *consensus* does not seem to be as permissive as in the past, because it is very much influenced by the major political and economic events.

European support for European integration is influenced by contingent events. If international migration flows, environmental disasters, economic crises and unemployment, constitute a threat to Europeans' interests and lives, they might negatively influence the attitudes towards European integration. Unless the EU will be able to find a solution in the direction of tangible economic benefits and higher standards of living, European nationals as an attractive alternative could consider nationalism or local separatism. Europeans are clearly not ready to sacrifice themselves for Europe.

A Public Debate on European Integration: The Treaty of Maastricht Judged by the Europeans

Due to the adoption of the TEU, a large public debate has arisen on European integration, and the referenda highlighted the distance existing between citizens and the EU. It was then clear that a good deal of the population fears that the EU would threaten their national interests acting in fields previously regulated by national governments.

However, when explaining the reasons why the respondents are hostile to the treaty, they describe a Community that is basically organized according to the treaty itself. The Europeans fear that the EU as described in the TEU would threaten national identity and cultural diversity, that their governments would be forced to carry out decisions they do not want. They do not like a too centralized European decision-making process guided by bureaucracy in Brussels. To sum up, they are against a community that is distant from the citizens. They want different cultures and identities to be respected, their governments to play an important role in the decision-making process and sovereignty not to be transferred completely to the common institutions. They do not know, then, that they are in favour of the system that is established in the TEU, where the principle of subsidiarity disciplines the level of intervention.

Those who are traditionally against an 'ever closer Union' and the increasing of common policies, mainly the Danish and British but also the

Finnish, are those who prefer the EU to be responsible only for matters that cannot be effectively handled by national, regional or local governments.[14] But supporting the EU does not necessarily mean having a precise knowledge of the EU machinery or of the EU agenda. The Italians, for example, have always been pro-Europe and the most in favour of the creation of a European government directly accountable to the EP and of the increasing of EP powers, including legislative powers. Nevertheless, they do not know the decision making process well and wrongly indicate the EP as the most powerful institution in adopting EU legislation. On the contrary, despite their slight opposition to the EU, the Danish are better informed about the distribution of normative powers.

Analysing the most recent data on support of European integration, there is evidence for two groups of member states with completely different attitudes. On the one hand, Italy, Luxembourg, Ireland and Netherlands are the most in favour of European integration. On the other, in Austria, United Kingdom, Sweden, Finland and Denmark support is much lower.[15]

National Identity and European Identity: Conflict or Compatibility?

Moving from the above severe public judgement on the European Union, mainly stemming from economic considerations and dissatisfactions, to a sociological level, the EB surveys offer a different picture of European public opinion: half of the EU peoples feel to some extent European.

The 'feeling European' survey indicates that in spring 1997 the majority of the Europeans declared having a European identity.[16] This majority is divided into three categories of identity: 'national and European' (40 per cent); 'European and national' (6 per cent); 'only European' (5 per cent). Forty-five per cent of the respondents declared having only a national identity.

The same survey has been regularly conducted and the trend 1994–97 shows a slight but constant increase in 'only national' responses. But the most interesting data emerges from a distinction in responses according to the nationality. As a matter of fact, it is in the three new member states, in United Kingdom, and in Denmark, but also in Portugal, that the 'only national identity' category is more consistent. While three original member states, France, Italy and Luxembourg, are much above the average EU rates.

The variables influencing the 'feeling European' are first of all age, sex and political ideas. In general young people, men and leftists are more pro-European than elderly people, women and rightists.

The survey on a sample of Italian students I personally conducted indicates that a high level of education implies a full comprehension of the compatibility between national (Italian) and European identity (only one student out of 50 considered himself/herself only Italian). Moreover, to a large extent respondents rely upon EU to protect cultural diversities.

Though, if citizens are asked to choose between having a European identity and a national identity, they consider national ties stronger than the European ones. The attachment to one's nationality emerges from an EB survey about the rights and freedoms to be respected 'under all circumstances'; then, 80 per cent of respondents refer to the right to one's own language and culture.[17]

Although in the latter data the national identity prevails, I would stress rather the importance of the general coexistence of two identities, national and European, stemming from the surveys mentioned earlier In fact, the 'feeling European' question is based on the assumption that one does not need to give up one's national identification in order to adopt a European one. To feel European does not mean to 'die' for the EU (Attinà, 1995: 125). Even in the TEU the relationship between national identity and European identity is defined according to a principle of respect and compatibility. As a matter of fact. Title I, Art. F, states that: 'The Union shall respect the national identities or its Member States, whose systems of government are founded on the principles of democracy.' The EU clearly does not aim at substituting national and regional identities with a European one.

Undeniably, in Europe there are common historical origins and a common cultural heritage. But at the same time the EU is characterized by a plurality of cultures, languages, and ethnic groups. And, in view of any further enlargement, Europe is destined to be a continent of pluri-belonging. It is difficult to imagine a cultural 'unification', and in any case this is not the ultimate goal of the EU. Talking about a common identity cannot imply a uniformity of European cultural identities. The deepening of the common European values does not necessarily mean the removal of cultural specificity of the European peoples. This would be in contrast with the TEU articles giving way to a certain regional decentralization and establishing the right to respect local and regional identities (Art. 126–8).[18]

A comparison can be made between the coexistence of different levels of sovereignty and powers, and of identities. As a matter of fact, Europeans are used to democratic participation at different levels, as regional, national, European levels have each a special specific logic. Europeans are at the same time citizens of their town, their region, their nation, and of the EU. The EU does not aim at substituting the member state nations, and the principle of subsidiarity is the weapon aimed at protecting the different levels, and consequently, different identities.

The point of departure here is the 'evolution towards a *post-étatique* entity of the EU made up of different levels: local, national, and supranational' (Telò, 1995: 5). Wæver clearly points out that the complexity of the EU political system is strictly linked with the definition of European identity as 'the emerging complexity of various co-existing layers of identity forces us to rethink what kinds of identity might be possible to function here. In a post-sovereign space like Europe, identity cannot be connected to the idea of primacy, of the one "real" identity' (Wæver, 1996).

The emergence of a European identity does *not* imply the substitution of other identities. Dealing with identity we cannot think in terms of zero-sum games, instead sociological terms of reference are much more explanatory. As they are used to adapting to different social roles in their life, Europeans should get used to different belonging. Each human being often shares highly contradictory identities and social roles as a member of his family, of his locality, of his professional, social, political and religious adherence, of his region, of his nation and possibly, by the virtue of transnational links, of the world. It is a question of multiple allegiances. Sociologically, human beings can move between their multiple identities according to context and situation. Such identities may be concentric rather than conflictual and there is plenty of historical evidence for the coexistence of concentric circles of allegiances (Smith, 1992: 67).[19] Smith clearly describes the relationship between national and European identity in terms of compatibility stating that 'however dominant the nation and its national identification, human beings retain a multiplicity of allegiances in the contemporary world' (ibid.: 59).

However, several sociological analyses confirm that the lack of affection towards institutions exists at all levels: local, regional and national. In his research Dogan (1993 and 1994) gives evidence for a decline in the intensity of nationalism in Western Europe. Nationalism – which is traditionally considered as high national pride, confidence in the own country's army, readiness to fight for the own country – is declining among the upcoming generations 'because a supranational consciousness is rising, by a progressive interaction at several levels, economic, military, social, cultural, and political' (Dogan, 1994: 294). The existence and the perception of the EU are then responsible for the decline of nationalism because 'Western European counties having achieved their national integration a long time ago, find themselves today in a post-nationalistic phase' (ibid.: 281). Decline in nationalism is typical in mature western European countries which have experienced before others the creation of liberal states where now 'sovereignty of the nation-states is slowly but progressively reduced by a kind of loose confederal sovereignty, vaguely called "community"' (ibid.: 303).

A Constructivist Approach: The Necessity of Strengthening a European Identity

In constructivist terms state identities and interests are to a large degree constructed by social structures (Wendt, 1994: 385). Then, as in all democratic systems, EU institutions should act at EU level as identity producers. The EU institutions should help the Europeans to become aware of their belonging to a political common entity. At the same time they should help the development of a feeling of belonging to a common identity and to a common destiny. According to Wallace (1990: 55):

> political integration is a matter of identity and loyalty: of the emergence of a political community based upon shared values and mutual trust out of previously separate and mistrustful groups … There is no simple or inexorable transition from contact through trade to the emergence of political community.

For many years the Commission has stated the importance of stimulating the feeling of belonging to the same community by the use of symbols and the creation of the European flag, the European anthem or the European passport. But even the adoption of the Euro and the establishment of transnational rights of the union's citizenship can act as European identity creator. Also the development of communication between Europeans can be helpful in developing a mutual understanding. In this view mobility programs such as Erasmus, Comett, Lingua and Petra, now Socrates and Leonardo, have financed the mobility of a great number of students and workers since 1987 and proved to be successful in increasing public opinion awareness of movement rights (see above).

The necessity of keeping on spreading the idea of Europe is confirmed by the result of an EB survey on the attachment to different political levels: town, village, region, country, EU and Europe.[20] There is a big difference between the degree of attachment to towns or villages, regions and countries (about 90 per cent), and rates referring to European Union and Europe as a whole, which are much lower (about 40 per cent).[21] This might be due to the fact that we are just at the beginning of the *Europeanization* process.

Many scholars refer to 'top-down' strategies of state-building applied to the European integration process. As a matter of fact, a parallel can be made between the process of nation-building which occurred in the last century in many European states, and what is happening now at EU level. States used enormous resources and symbols to instill a sense of loyalty and identification with the national political community. After having learnt the sense of belonging to the nation (process of nationalization) it is now necessary to teach the EU citizens to live with an own (state) government and a common (EU) government (Attinà, 1995: 21). The process of nation-building is now affecting the supranational level (although it might seem a contradiction in terms) and has created the EU federal system made up of the 15 member states. A process of Europeanization is therefore binding. In this context, Europeanism – considered as mobilization of symbolic values – has to be spread in support of European integration.

The mobilization of public opinion in favour of the integration process is often regarded as an essential element. Telò (1995: 20) for instance refers to a 'learning' process which 'instead of teaching a national mythology, ethnocentrism and nationalism should be eradicated in the name of a political democracy, in order to give way to an equal European citizenship, independent from the nation, ethnic group and language' (ibid.: 48).

The importance of the 'top-down' strategies is stressed also by Neumann (1994: 58), who transfers the nation-building process to the regional level, and refers to a process of region-building: 'the existence of regions is preceded by the existence of region-builders, political actors who, as part of some political projects, imagine a certain spatial and chronological identity for a region, and discriminate this imagined identity to others'.

However, when arguing that the union 'top-down' strategies of state building have a role to play in altering perceptions of the political space to which individual Europeans belong, we do not mean that the Union should set out to replace national identities, but that 'the extension of political space beyond the nation-state provides a shelter for multiple identity, be they local, regional or national' (Laffan, 1996).

Conclusions

Dealing with European identity implies referring on the one hand to a convergence of cultural values among European citizens, on the other to a capacity of tolerating cultural diversity. Considering the growing danger of international instability, the EU and its institutions constitute a precious intermediate instrument between the local, regional, national and global level. But at the same time, there is an urgent need to build a European consciousness, to create a sense of community that can safeguard and nourish the basic elements of the European culture.

The analysis of the EB public opinion surveys indicates that the establishment of the European citizenship apparently has not stimulated a stronger European identity. Due to the difficult economic situation Europe has been faced with in the last few years, Europeans judge European integration in highly utilitarian terms (their main interest is to find a job!). Is it worth then to spread the idea of Europe in such a context? The answer would be yes. Defending and protecting diversities seem to be the only way for the EU to face, on the one hand, the challenges of the global world economy, on the other, the moves towards fragmentation and regionalization which might risk becoming separation and secession. The reason why public opinion is not aware of these constraints might be that we are experiencing the first phase of the *Europeanization* process.

Looking at the future of the EU, we should keep in mind Wæver's warning that:

> Europe can only be if we avoid renewed fragmentation ... integration/ fragmentation is not a question of how Europe will be, but whether Europe will be ... Security, politics, identity and Europe meet in something which is even, self-declared as a project of constructing a 'security identity' (Wæver, 1996).

Meehan (1993: 185) perfectly describes the present situation and indicates the path for the future:

> a new kind of citizenship is emerging that is neither national nor cosmopolitan but which is multiple in enabling the various identities that we all possess to be expressed, and our rights to be exercised, through an increasingly complex configuration of common institutions, states, national and transnational interest groups and voluntary associations, local or provincial authorities, regions and alliances of regions ... A multiple identity allows different identities to be expressed and different rights and duties to be exercised.

Coming back to the basic assumption of this essay that European citizenship and European identity are strictly interrelated, it appears extremely important to foster actions which spread the sense of belonging to the EU. It is not sufficient to entitle the Europeans to EU rights without instilling at the same time the *Europeanness*. If, as Kratochwil (1996: 181) points out, the concept of citizenship is based on the two focal points of belonging to a political community and of the status of enjoying distinctive rights, the entitlement of the new rights alone does not necessarily imply an increased allegiance to the EU. The identity formation is an 'instituted process' based on the boundaries existing between the group and the outsiders, in our case the difference is between EU and non-EU citizens.

Notes

1 The Council Directive 93/109/EC, OJ L 329, 30.12.1993 specifies that citizens may choose to exercise their right to vote either in their member state of residence or in their home member, but they may neither vote nor stand as a candidate more than once for the same election.

2 The entitlement to diplomatic protection further develops the external dimension of European citizenship launched many years earlier by the adoption of a uniform passport.

3 The citizen's right to address petitions was already established by the EP rules of procedures in 1989, but the TEU implied its effective constitutionalization.

4 The first Ombudsman, Mr Jacob Soderman, was appointed only in July 1995 for some hostilities of the EP that considered a powerful ombudsman incompatible with its petitions committee.

5 According to Eurostat data (1992) roughly 5 million Europeans reside in an EU country which is different from their own country.

6 IEB 48, Autumn 1997, Table 3.11.

7 An EB survey conducted in 1996 highlights that in general there is a high level of trust in people from the smaller countries of northern Europe and a lower level for southern Europe – Greek and Italians in particular (EB 46, Autumn 1996, Figure 4.3).

8 EB 48 indicates that in 1997, 52 per cent of the respondents were in favour of the right to vote, 43 per cent were in favour of the right to stand as candidate, while 69 per cent and 63 per cent respectively supported a common defence and a common foreign policy.

9 EB 47, Spring 1997, Figure 5.5.

10 In 1997 half of the interviewed considered EU membership a 'good thing', and three out of ten 'neither good nor bad', while only 14 per cent judged it a 'bad thing' (EB 48, Autumn 1997, Figure 3.1).

11 EB 39, June 1993, Figure 1.7.

12 EB 43, Autumn 1995, Figure 1.7.

13 EB 44, Spring 1996, Table 7.6.

14 EB 43, Autumn 1995, Figure 3.4.

15 A country-by-country analysis gives evidence for the great differences that are hidden by average data. If eight Irish respondents out of ten support EU membership, only three Austrians and Swedes out of ten do (EB 48, Autumn 1997, Table 3.1a).

16 EB 47, Spring 1997, Figure 5.1.

17　EB 47, Spring 1997, Figure 5.9.
18　With the creation of the Committee of the Regions (Art. 198A), regions gained a consultative power they did not have before. It is not possible here to refer to the difficulties the Committee is faced with, such as the different status of the European regions, or the different composition of the assembly (some members are directly elected, but not all), to mention just a few. But here I would stress rather the high symbolic value of this lastly created institution that gives the opportunity to express regional interests at EU level.
19　In the book edited by Garcia (1993) the European citizen is seen as a human being with variable geometry, used to living in a complex world, and the potential development of multiple identities in concentric circles should encourage compatible loyalties from the local to the European level.
20　EB 44, Spring 1996, Figure 7.1.
21　Again, the survey on Italian students gave different results. In this case, the feeling of belonging to Europe at large was even stronger than the belonging to town, region or Italy. In accordance to the basic principle of compatibility of the different levels, I have asked one question for each specific issue; then respondents were not forced to indicate their strongest feeling of belonging in exclusive terms (*either* local, regional, national *or* European); they could then consider every single case on its own. The comparison between the different answers can be then made at the analysis stage.

References

Attinà, F. (1995), 'Nazionalismo e europeismo', in F. Attinà, F. Longo and S. Panebianco (eds), *Identità, partiti ed elezioni nell'Unione Europea*, Cacucci, Ban, pp. 7–30.

Attinà, F. (1997), 'Nationalism and Europeanism: The European Union and the Question of Multiple Identity', *The European Union Review*, Vol. 2, pp. 25–41.

De Guttry, A. (1995), 'I nuovi diritti in materia elettorale del cittadino dell'Unione Europea', *Quaderni dell'Osservatorio elettorale*, Vol. 33, pp. 61–91.

Dogan, M. (1993), 'Comparing the decline of nationalisms in Western Europe: the generational dynamic', *International Social Science Journal*, Vol. 736, pp. 177–98.

Dogan, M. (1994), 'The Decline of Nationalisms within Western Europe', *Comparative Politics*, Vol. 26, pp. 281–305.

Eurobarometer 48 (Autumn 1997); 47 (Spring 1997); 45 (Spring 1996); 44 (Spring 1996); 43 (Autumn 1995); Trends (December 1994); 41 (July 1994); 39 (June 1993).

Franklin, M., Marsh, M. and McLaren, L. (1994), 'Uncorking the Bottle: Popular Opposition to European Unification in the Wake of Maastricht', *Journal of Common Market Studies*, Vol. 32, pp. 455–72.

Gabel, M. and Palmer, H.D. (1995), 'Understanding Variation in Public Support for European Integration', *European Journal of Political Research*, Vol. 27, pp. 3–19.

Garcia, S. (ed.) (1993), *European Identity and the Search for Legitimacy*, Pinter RITA, London.

Handley, D. (1981), 'Public Opinion and European Integration: The Crisis of the 1970s', *European Journal of Political Research*, Vol. 4, pp. 335–64.

Inglehart, R. (1970), 'Public Opinion and Regional Integration', *International Organisation*, Vol. 24, pp. 764–95.

Kratochwil F. (1996), *Citizenship: On the Border of Order*, in Y. Lapid and F. Kratochwil (eds), *The Return of Culture and Identity in IR Theory*, Lynne Rienner Publishers, London.

Laffan, B. (1992), *Integration and Co-operation in Europe*, Routledge, London.

Laffan, B. (1996), 'The Politics of Identity and Political Order in Europe', *Journal of Common Market Studies*, Vol. 34, pp. 81–102.

Lindberg, L.N. and Scheingold, S.A. (1970), *Europe's Would-be Polity: Patterns of Change in the European Community*, Prentice Hall, Englewood Cliffs, NJ.

Meehan, E. (1993), 'Citizenship and the European Community', *The Political Quarterly*, Vol. 64, pp. 172–86.

Neumann, I.B. (1994), 'A Region-building Approach to Northern Europe', *Review of International Studies*, Vol. 20, pp. 53–74.

Reif, K. (1993), 'Cultural Convergence and Cultural Diversity as Factors in European Identity', in S. Garcia (ed.), *European Identity and the Search for Legitimacy*, Pinter RITA, London.

Reif, K. (ed.) (1985), *Ten European Elections. Campaigns and Results of the 1979 First Direct Elections to the European Parliament*, Gower, Aldershot.

Shepherd, R.J. (1975), *Public Opinion and European Integration*, Saxon House, Westmead.

Slater, M. (1982–83), 'Political Elites, Popular Indifference and Community Building', *Journal of Common Market Studies*, Vol. 21.

Smith, A.D. (1992), 'National Identity and the Idea of European Unity', *International Affairs*, Vol. 1, pp. 55–76.

Telò, M. (ed.) (1995), *Démocratie et construction européenne*, Editions de l'Université de Bruxelles, Bruxelles.

Wallace, W. (1990), *The Transformation of Western Europe*, Pinter RITA, London.

Wæver, O. (1996), 'European Security Identities', *Journal of Common Market Studies*, Vol. 34, pp. 103–32.

Wendt, A. (1994), *Collective Identity Formation and the International State*, American Political Science Review, Vol. 88, pp. 384–96.

Chapter 3

European Citizenship and the Se
Legitimacy:
The Paradox of the Danish Case*

Camilla Hersom

> Everyone nowadays recognises the sky-blue banner with 12 gold stars symbolising European unification, which we see more and more often flying alongside national flags in front of public buildings. Is there anyone who can fail to be moved on hearing the Ode to Joy ...? What Community national does not enjoy following the 'European Community' sign in the airport arrival halls, and passing through simply by showing the uniform passport adopted in 1985? (Fontaine, 1991: 7).

Prologue

This quotation is drawn from an information booklet on the European Union. However, it would be wrong to assume that it is an eloquent characterization of most peoples' feelings towards the EU. There is a stronger case for arguing that if the European Project is to succeed, a *development* of such feelings is both desirable and necessary. One way the Community has tried to address the problem has been through the development of a notion of European Citizenship. The underlying idea is that by granting the peoples of Europe political and social rights in relation to the Union, the Community would be more visible and relevant in people's everyday life, thereby countering the legitimacy deficit which the Community apparently suffers. Ideally, it would indeed make people *feel* European, fostering the group-identity that could glue the Community together, because it would work the same way as the national identity in the nation state.

The discussion in the present article will evolve around the 'Danish case' After the Danish 'no' to Maastricht in the referendum of 1992, the Community and Denmark agreed on a 'decision' giving Denmark four opt-outs of the Maastricht Treaty. European Citizenship was one of the opt-outs guaranteed.[1]

The Danish referendum results are naturally complex and multicausal in character, and all of the 'opt-outs' had their share in the change of attitude. The focus here will, however, be on the 'opt-out' on European citizenship. The aim is to draw some conclusions on the apparent paradox that an initiative – European citizenship – which was meant to establish legitimacy in the European Union has had the opposite effect in one of the member states. That the Danish case has relevance for the European Community as such should be apparent, when it is remembered that the wording of the Danish opt-out on citizenship has been written into the new Amsterdam Treaty.

Citizenship and Identity

Most people possess a variety of identities according to gender, professional occupation, personal relationships, political observance, special interests, and nationality. It is the latter that is of interest in the present context.

The feeling of identity that people have towards their nation generates a community feeling which in the modern state provides the legitimate basis of representative democracy, and leads people to be willing to make great economic as well as personal sacrifices. This is most powerfully manifest in the fact that people are willing to pay taxes and go to war for their nation. National identity can, to an extent, be viewed as the glue that knits society together. In the words of Anthony D. Smith '*national* identification has become the cultural and political norm, transcending other loyalties in scope and power' (Smith, 1992: 58, emphasis in original).

In most cases, the feeling of national identity is linked to the citizenship of a particular state. There are obviously numerous examples of nations that do not have their own state, and many examples of nations that feel oppressed in the state in which they hold citizenship. However, for the former, the state creates a common public culture open to participation of all citizens (ibid.: 62). For the latter, the desire – in some cases even struggle – is to *obtain* their own state, which further emphasizes the powerful feelings attributed to the national identity and the link between citizenship and national identity.

At present the European Community is neither a state, nor an ordinary international organization. The latter is, among other things, apparent in the fact that enforcement of Community law must take precedence over national laws, even in the case of conflicts, and that private parties may refer to provisions of Community law before the national courts.[2] These legal doctrines place European law as the supreme law of the land, and have indeed by some commentators been viewed as founding a *new constitutional order*.[3] Still, as Joseph Weiler points out (1996: 518–19), this new constitutional order has come about with very little constitutional debate, not to mention citizen participation.

By definition, a problem necessarily arises in the context of the European Union: the conception of citizenship – as characterized in the traditional nation state – *cannot* be transferred to the Community level, when it comes to the identity-feeling that people have towards their state *qua* their nationhood. On a European level, the notion of citizenship must necessarily include a variety of political and cultural identities, and the common features must be nested in something different than the 'cultural homogeneity', which is the foundation of national identity.[4]

The Legitimacy Deficit

In recent years there has been much debate over the democratic and legitimacy deficit of the European Union. But the democratic and legitimacy deficit is *precisely* a problem because the policies of the European Union are agreed and implemented within a binding 'constitutional' order. If the European Union was an ordinary intergovernmental organization, nobody would lift an eyebrow as to the secrecy of the Council of ministers or the inferior role of the European Parliament (Weiler, 1996: 518–19).

Provided that the Union is forming a binding constitutional order, it is quite clear that this constitutional order in turn does not live up to the requirements of democracy and accountability as they are secured in liberal, democratic states. Therefore, the lack of democracy and legitimacy is often considered as an institutional problem, where the solution envisaged is developing the Union towards some kind of federal system. However, it does not seem likely that a federal-type system is the end result envisaged by the governments of the member states at the present stage of integration. Consequently, the challenge of the 'democratic deficit' has to do with how to create and secure democracy in a non-state entity, rather than addressing the question as if the Union was to become a state (Weiner, 1996: 2).

If the question of legitimacy had not been considered a crucial problem before, it certainly became one after the Maastricht referendums in 1992, when the Danish population rejected the Treaty and the French only barely accepted it – the votes were very close in both countries (Laffan, 1996: 23).[5]

The 'legitimacy deficit' is here to be understood as relating to the debate that arose in the aftermath of the ratification of the Treaty. In the words of

Juliet Lodge (1994: 343), it 'became clear that not only were people mystified by some of its [the Treaty's] terminology ... but that they were becoming increasingly alienated from the idea of the European Community'. Given that the 'democratic deficit' is a serious problem of the Community in its own right, it therefore seems as if the most fundamental problem is the 'legitimacy deficit' linked to it. Indeed, it has been argued that legitimacy rather than democracy seems to be the critical condition for integration.[6]

Analogously, Joseph Weiler (1997) argues that the Community enjoyed legitimacy *until* the Maastricht referendums, despite serious democratic deficiencies in the governing of the Community. When integration gained momentum in the mid-1980s after years of stagnation, both the national political institutions and public opinion supported the expansion of Community powers notwithstanding the lack of democratic control (Weiler, 1997: 254).[7] This did however change considerably in the run-up to Maastricht and after, when the public opinion turned to be much more critical and sceptical of European integration than previously. This legitimacy deficit is not only recognized by a number of academic scholars[8] but also by the Community itself, as the initiatives on European citizenship clearly show.

Weiler links the change of public opinion to the lack of a European *demos*, since the citizens do not constitute the political subjects of the *polity* in a European context the way they have traditionally done so in Western, liberal democracies.[9] The implication of the missing participatory role for the citizens is that countering the deficit of legitimacy will not only demand measures aimed at the institutional structure of the Union, but it must also address the problem of the lack of *political community* (Laffan, 1996: 198–9). Unless the people of Europe gain a role in, and feel attached to, the project of integration, they will not consider further integration to be legitimate.

The Community itself is all too aware of the lack of public support. Thus, in the last three decades, a number of initiatives have been taken aimed at collective identity formation by including the people of Europe in the integration process and fostering a sense of belonging. This enterprise is taking place under the heading of 'a Citizen's Europe', 'a People's Europe', and, finally, with the creation of 'a European Citizenship'.

That the Community has linked the question of legitimacy to a lack of common identity, and has tried to promote the latter through measures creating a 'European citizenship', is by no means a coincidence. The blue-print used is the modern nation state, where citizenship can be regarded as the legal expression of *belonging* to a particular state.

European Citizenship

The concept of European citizenship is intimately linked to the idea of the European Union as a *political union*. Forming part of the political agenda directed towards Political Union, citizenship addressed the question of what constitutes a polity and who it is to be included in the creation of a constitutional system in a non-state entity (Wiener, 1996: 2–3). Arguably, the most important step concerning Union Citizenship was bringing together the already existing freedoms and the new rights in a new separate part of the Treaty, thereby creating a coherent concept labelled 'European citizenship'. The new elements in 'European citizenship' count the right to vote and stand as a candidate at municipal elections and in elections to the European Parliament, establishment of an ombudsman institution and the entitlement to diplomatic protection of any member state in a third country in which the national's own country is not represented. With respect to the substance of the provisions, the creation of political rights – hitherto unprecedented in international organizations – was undoubtedly most significant. There is no doubt that the Community itself assigns huge symbolic importance to the new concept of European citizenship. This is apparent in the preamble, which explicit states that the member states will 'establish a citizenship common to the nationals of their countries' as well as in the placement of Art. 8 to 8E concerning citizenship immediately after the introductory provisions of the Treaty of Rome. Likewise, the importance shines through in the rhetoric of the Commission, which in its initial report on Citizenship of the Union states that it 'welcomes this opportunity to set out its conception of these new provisions, the importance of which cannot be sufficiently stressed' (COM (93) 702: 1–2).

Union Citizenship Additional to National Citizenship

Notwithstanding the initial ambitions, the Treaty of the European Union does not create a new political subject. However, the civic and political rights now included in the Treaty represent a challenge for the understandings of citizenship and nationality in a number of member states, as the rights touch on the participatory role of the individual in the state and his or her relationship with other states (Guild, 1996: 32). What lies at the core of the discussion is how European citizenship might transform the concept of nationality.

The wording in the Treaty runs as follows: 'every person holding the nationality of a Member State shall be a citizen of the Union'. Thus, Union citizenship has member state citizenship as a necessary prerequisite. This restrictive interpretation of citizenship of the Union is the result of vigilance of the member states in assuring that the new citizenship would in no way undermine the concept of nationality. From a political point of view it concerns that decisions regarding nationality are commonly understood as being an essential part of a state's sovereignty. (O'Keeffe, 1994: 92). It is explicitly stated in the declarations of the intergovernmental conference that:

> wherever in the Treaty... reference is made to nationals of the Member States, the question whether an individual possesses the nationality of a Member State shall be settled solely by reference to the national law of the Member State concerned (reproduced in Rudden and Wyatt, 1994: 209).

In addition, the European Council has, in two declarations, made it clear that the present content of European citizenship does not in any way challenge nationality. The first of these, the Birmingham Declaration, clarifies that 'citizenship of the Union brings our citizens additional rights and protection without in any way taking the place of their national citizenship' (Bull-EC 10–1992 pt I.8, 9). This statement was later repeated at the European Council meeting in Edinburgh, when it was asserted that rights and protection granted by the citizenship do not substitute national citizenship (Closa, 1994: 114–15). This has also been confirmed in the new Amsterdam Treaty 'which adds that: 'Citizenship of the Union shall complement and not replace national citizenship' (Art. 17, 1). At the time of Maastricht, the guarantees set forward were, however, not sufficient to satisfy the Danish government which made a unilateral declaration on the same issue after the Maastricht referendum in 1992.

Since Union citizenship is bound to being a national of one of the member states and since it is the prerogative of these to decide their own rules genuine new kind of citizenship. Nobody can be a Union Citizen in their own right, so the term must be considered as a supplement to national citizenship.

The Challenge of European Identity

The concept of European citizenship has, as its clearly stated goal, the increasing of legitimacy of the Union through the notion of citizenship and an explicit policy of stimulating a European identity. Whether European citizenship holds promise for the development of a European identity or not obviously depends on whether Union citizenship is conceived as making a difference in its own respect. The limitations of the present article do not permit us to enter into a discussion of whether a genuine new citizenship with a corresponding identity is emerging, being neither national nor cosmopolitan in character or, whether European citizenship is without significant substance. Suffice for the present to note that for the advocates of the former viewpoint, European citizenship is evaluated as a process, a step-by-step formation of expectations, perceptions and behaviour, which in their turn stimulate a European identity. This is contested by authors who compare European citizenship with national citizenship and find serious shortcomings in the former. This leads them to argue that it is unlikely that European citizenship will ever develop into a genuine new citizenship, let alone be a way of promoting a European identity.[10] The determining factor in evaluating the prospects for a European identity in the discussion outlined above is the importance ascribed to *homogeneity* of a community. If homogeneity is regarded as the *crucial* factor for collective identity formation, a collective European identity formation based on the co-operation in the community would have poor prospects. However, if homogeneity is *not* considered an *indispensable* building block of a given community, the conclusion reached about the prospects of a European identity are different.

For the purposes of the present chapter, there can be no doubt that collective identity formation in Europe must overcome the challenge inherent in a heterogeneous, multicultural community. In this thinking, a European identity must be constructed along civil and political lines. But is this development a manifestation of the *will* of the European peoples? The answers to this question would certainly have great implications for the use of Union citizenship in the search for legitimacy.

The Will of the Peoples?

A striking feature when evaluating the European Community in general and European citizenship in particular is that it is inherently a *top-down* construction. Even when it comes to such fundamental questions as the foundation of a constitutional system – enshrined in the Courts claim of founding a new legal order – this has come about with literally no public debate at all. Indeed, this situation has led Joseph Weiler to conclude that 'the condition of Europe is not ... that of constitutionalism without a constitution, but of a constitution without constitutionalism' (Weiler, 1996: 518). Similarly, authors such as Soledad García (1992) and Paul Howe (1995) who are optimistic about the possibilities for development of a European identity. They both recognize that a Europe promoted and driven by elites will hardly gain the support of the peoples. Thus García states that:

> there is a danger in trying to construct a Europe in which public opinion is left
> behind by national or European elites. Such a legitimation deficit indicates that
> the European enterprise is not clearly justified in terms of citizens' beliefs and
> expectations (García, 1992: 2).

Likewise Howe argues that:

> the last 35 years may have seen the entrenchment of the European Community,
> but it is evident there has not yet been a parallel forging of a community of
> Europeans ... given the Community's emphasis on economic affairs and
> its generation of elite association, rather than interaction among ordinary
> Europeans. While there are plenty of Eurocrats comfortable with the idea of a
> community of Europeans, the cultural and social face of Western Europe has
> not changed dramatically since 1957 (Howe, 1995: 28).

The divide between the elites and the peoples is regarded as a major obstacle
for the development of a European identity, even by the authors who believe
that a European identity *is* imaginable. This observation prompts the question:
is the illegitimacy of the European construct solely or mainly linked to its
elitist character? Trying to answer this question involves great problems in how
to measure peoples' support for or attachment to political constructions. The
following will try to come around this through a combination of quantitative
and qualitative analysis of the Danish case. Notwithstanding the Danes'
reputation for being 'reluctant Europeans', the hope is that the outcome of
the reputation for being 'reluctant Europeans', the hope is that the outcome of
the analysis will not only characterize the Danish population, but in addition
point to some common features of the European peoples' perceptions, beliefs
and fears in relation to Europe.

The 'Danish Case' – The Odd Man Out?[11]

Denmark is a representative democracy where referendums are not widely
used, but somewhat of a political tradition have been established in the specific
case of the European Community. So far there have been four referendums on
this issue: in 1972 on joining the Community; 1986 on the Single European
Act; 1992 on the Maastricht Treaty; and 1993 on the Maastricht Treaty with
the opt-outs provided for in the so-called Edinburgh-agreement.[12]

Since joining the Community, the Danes have been divided on the issue. In 1992, the referendum on Maastricht turned out a 'no'. With a participation of 83.1 per cent of those entitled to vote, a majority of 50.7 per cent as opposed to 49.3 per cent voted against Maastricht (Svensson, 1994: 75; Haahr, 1992: 2).[13]

Whereas the immediate reaction of the Community was to continue the ratification process as foreseen, this mode of conduct was seriously challenged as the referendum started a debate highlighting the gap between the elites and the electorate and manifesting the public disquiet of the European 'project' (Laffan, 1996; Moxon-Browne, 1996; García, 1992; Curtin and van Ooik; 1994). The Danish referendum did not only cause turbulence in the Community as such, it also created problems domestically in several member states. Referendums on Maastricht were as mentioned held in both Ireland and France. In the former, the support was convincing, but in the latter there was a very small majority in favour of the Treaty. In the United Kingdom, John Major was forced to assure dissidents in his own party that the final decision on ratification would wait until after the second referendum in Denmark – a position that according to Elizabeth Meehan, caused 'dismay [among] his continental partners who believed that he as President of the European Council, should not imply that the UK position hinged upon that of the most reluctant ratifier' (Meehan, 1993: 42).

The Danish problem was addressed at the European Council meeting in Birmingham on 16 October 1992 (Curtin and van Ooik, 1994: 350). Here, the 'Birmingham Declaration on a Community close to its citizens' was issued, democracy, openness, and transparency in the Union.[14] The Declaration was followed up by the Danish so-called 'national compromise', a memorandum drafted by the Danish Parliament and dealing with the most important aspects of the public rejection of Maastricht (Curtin and Ooik, 1994: 350).

At the following European Council Summit meeting in mid-December, a 'decision' giving Denmark four opt-outs of the Maastricht Treaty reached agreement. The legal status of this 'Edinburgh agreement'[15] has been subject to discussion and will be addressed below. The decision on a second referendum on Maastricht was fixed for 18 May 1993 after the 'Edinburgh agreement' had been reached and a domestic turbulence leading to a change of government had been solved (Siune et al., 1994: 25–7).[16] This second referendum in 1993 increased the turnout to 86.5 per cent of the voters, with a majority of 56.7 per cent voting in favour and 43.3 per cent against (Svensson, 1994: 74–5). Denmark could finally ratify the Maastricht Treaty, albeit it in an atmosphere of severe turmoil.[17]

The 'National Compromise'

The domestic solution to the situation after the first referendum was the drafting of a memorandum by seven out of the eight parties in the *Folketing*[18] with only the extremely right (the Progress Party) standing outside. The decision making process leading up to the so-called 'national compromise' has been described as 'an extreme manifestation of the peculiar arrangements of Danish minority parliamentarism' (Svensson, 1994: 71).[19]

The key to the 'national compromise' lay with the Socialist People's Party, one of the two political parties that had been clearly against Maastricht in Parliament. Together with the Social-Democratic Party and the Social-Liberal Party an agreement was reached and presented to the government more or less as a *fait accompli* (ibid.; Siune et al., 1994: 23). The content was very much the common denominator of the views of the anti-Unionist People's Socialists and the lukewarm Social-Democrats and Social-Liberals combined with the presumed position of the Danish population (Petersen, 1993: 13). It demanded four exemptions from the European Union formulated as follows:

> (1) Denmark does not participate in the so-called defence policy dimension involving membership of the Western European Union and a common defence policy or common defence;
> (2) Denmark does not participate in the single currency and the economic policy obligations linked to the third stage of the EMU;
> (3) Denmark is not committed in relation to union citizenship; and
> (4) Denmark cannot accept the transfer of sovereignty in the area of justice and police affairs (quoted from Svensson, 1994: 71–2).

The exemption on Union citizenship which is of special interest here turned out to be particularly difficult to explain abroad. This was not least due to the fact that Denmark *already* allowed foreigners to stand for and vote in local elections; but in addition Denmark had no objections whatsoever to giving EC residents the right to vote and stand for European elections, just as it was unthinkable that EC citizens would not get diplomatic protection in third states if needed (ibid.: 15). This exemption on European citizenship was much more of a symbolic expression of the opposition to the creation of some kind of federal system in Europe, complete with citizenship and the like. The negative symbolic value attached to the concept of Union citizenship in public carried considerable weight in relation to the outcome of the second referendum in 1993.

The Legal Status of the Edinburgh Agreement

The most important legal question in relation to the 'Edinburgh agreement' is how the substance of the 'opt-outs' was evaluated. It was clearly indicated by the member states that the decision *is* meant to be legally binding, even if it is remarkable that the consent of the member states was not to be expressed by means of ratification insofar as signature was found sufficient. Denmark can at any time unilaterally revoke the decision or parts of it (Curtin and Ooik, 1994: 354). The four 'opt-outs' in the decision concerns justice and home affairs; foreign and security political; economic and monetary union; and union citizenship.

Justice and home affairs makes up the so-called third pillar of the Maastricht Treaty. The cooperation is mainly intergovernmental, and these provisions are fully applicable to Denmark. What the opt-out concerns is to a much larger extent the future of this cooperation. The Danish unilateral declaration states that since unanimity is required for the adoption of any decision in this field, such a decision therefore will have to be adopted in each member state in accordance with its constitutional arrangements (ibid.: 363; *Unilateral Declarations of Denmark*, reproduced in Rudden and Wyatt, 1994). That this should be the consequence is hardly surprising to anyone. The real significance of this opt-out is that before sovereignty is transferred in this field, a referendum will be held in accordance with the political tradition established.[20]

The co-operation in the field of *foreign and security policy* is contained in the second 'pillar' of the Treaty, and links the future development of a common defence policy to the Western European Union (WEU). However, Denmark is not a member of the WEU, and the decision states that nothing in the Maastricht Treaty commits it to *becoming* a member. As argued by Curtin and Ooik, this seems to follow implicitly from the Maastricht Treaty itself, and indeed at the time Denmark was not the only member state where the possibility of a compulsory membership of WEU would have been a problem, as Ireland is not a member either. Consequently, the opt-out serves first and foremost as a clarification of the Maastricht Treaty itself (ibid.: 363).

A similar interpretation applies to the opt-out on *economic and monetary union* (EMU). Denmark has stated that it will *not* participate in the third stage of the EMU. There is however, nothing in the Maastricht Treaty that obliges any member state to do so. The decision merely stated at this early point that Denmark would definitely not participate in the third stage of the EMU (Svensson, 1994: 72). Again, the opt-out serves the role of clarification rather than changing anything in substance (Curtin and Ooik, 1994: 361).

The picture is even more obscure when it comes to the opt-out on *citizenship*. As this is of special interest here, it seems worth quoting the wording of the decision in full:

> The provisions of Part Two of the Treaty establishing the European Community relating to citizenship of the Union give nationals of the Member States additional rights and protection as specified in that Part. They do not in any way take the place of national citizenship. The question whether an individual possesses the nationality of a Member State will be settled solely by reference to the national law of the Member State concerned (Decision of the Heads of State and Government, reproduced in Rudden and Wyatt, 1994: 213).[21]

In addition, Denmark stated that:

> Union Citizenship does not give a national of another Member State the right to obtain Danish citizenship or any of the rights, duties, privileges or advantages that are inherent in Danish citizenship by virtue of Denmark's constitutional, legal and administrative rules. Denmark will fully respect all specific rights expressly provided for in the Treaty and applying to nationals of the Member States (ibid.: 216).

As is apparent there is no reference made to *any* kind of exception from the provisions contained in Union citizenship. Denmark is *fully* bound to the whole of article 8-8E, and as mentioned some of the new provisions were indeed already established in Denmark before the Maastricht negotiations. All this leads Curtin and Ooik (1994: 350) to the conclusion that 'it is submitted therefore that the oft-repeated assertion that "Denmark does not accept the idea of European citizenship" is not correct'. This is surely the case when it comes to the legal implications of the decision, but it is a quite different matter when it comes to the political implications. The decision is first and foremost a symbolic rejection of the *idea* (Svensson, 1994: 72).

That the opt-out on citizenship served a purely political purpose is recognized by Curtin and Ooik, who furthermore suggest that the opt-out gave an entirely *different meaning* to citizenship in the public debate (Curtin and Ooik, 1994: 350). As will be seen shortly, this argument holds a strong value. This notwithstanding, there is one legal problem of the Danish unilateral declaration. It also states that:

> Nothing in the Treaty on European Union implies or foresees an undertaking to create a citizenship of the Union in the sense of citizenship of a nation-state. The question of Denmark participating in any such development does,

therefore, not arise (Unilateral Declaration of Denmark, reproduced in Rudden and Wyatt, 1994: 216).

This statement is problematic insofar as European citizenship continuously is being described as a dynamic concept and because there *are* voices advocating a seriously expanded European citizenship.[22] However, if concrete proposals should arise under Article 8b or 8a, these can only be adopted with Denmark's consent, as such a measure requires unanimity (Curtin and Ooik, 1994: 350–51). Here, the Danish declaration clearly states the very firm oppositions to any such development.

In the run up to the second Maastricht referendum, the 'Edinburgh agreement' was very much presented to Danish population by the supporters as containing important concessions. However, the Maastricht Treaty itself was not amended, and consequently no change of the text had to be carried out. The 'Edinburgh agreement' merely interpreted or clarified the Treaty on the issues of citizenship, foreign and security policy, and justice and home affairs. As for the EMU, the agreement 'activated a right that was contained in the Treaty' from the outset. As Curtin and Ooik argue (1994: 364), the fact that no national parliamentary ratification of the decision took place. demonstrates that the decision did not give Denmark any right that was not already contained in the Maastricht Treaty itself. The text the population had to vote on in the second referendum was exactly the same as in the referendum of 1992 – the Maastricht Treaty.

Nevertheless, the second referendum brought about the 'desired' result – a 'yes' to the Maastricht Treaty. The question that arises is how important the 'opt-outs' in general, and the opt-out on citizenship in particular, were for this outcome.

The Maastricht Referendums 1992 and 1993

The debate before the first referendum in 1992 was heavily preoccupied with political cooperation in the Community. This embraced the discussion of surrender of sovereignty as opposed to 'influence' on European affairs, and counted the 'Union' as the single subject most referred to. However, during the course of the campaign there was a growing debate about the economic consequences if the referendum turned out a 'no' (Siune and Svensson, 1992: 41).

In the short campaign before the second referendum in 1993, the supporters maintained that Denmark had obtained important exceptions to the Maastricht

Treaty. The supporters included at this point basically the whole political establishment as all political parties in Parliament but one advocated a 'yes' following the changed position of the People's Socialist Party. In addition, those in favour included almost all major interest organizations and all the major newspapers (Svensson, 1992: 73). Against this, the Progress Party and the two anti-Union grassroots *organizations, the June Movement*[23] and *the People's Movement against the* EC, argued that the agreement did not represent anything new and that more integrative initiatives would emerge shortly, forcing Denmark to 'take it or leave it' (ibid.).

The net change between the two referendums was no more than 7.4 per cent, and this obviously has to include people that did not participate in both elections, so half of the population was still opposed to the Maastricht Treaty – with or without opt-outs (Siune et al., 1994: 95). It is not the purpose here to give a very detailed explanation of the pattern of the votes. Suffice it to point to the general socioeconomic divides within the population as well as the main reasons behind the turn-out.

Reluctant Europeans

The Danes are often referred to as 'reluctant Europeans'. This has not least to do with the lack of identification with Europe. In a number of studies carried out in 1992 and 1994, the Danes are described as having a very limited sense of European identity and community, and that the basic orientation towards the EU is a feeling of powerlessness, almost amounting to fatalism (Goul Andersen and Hoff, 1992; Nielsen, 1992; Worre, Nielsen and Goul Andersen, 1994). Thus, when asked about whether they felt as much as Europeans as Danes, an overwhelming majority of 75 per cent disagreed, and 52 per cent believe that '*no matter which government is in office, it will be the EC that determines what shall happen in this country in the future*', with only 33 per cent disagreeing (Goul Andersen and Hoff, 1992: 11–12). The lack of European identity is however not a purely Danish phenomenon. In a *Eurobarometer* from 1991 the Germans, the Dutch, the Irish and the British had an even smaller score than the Danes on European identification (*Eurobarometer*, reproduced in Nielsen, 1992: 379). In addition, there is nothing that suggests that the Danes should be *poorer* Europeans in terms of interest in or knowledge of the EU than other European populations, as the Danes continuously have been among the populations that knew most about the Community (Goul Andersen, 1994: 55–6).

What seems to set the Danes apart from the rest of Europe is thus not the lack of identification or knowledge of the Community. Rather, it has to do with a very strong attachment to their own country – 84 per cent feel a strong attachment to Denmark. This percentage tops the list, together with the Greeks, whereas the French and the Germans have 46–47 per cent feeling strong attachment, and the Belgians only 30 per cent (ibid: 56–7). A number of possible explanations for this strong attachment is dealt with below. Here, the question is how this population of reluctant Europeans voted on Maastricht. A number of studies have dealt with this question, and the data show the pattern in Table 3.1 when it comes to the behaviour of major social and political groups. It shows how the tendency to vote 'no' is more widespread among women than men; middle aged more than young or older; workers and public employed more than private and self-employed (Siune, 1992; Svensson, 1994; Siune and Svensson, 1992; Siune, Svensson and Tonsgaard, 1994).

These data supplied are clearly tendencies rather than clear-cut divisions according to socioeconomic criteria. The difference between men and women and various age-groups do not sum up to more than 13 percentage points. Also remarkable is the fact that education has no relevance for how people vote. The most significant division is found when it comes to political affiliation and interest. As regards the former, there is a tendency for voters on the left side of the spectrum to be more opposed than on the right, provided that the Progress Party is left out of consideration.[24] What is interesting in this picture is the extent to which the voters followed the recommendations of their party. The Socialist People's Party was in line with its voters in the first referendum, where it as mentioned advocated a 'no', but it hardly convinced any of its voters to follow the change as regards the second referendum. In addition, the Social-Democratic Party, the centre parties and the Progress Party all had huge problems convincing their voters to follow the party line. Overall, the voters behaved quite independently of their party in the referendums.

An interesting aspect in Table 3.1 is the parameter measuring political interest. Where the difference between the most and the least interested according to the 'no' percentage in the first referendum was almost 30 percentage points, there is almost no difference at all in the second, first and foremost because of a significant shift among the least interested from 'no' to 'yes'. Apparently this group was the most receptive to the arguments of the 'establishment' stating that the 'Edinburgh agreement' did constitute something new, and that the consequences of a 'no' would be severe.

Another important trend can be found in individual attitudes of the voters towards EU integration. Table 3.2 identifies the main ideological attitudes towards EC integration according to areas to be included in EC cooperation.

Table 3.1   Referendum behaviour of social and political groups 1992 and 1993. Percentage voting 'no'

	1993	1992
All	50 (N=699)	42 (N=905)
Men	47 (N=376)	39 (N=444)
Women	54 (N=323)	44 (N=461)
18–29 years	44 (N=172)	43 (N=206)
30–49 years	57 (N=225)	46 (N=398)
50 years	49 (N=301)	35 (N=300)
Basic school	52 (N=286)	41 (N=348)
Grammar school/O-levels	47 (N=240)	42 (N=329)
High school/A-levels	52 (N=171)	42 (N=226)
Unskilled workers	65 (N= 84)	51 (N= 85)
Skilled workers	46 (N= 88)	48 (N=131)
Public white collar without high school	60 (N= 70)	48 (N= 87)
Public white collar with high school	54 (N= 48)	47 (N= 57)
Private white collar without high school	36 (N= 74)	25 (N=109)
Private white collar with high school	39 (N= 37)	20 (N= 51)
Self-employed	34 (N= 48)	27 (N= 64)
Very much interested in politics	47 (N=125)	39 (N=151)
Somewhat interested in politics	49 (N=317)	42 (N=527)
Only a little interested in politics	51 (N220)	42 (N=204)
Not at all interested in politics	76 (N= 34)	37 (N= 22)
Socialist People's Party	92 (N= 79)	81 (N=100)
Social Democrats	64 (N=207)	50 (N=263)
Centre parties	38 (N= 33)	37 (N= 78)
Conservatives	13 (N= 68)	18 (N=156)
Liberals	18(N=144)	12(N=161)
Progress Party	55 (N= 24)	69 (N= 38)

Note: The centre parties comprise the Social Liberals, the Centre Democrats and the Christian
     People's Party.

Source: Svensson (1994: 78).

Table 3.2 reveals two important features. There is a clear pattern in the overall orientation towards integration, showing economic integration to be favoured by a majority of the population, whereas the level of support declines the more political the integration becomes. In addition, this orientation is very

Table 3.2   Areas to be included in EC cooperation. Percentage

	May 1993	May 1992	June 1992
Breaking down barriers of trade/customs tariffs	61	69	65
The Single Market	59	74	71
The Economic and Monetary Union	45	53	42
Levelling economic differences between EC countries	42	49	43
Common foreign policy	38	38	37
Common defence policy	37	30	34
Single currency	35	34	23
The social dimension	33	39	41
Establishing the United States of Europe	23	19	21
Common citizenship	15	13	14

Source: Svensson (1994: 79).

stable over time. The support for a single market is the only single parameter, where the support changes more than 10 percentage points.[25]

The single point of most interest here is the orientation towards a common citizenship. As the table shows, more than 85 per cent of the population rejects the idea. The opposition is much stronger on this issue than on the other opt-outs included in the table; economic and monetary union, where there actually was a majority in favour at the time of the first referendum; and common foreign and security policy, which is opposed by 62 per cent to 70 per cent of the population in the period starting just before the first referendum to the time of the second.[26]

This might lead to the conclusion that the politicians were right when they pointed to these areas as something that had to be clarified if the population was to support Maastricht in the second referendum. It seems worth investigating whether the explanation is really that straightforward.

The Significance of the 'Opt-outs'

When discussing the relevance of the opt-outs for the second referendum, it has to be kept in mind that only a very small group of people changed their voting behaviour. As mentioned, the net change was only 7.4 percentage points, which covers the fluctuations shown in Table 3.3.

Table 3.3   The voters according to behaviour in 1992 compared to 1993. Percentage

No–No	35%
Yes–Yes	41%
No–Yes	10%
Yes–No	2%
Other	12%

Source: Siune et al. (1994: 95).

As can be seen, it was not more than 10 per cent who changed their view from 'no' to 'yes'. This group is obviously the key to the outcome of the second referendum, since the vast majority of the population – 76 per cent – did not change its views on Maastricht after the 'Edinburgh agreement'. The question is which reasons the decisive 10 per cent had for changing opinion. These are listed in Table 3.4.

Table 3.4   Reasons for changing from 'no' in 1992 to 'yes' in 1993. Percentage that had the answer as first reason, and percentage that mentioned the answer in all. Number in all = 948

	In all	First reason
Employment	20	28
Additional economic reasons	15	25
'Edinburgh agreement'	19	19
Otherwise we would have been isolated in Europe	16	20
We cannot continue voting 'no'	5	6
Regret without further explanation	2	2
1992 'no' has had its effect	–	1
Other	19	24
Do not know	4	*
Do not want to answer	–	*

Note: * = the figure cannot occur.

Source: Siune et al. (1994: 132).

It follows from Table 3.4 that for 35 per cent of the voters the most important reason to change opinion was out of economic considerations, whereas for 19 per cent it was determined by the 'Edinburgh agreement'. For almost a quarter of the people changing from 'no' to 'yes' the reasons were more diffuse, insofar as it had to do with feeling insecure about the future of Denmark in a European context if it was to be a 'no' again. This leads Karen Siune, Palle Svensson and Ole Tonsgaard to conclude that the 'Edinburgh-agreement' had the effect of making the political aspects of the Maastricht Treaty less frightening, so that the priority made between economic gains and sovereignty changed between 1992 and 1993 for a decisive group of voters (Siune et al., 1994: 135–6). In the words of Karen Siune:

> The opt-outs did matter, because the Danes felt they could dig their heels in. In this way, the opt-outs had a very strong psychological effect in areas that were sensitive for the population. But it was only a limited number that changed their opinion, because the confidence in the politicians was limited. So there was a big group of very concerned people [about political cooperation], but also some that were only modestly concerned. And it was some of the latter who changed their minds (Karen Siune, interview).

This view is shared by Ove Fich, spokesman for the Social-Democratic Party on European Affairs and present chairman of the parliamentary committee on the EU. As shown in Table 3.1, the major shift in 'no' percentage between the two referendums took place within the Social-Democratic Party. As this is the biggest Danish party, it also made up for the greatest shift in real figures:

> The areas of the opt-outs were considered as three blank cheques which the population did not want to sign. The EMU was the only thing that was not considered as such. In addition, there had been a change of government between the referendums, which possibly played a great role for the social democratic voters. Do they have confidence in the person who advocates a yes? They had no confidence in Uffe [Ellemann-Jensen] (Ove Fich, interview).[27]

The four opt-outs were to a certain extent dictated by the Socialist People's Party that viewed them as 'not only symbolizing, but also carrying the development of the Union. If these four areas were taken out, there would be no development towards a Union' (Gert Petersen, interview). However, the party had as seen severe difficulties convincing their voters to vote 'yes' in the second referendum. Table 3.1 shows that only 11 percentage points supported the line of the party and changed their vote. This is explained by former party leader Gert Petersen in the following way:

> [Our voters] were apparently more occupied with bloodying the EU's nose. They do not like the EU. It is as simple as that. This view has been developed over 20 years or so. So they were not ready to compromise and accept a development with strong integrative elements … the opt-outs stand firm, but the question is whether they are sufficient for people (Gert Petersen, interview).

That the opt-outs are indeed insufficient is a view held by the opponents, counting the Progress Party – 'the opt-outs are not worth the piece of paper they are written on' (Annette Just, interview) and the List of Unity, the latter entering into parliament after the general election in 1994.[28] These two parties make up the extreme wings in the Danish Parliament. Also the two major anti-EU grass-root organizations (the June Movement and the People's Movement against the EC), both non-parliamentarian, share the perception of the in-sufficiency of the opt-outs. Hence, to a question on whether the List of Unity regarded the four opt-outs as covering the most important areas, Keld Albrechtsen (the List of Unity) replies:

> The reason why we could not support the 'Edinburgh agreement' was that it still included the Maastricht Treaty and that it did not hinder the other member states in integrating further in the four areas. The opt-outs are decisive and important because a common coin, military, and police are the core of national sovereignty – which of course goes for citizenship as well. Thus, for us it is of vital importance that the EU cannot regulate these areas. But there are a range of other things in relation to the Union which are not acceptable (Keld Albrechtsen, interview).

Similarly, Drude Dahlerup from the June Movement reasons:

> It is clear that for the opponents the development towards a common defence and a common military has always been a vital point, because these are the characteristic of building a new state … And that is what is being build even if it is called something else. It is of course not a state as yet, but it is starting to look like one. This was why we were opposed to Maastricht … When the opt-outs were on the table, we answered that it all looked very well, but that we were not sure that they would be kept. And that is exactly what we see today. This is the time to stand tall. But the new Treaty is undermining all of these areas (Drude Dahlerup, interview).

A very different view is found among the centre and bourgeois parties, where the opt-outs are considered as having a *symbolic* value, rather than real substance – especially regarding the opt-out on citizenship. Thus Henning Grove, member of the European Committee for the Conservative People's Party argues:

> I believe a number of conservative voters, had the feeling that a Union Citizenship would take over Danish citizenship the minute it was introduced. And that was not acceptable. People are supportive of political co-operation. but they do not want to be part of the United States of Europe. They had fear. I can for my part try to explain that it has nothing to do with that. but people do not believe me. They say it is too close to Danish citizenship and that they do not want it (Henning Grove, interview).

A similar observation is made by the EU spokeswoman for the Social-Liberal Party, Elisabeth Arnold:

> There has been a lot of psychology involved for the Danes. I must say I was surprised when the Socialist People's party had the opt-out on Union citizenship as a condition for advocating a 'yes'. I wondered why, since we had already implemented all the rules as regards voting rights … But later I realized how much it had to do with the symbolism. It has to do with that citizenship spells creation of a state. And those overtones have of course been used vehemently by the People's Movement Against the EC and the June Movement (Elisabeth Arnold, interview).

It is interesting that representatives for *all* political parties and the two grassroots-movements agree with the view that the opt-outs had a totally different meaning in public than what was the real content. This goes for both opponents, who viewed the opt-outs as insufficient and supporters, who regard the significance as symbolic more then anything else. Bent Brier (the People's Movement against the EC) formulates it the following way:

> It was psychological factors much more than the opt-outs as such that made the difference. But the opt-out were maintained cleverly – there is no doubt that the 'Edinburgh-agreement' was sold [to the people] as having decisive importance for Denmark. The opt-outs had a different meaning in public. They gained a market value they did not deserve (Bent Brier, interview).

This is acknowledged among the supporters as well. Hence, Ove Fich (the Social-Democratic Party) replies to a question on whether the opt-out on citizenship had a distinctive different meaning in public as follows:

> Yes, I believe this is true. In fact I believe it was decisive. When I explained the real content of citizenship, people replied 'is it nothing else?'. Many thought that citizenship was a replacement for national citizenship (Ove Fich, interview).

In this way, the supporters regard the symbolic value as signifying a kind of assurance for the population that European integration would not get out of control, where the opponents very much view it as a way of luring the population into changing its vote. The 'opt-outs' were the main reason for the shift from 'no' to 'yes' for 10 per cent of the voting population. The idea of European citizenship is rejected by more than 85 per cent of the whole population – it is thus the most unpopular integrative proposal included in Table 3.2, also when compared with the two other opt-outs listed. It therefore seems very likely that this particular opt-out had an importance of its own, even if the data do count the opt-outs as *one* in Table 3.4.

However, when it comes to evaluating *why* European citizenship is an important opt-out, there are two lines of arguments. For the opponents to Maastricht, Union citizenship is a significant element in the building up of a state-like entity. When Maastricht was still rejected after the 'Edinburgh agreement' it was because this group did not regard the agreement as sufficient.

Among the supporters, the evaluation is quite different. Here, the view is that the opt-out on Union citizenship first and foremost is of symbolic relevance, as it lowered the fear among the voters that the introduction of Union citizenship would constitute the first step on a slide towards a United States of Europe, if not even a manifestation of it. This argument is summed up by Karen Siune as follows:

> It was a reaction against Union citizenship as a symbol. It is not the substance that people react against – it is wholly citizenship as a symbol. So when investigating the causality, you need to go via the negative perception of the political union. It is not only a step towards the Union; it is viewed as the result of a political union. You get an extreme reaction on something that in substance is nothing. It becomes a concrete manifestation of the negative evaluation of the Union. It is the supranational aspect that people are reacting against (Karen Siune, interview).

As has been argued, Denmark is fully obliged as regards the provisions in European citizenship. The opt-out on citizenship is therefore nothing more than an rejection of the *label* 'European citizenship'. If this is held against the motives and ambitions laying behind the initiatives in the field of European citizenship, somewhat of a double paradox seems to appear.

The Paradox

It has been maintained that the initiatives on European citizenship can be viewed as a strategy for strengthening the legitimacy of the Union. But European citizenship was still rejected by the Danish population. This constitutes the first part of the double paradox that arises out of the Danish case. Why did an initiative explicitly aimed at creating legitimacy turn out to have quite the opposite effect in one of the member states?

The question does not become less intriguing when it is remembered that Denmark 'will fully respect all specific rights expressly provided for in the Treaty and applying to nationals of the member states' (*Unilateral Declaration of Denmark*, reproduced in Rudden and Wyatt, 1994: 216). Indeed, Denmark has been a strong advocate for granting the right to vote and stand for local and European elections. The previous section has pointed to the fact that citizenship is being rejected because of the *symbolism* inherent in the concept. This points to the second part of the paradox. Where does the strong reaction against the *label* 'European citizenship' originate?

The two sides of the paradox will be addressed in reversed order below, as it seems that the answer to the latter will provide some of the explanation for the former.

Rejecting a Label

When addressing the question of why European citizenship had to be one of the four opt-outs to convince a sufficient number of Danes to change their view on Maastricht, the political actors all evaluate the significance of this particular opt-out as one of *symbolic importance* more than anything else. There is a difference between supporters and opponents when it comes to evaluate the symbolism – for the former it has to do with a groundless fears in the population, whereas the opponents view citizenship as a symbol of a Union aiming at the creation of a new European state.

One aspect that needs to be pointed out when discussing the strength of the word 'European citizenship' in a Danish context is linguistic. There is no direct translation for the word 'citizenship'. In Danish, a national citizen is a 'burgher of the state' [*statsborger*]. Consequently, the first translation of European citizenship into Danish was 'burghership of the state of the Union' [*unionsstatsborgerskab*], later modified to 'burghership of the Union' [*unionsborgerskab*]. This sheds some light on how the concept could be misinterpreted as meaning that one had to be citizen of Europe rather than of Denmark.

But pointing to the symbolic importance does not answer why the symbolism is so strong. What are the Danes afraid of losing? The elements pointed to by the political actors cluster around three areas; state-culture, the welfare system and the national identity. The sum of these elements can to a certain extent be viewed as a description of the particularity of the Danish society – what makes Denmark *Denmark* in the eyes of the people. The strong attachment that the Danes feel towards Denmark can therefore be sought in the values described below.

The state-culture In an article arguing that the Danish rejection of Maastricht in 1992 has to be found in the specific way the Danish state was built historically and the culture surrounding it today, Tim Knudsen (1992) links these features to the concept of 'state-culture', which he defines the following way:

> 'State-culture' is here understood as not only the political and administrative institutions (including the informal, nonverbalized 'givens' surrounding these), but also as the relationship of political-administrative institutions and the culture of a country (Knudsen, 1992: 263).

In this understanding the state-culture for each country influences the approach which the country takes toward European integration (ibid.). The historical development of the Danish state-culture has developed from an era of absolutism (1660–1848), marked by heavy rearmament and a strong state-building process to later stages characterized by 'liberalization, popular participation, reorientation from warfare to welfare, decentralization, and tightly knitted connections and integration between the public and the private sector' (ibid.: 290). This has resulted in a state that can be portrayed as characterized by continuity, homogeneity and with a strong tradition for consensual democracy, where a maximum agreement is sought before political decisions are taken. It is a state with high welfare ambitions paid by high rates of tax (ibid.: 288–9).

According to the political actors, the Danish history in general, and the national tradition of state and democracy in particular, are part of the reason for the strong reaction towards European citizenship. Hence, Peter Duetoft, spokesman on European Affairs for the Centre-Democratic Party, argues:

It is only eccentrics that fly the EU flag in Denmark, unless there is a commercial reason to do it. [The other Europeans] have another perception, another cultural tradition. In addition, they have historical experiences that make them more supportive of the Community than us – they had to pay at the time when there was no Community. So my vicious comment to the Danish view is that it is bloody easy, when all that happened here was that we most graciously were saved from a position as the Germans helpers … For them the Community is necessary, whereas it simply denotes something troublesome with a bureaucracy for the Danes. It most certainly has to do with our 'easy' history (Peter Duetoft, interview).

For the opponents, the main issue is the lack of democracy in the EU and the limited role of the people. Drude Dahlerup, spokeswoman for the June-Movement, argues:

Not only people's perception of, but also their real influence on decisions that affect them, is being undermined. The political power has been transferred from elected politicians to bureaucrats … Here, there is a historical balance in the national context … In addition there is the lack of transparency [in the Union]. Legislation is taking place behind closed doors, and secret protocols interpreting the legislation are being made. It constitutes a very severe attack on the rule of law. And it feeds the powerlessness that many people feel as regard the EU (Drude Dahlerup, interview).

A similar argument is adduced by Keld Albrechtsen (The List of Unity) and Bent Brier (the People's Movement against the EC):

If the goal is a federation or a union, the minimal requirement in my view is a genuine constitutional debate, so the union develops because the people wants it to develop … But such a debate is impossible in Europe, when the Treaties are created the way they are. Therefore the risk is that the integration process carries on and the people feels more an more alienated. And this will by guaranty not stimulate any kind of loyalty or identity. On the contrary, it will stimulate a deep and profound and increasing opposition (Keld Albrechtsen, interview).

There is a big group of people, who are worried about the rule of the people [*folkestyret*]. The *Folkestyre* depends on the existence of a people – a people that feels like a people. And a number of very politically interested people feel that this is being undermined … I believe our existence as an independent people is at stake … If the democratisation of the EU, as it is called, is continued with more power to the European Parliament, then you only have to look at the numbers. Our possibility for organizing the society the way we want to would disappear (Bent Brier, interview).

The strong emphasis on the lack of democracy and public debate held by the opponents touches on very sensitive issues in a Danish context, as the self perception is one of a state-culture characterized by extensive public participation and consensus. The strong criticism on these issues has been very hard to counter for the supporters, as the arguments for supporting European integration always have been set forward in terms of economic interests and benefits. Ideological reasons for uniting Europe has never played a significant part. In fact, the debate before the first Maastricht referendum was the first were the Community as such was defined in political more than economic terms.

The welfare system It is well-known that Denmark has a wide-ranging, tax-based welfare system. According to the interviews conducted with the political parties and the grass-roots organizations, there is a strong fear among certain parts of the population that European integration will lead to a undermining of the social rights in the welfare state. This view is supported by a survey carried out in 1991 and 1993, where a percentage of 45 per cent going down to 43 per cent in 1993 agreed that it will be difficult to sustain the Danish welfare system in the EU (Goul Andersen, 1994: 56). In the referendums, this fear was primarily found among the voters on the political left. Ove Fich (the Social-Democratic Party) argues:

> People guard the welfare system, and those that find themselves on the margin of the labour market or of a social context know they need it fundamentally. Two aspects were regarded as posing a danger – one was Union citizenship, because the perception was, to be quite blunt, that a great number of people could use our system and thereby undermine it. There they were wrong, but this was the perception. The other factor was the EMU. People were not against a common coin or a central bank. It was an instinctive reaction ... They asked: What will happen in hard times? Will I get any pension? (Ove Fich, interview).

This view is supported by Keld Albrechtsen (the List of Union) and Gert Petersen (the Socialist People's Party), both representing left-wing parties:

> I am convinced that the reason why the opposition to Union citizenship was so massive has to do with that people do not consider themselves to be citizens of the Union, but of Denmark, and they do not want to consider the Union as their country neither legally nor symbolically. There is a strong element of

fundamental values buried here ... In addition they fear that Union citizenship will comprise rights and duties – especially social rights. If social rights became a part of Union citizenship, then this would render the tax-financed systems impossible. This would have great implications for Denmark, where the tax-financed system has had such an impact and where the support of the welfare state with a tax-based pension for all is so strong. The lowest common denominator would prevail if social rights were part of Union citizenship. The fear of this has been decisive in a Danish context (Keld Albrechtsen, interview).

[The population] thought that Denmark would have to finance the social rights throughout Europe in countries that had done nothing about it themselves. This is obviously a very primitive line of thought, but so was the perception (Gert Petersen, interview).

The fear of losing social benefits is the element that makes the clearest distinction between people on the left and right wing of the political spectrum, insofar as it is most outspoken by the socialist parties. This is not very surprising considering that the political agenda of these parties is based on safeguarding the welfare state. For the bourgeois parties, concern for the welfare state is not considered an essential element of the negative reaction towards Union citizenship.

National identity A final element in the rejection of Union citizenship as a symbol involves national identity. A number of the representatives from the political parties notice a fear of being absorbed as a nation in the Danish reaction. This fear seems to have very much to do with the tiny size of the Danish nation. Gert Petersen (the Socialist People's Party) describes it the following way:

There is a historically founded fear of being absorbed. We are a small people. From a historical point of view it is quite amazing that Denmark is a sovereign state. Jutland is literally a peninsula on Germany, and the islands have so often been part of Sweden, that is it a miracle they are now Danish. It is quite simply a fear of disappearing (Gert Petersen, interview).

Elisabeth Arnold (the Social-Liberal Party) links this view to a certain amount of nationalism among the opponents:

The fact that we are a small, homogenous population is very important. This is a small country with a big neighbour, which existence has not always been guaranteed. We have been occupied and under threat of being absorbed. It

also links to the Danish history of the 'high school'[29] movement. It is built
on broad-mindedness, vision and knowledge and that the whole people should
be educated. But it is also very nationalistic. It is well known that some of the
outstanding people from the 'high school' movement are fierce opponents. They
are also very nationalistic. So there is a core of nationalism in the opposition
(Elisabeth Arnold, interview).

The spokespersons on European affairs of the Progress Party and the
Conservative People's Party speak of concerns for Danish identity in an
even more direct way. Insofar as the people's concern on this issue is being
acknowledged by a number of the political actors, it is most clearly spoken of
as a *threat* by the Conservative People's Party and the Progress Party. Annette
Just (the Progress Party) states:

> We do not want to be absorbed by the Union. We want to preserve King and
> Country. We want to maintain our sovereignty (Annette Just, interview).

Similarly Henning Grove (the Conservative People's Party):

> People are afraid of the United States of Europe ... The larger countries'
> cultures will be dominating. Think of the Baltic States and the Soviet Union
> ... They have just dissolved a Union and everybody is happy (Henning Grove,
> interview).

The rejection of European citizenship as a *label is* partly grounded in the
state-culture with its historical experience and its tradition of participatory
democracy, a fear of the future of the welfare system and – to a lesser extent
– a fear of being absorbed as a nation. This has obviously nothing to do
with the actual content in Union citizenship – it is a reaction founded on the
associations people get from the word 'citizenship'.

In this respect the opt-out on citizenship certainly had significance. Being
described as a legal mirage (Curtin and van Ooik, 1994: 364), it nevertheless
underlined the point that Union citizenship was not to replace Danish
citizenship. There is strong reason to believe that this particular opt-out had
a totally different meaning in the public perception than in reality. Indeed, this
is a view supported by *all* those interviewed. Ove Fich (the Social-Democratic
Party) formulates it this way:

> The name was decisive for the outcome ... I believe that if the label had been
> more cleverly worked out there would not have been any problem. It was

purely the symbolism in the name that people reacted against. The failure lay in the name (Ove Fich, interview).

One side of the paradox – why the Danes rejected a label rather than the substance of European citizenship – must accordingly be explained in terms of symbolism. What remains to be addressed is why the Danes reacted with rejection towards a Community policy that was aimed at promoting legitimacy among the peoples of Europe.

Rejecting a Policy

When asked how come a policy initiated to promote legitimacy had the opposite effect in Denmark, David O'Keeffe replied that it had to do with the process itself being constructed 'top-down'. Where citizenship rights had historically been achieved through struggle, this was not the case in the Community. At the Union level, the situation was one where the institutions granted the rights to the citizens – the rights did not arise out of any demand.[30] As will be apparent shortly, this explanation is most probable true. The task here is therefore to try and answer the question set out earlier in this article. Is the Union a result of the will of the people?

An elitist project That the illegitimacy of the integration process in a Danish context has to do with its top-down construction is a view clearly expressed in the vast majority of the interviews conducted for this study. It is interpreted as one of the most fundamental problems of the integration process. Elisabeth Arnold (the Social-Liberal Party) argues that this point constitutes the fundamental divide in a Danish context:

> It is a tremendous problem that the EU has become such an elitist project. Even here, in the *Folketing*, it is primarily the political elite that is supportive … Part of the difficulty is that the pattern in the population is not found in the *Folketing*. The fierce opponents are found on the extreme wings, it is not the broad opposition found among half of the population (Elisabeth Arnold, interview).

Keld Albrechtsen (the list of Unity) notices the same line of division between the elite and the population at large:

> The elite of the society has a fundamentally different view on European issues than the majority of the population, and the divide becomes increasingly bigger,

as the elite consists of civil servants, people from the major organizations and all sorts of experts agree that we need a common coin and a common policy of justice and so forth, even if the public opinion is totally different ... The lesson from previous years is that the people, with reason, are very sceptical and become accordingly aggressive, when they realize that the signals sent in the referendums are not being taken note of – they are simply not being perceived and the elite is carrying on regardless, using an argumentation that is totally foreign to the population ... This causes an irritation and an opposition that makes the dialogue wither away. I feel it at meetings of electoral colleges – the population stuff their ears with straw when the politicians talk about the EU, it does not believe what we say. I feel this even though I am an opponent (Keld Albrechtsen, interview).

The problem of a lack of democratic debate pointed out by Keld Albrechtsen is also being recognized by Drude Dahlerup (the June Movement) and Gert Petersen (the Socialist People's Party). Drude Dahlerup argues:

One of my main objections is that there is no European public. There is no dialogue between the European peoples and the people in power. It is sending us 200 years back in time to when the people had no say at all (Drude Dahlerup, interview).

Gert Petersen argues that the lack of democratic debate is the *primary* reason why a European identity in his view is impossible in the foreseeable future. Responding to a question on whether he can envisage the formation of a European identity along civic lines and promoted through European citizenship, he replies:

It is an impossibility. The system would break down under the process. Why? Simply because there are fundamental differences of language that are much more far-reaching than most intellectuals and semi-intellectuals, who are occupied with this and who all speak English, imagine ... The prerequisite for a nation-wide debate is that people understand each other, that they can communicate. We cannot communicate in the same way with Italians and Spaniards ... The '*folkelige*' [public] debate cannot keep pace. It will not emerge. It is not there. It is a top-down process and I believe it is impossible. As you mentioned, it is a problem for the EU that people do not feel it concerns them. But you cannot force it to happen through legislation. This was neither the way it happened in our democracy. Here, it emerged out of popular movements and debates. There is no European movement among the majority of the people. It may happen among the best educated, the most knowledgeable, the most well-read 5–10 per cent, but not among the rest. Maybe in a hundred or two hundred years. But not today (Gert Petersen, interview).

The analysis provided by these politicians demonstrates that the European Community is regarded as an elitist project among a very big part of the population, and that this to a great extent is grounded in the lack of public debate. According to Gert Petersen, this debate is very unlikely to emerge. This is a vital point. If the lack of a common language in the broad layers of the European peoples constitutes the core of the problem, this would have devastating consequences for the future political, and democratic integration in Europe.

There seems to be little doubt that the EU, at least in a Danish context, is considered an elitist project, having nothing to do with the will of the people. The process is entirely top-down leading to situations where a Treaty is presented to the population as a *fait accompli*. In this respect European citizenship did not merely constitute a policy that the population was indifferent towards, as has been suggested by Hans Ulrich Jessurun d'Oliveira (1995). In a Danish context, it symbolized a *policy* that large parts of the population were fiercely opposed to. This link to the last point that needs to be evaluated, which is whether the Danes want to be Europeans.

European identity undesired   It has been argued that Danes do not identify strongly with Europe. In addition, the clear conclusion drawn by the studies of the Maastricht referendums by Karen Siune, Palle Svensson and Ole Tonsgaard referred to above was that the Danes in general evaluated the EU according to two parameters – the political and the economical aspects of European cooperation – where the former as a general trend was regarded negatively and the latter positively. The decisive factor in how people voted was the priority between the parameters. Together, these two trends seem to suggest that the Danes consciously do not want to become 'Europeans', which they understand as identifying themselves as Europeans. And they certainly do not want to have European symbols imposed on them. This view is supported by a number of the political actors. Elisabeth Arnold (the Social-Liberal Party) formulates it the following way:

> I am an opponent of a community-feeling that is being imposed on people. This has been on the agenda from the early years where an anthem, and a European sports-team and other forms of catchpenny were supposed to encourage a community-feeling. I believe it will have the effect of a boomerang insofar as

it will have the opposite result. People become irritated when a community-feeling is being forced upon them, it is regarded as propaganda. Especially the Danes do not like this kind of symbolism. They want *Dannebrog*[31] and nothing else. A soccer team is also OK, but it has to be Danish. It is not supposed to be a EU-team (Elisabeth Arnold, interview).

Her view is supported by Bent Brier (the People's Movement against the EC) answering a question on the Danish reaction on the attempts at creating a European identity:

> [Such attempts] will have the opposite outcome in a Danish context. We know that the EU was working on organizing a common entry at the Olympics, and there has been plans of creating a EU-team. But imagine that such a team would replace the individual countries – you would find the Danes on the barricades immediately. Indeed we [the opponents] would not need other cases. The minor part of the population we still need would support us (Bent Brier, interview).

A more forceful view is taken by Drude Dahlerup (the June Movement) that regards the policy of symbolism as pure terror:

> I call it EU-nationalism. They are trying to construct a European identity using immense commercial means. In 50 years time, this period will be regarded as an époque in European history, where the goal was to make people think European by using enormous means of propaganda … I am an opponent, and I have to look at all the blue flags with yellow stars. That has nothing to do with a dialogue. It is an attempt at buying people with money for projects and the like. Sometimes I feel totally powerless. It is truly a terror of symbols, if you are an opponent. And they are spending my money, the tax-payers money (Drude Dahlerup, interview).

The rhetoric of a 'terror of symbols' manifest in the quote by Drude Dahlerup is outspoken in the views of both grassroots organization against the EU. And the public opinion towards the symbols of the Union are very much regarded as something being imposed from above (or even from abroad) against the people's will.

In sum, it seems that the Danish opposition to Maastricht in general – and Union citizenship in particular – is not merely a reaction born out of the fear of losing the perceived benefits of being Danish. It has as much to do with · a conscious opposition to political integration. As a general rule, the Danes prefer a strictly economic cooperation, and they are only willing to agree to a minimum of political integration with a Community that in their view is strongly elitist. As this is the general view, it is not surprising that the Danes react very strongly, and quite opposite the intention of the Community, to the politics of symbolism that has been part of the construction of Union citizenship. It seems as if the people of Denmark consciously *do not want* a European citizenship.

Conclusion

That a sense of identity is an indispensable factor in achieving and maintaining European unity was recognized by Jean Monnet when he said that if he had to begin again he would start with *culture* (reproduced in Wistrich, 1991: 79). This has also been long recognized by the Community. Since the early 1970s the Community has launched a number of projects, proposals and policies aimed at stimulating a collective identity among the peoples of Europe, most notably through the introduction of a European citizenship in the Maastricht Treaty of 1992.

The European Community cannot do without legitimacy for one fundamental reason. It is made up of democracies, and the basic rule of democracy is that the people rule. This can be arranged in various ways, most often through some form of representation. But unless the people regard the arrangement of representation as legitimate, there *is* no democracy. Today, the Community takes a vast number of decisions which have a profound effect on people's lives. In addition, supranational decision-making in the Community is not likely to diminish in the course of development towards an 'ever closer Union'. The fundamental problem is that the Community lacks a decisive element: a *European demos.* This is not merely an institutional question that can be solved through, say, granting more legislative power to the European Parliament. On a more fundamental level it has to do with the fact that the peoples of Europe do not regard themselves to be a united people. This is not only a Danish problem – a number of the European national populations do not feel European – they consider themselves to be Germans, Dutch, Irish or British. It should be obvious how this is likely to pose severe problems in the future, when increased majority voting will ensure more cases of a national people being outvoted by a majority which is not considered to be part of their own community. This is why Europe needs a demos with a collective identity. And this is why the Danish case is not only interesting in a purely theoretical discussion. The new Amsterdam Treaty incorporates the wording of the Danish opt-out on citizenship in the text of the Treaty. This must be considered as a clear signal of the reluctance, or even fear, among other populations that the Danes towards the construction of *one* political community in Europe.

The fundamental question is here, whether the development of a European citizenship is a viable answer to the legitimacy deficit of the European Union, insofar as it could provide the feeling of community that the EU so strongly needs. If homogeneity is not considered as an *indispensable* factor for collective identity formation a community-feeling should be possible to forge in a heterogeneous, multicultural entity such as the EU. In this scheme, the identity itself would be based on *demos* rather than *ethnos*, where the demos in turn would depend on civil, political and social rights, shared expectations and the feeling that others are equal members of the society. Following this line of thought it would seem as if the endeavours on European citizenship by the Community could stimulate a European identity. However, the case study of Denmark indicates something different.

The Danes are reputed to be reluctant Europeans, and they certainly have a very low score when it comes to identification with Europe. But the Danes are not alone at the bottom of the list. Hence, this can not be the main factor in explaining why the Danes cut up rough when it comes to the EU. Rather the joker seems to be the high degree of attachment of Danes to Denmark, a feeling that may have to do with the particular state-culture, with the extensive welfare system or with the fact that the Danes are a small and very homogenous population born out of a history of shrinking territory. The case-study at least seems to indicate that these factors adds in the explanation of why the Danes reacted so fiercely to the label of 'European citizenship'.

It may well be that the Danes are extreme in their reaction. But as the French Maastricht referendum has shown in no uncertain manner, the Danes are not the only population divided over Europe. What the case would be for the Germans, the British, the Belgians or the Italians is not known. They were not asked. This is why a case study of 5 million Danes has relevance for the whole of Europe.

The case study points to the conclusion that the deep-rooted reason for Danish opposition to Europe has to do with a dislike of political integration in general, and a non-desire to become Europeans in particular. The problem seems to be that the Community is regarded as an elitist project, which has a strong alienating effect in the broad population – a problem that certainly is not restricted to a Danish context and which has been recognized by a number of commentators for causing a major European problem (Weiler, 1996; García, 1992; Howe, 1995).

Again, there can be no doubt that what Europe needs is a sense of Community among Europeans. However, it does not seem as if the present top-down construction of the European Community and the initiatives trying to promote a collective identity has lead to the desired outcome. Europe need to involve its people in the process. Offering the people a citizenship they did not ask for will not be sufficient.

It would seem as if the Community faces somewhat of a dilemma. On the one hand, a sense of European identity is the inescapable and necessary condition if further integration is to be legitimate. On the other hand it seems as if the means available for the Community to promote this collective identity feeling are scarce. The forceful reaction in Denmark against the introduction of 'European citizenship' was rooted in a fundamental opposition to political integration, but it was *also* a reaction against the symbolism inherent in the name, as it had nothing to do with the actual content. This indicates that a strategy resembling the processes leading to collective identity formation in a national context is *not* an option for the European Community. A pan-European history taught through the mass education system, some kind of compulsory European service, the introduction of English, German, French or Esperanto as a second official language in the various member states; none of these measures are prognosticated to fall on fertile ground in countries like Denmark and France, where half the population was against Maastricht, and it might indeed cause upheaval in other member states as well.

The conclusion regarding European citizenship seems sinister. It is a hard case to believe that the voices emphasizing a European identity on the basis of the *present* situation are right. As much as a European identity is needed, and as much as it can be rightly argued that it can be *thought* theoretically, the Danish case is a rejection of the basic assumption – European citizenship does not constitute the will of the people; and it has certainly not arisen out of public demands.

At the end of the day, it seems that Europe's only option is to bring the people back in – to take its citizens seriously and include them in the debate of the future of Europe. This is not an easy task, which the language problem alone should be a clear indicator of, does not make it less fundamental. Provided that the peoples of Europe would gain a more important role in the debate on the construction of the Union, a sense of common civic identity might develop in the course of the next generations, as public involvement and public demands would be mutually enhancing. But it seems inconceivable that such a debate could develop from the top-down policies inherent in the Community at present.

In this respect the outcome of the first Danish Maastricht referendum in 1992 constitutes the closest the Community has been to a situation with a *European* public debate. It may be the first[32] example of a situation where the populations of Europe have been discussing the same issue at the same time. And for the future of Europe, a crisis-ridden debate is supposedly better than no debate at all.

Notes

*   This article is drawn from a dissertation submitted for the degree of Master of Philosophy in European Studies at the University of Cambridge, 1997.

1   The three other 'opt-outs' were on common foreign and security policy; justice and home affairs; and the economic and monetary union.

2   In legal terms, these doctrines are known as *supremacy* and *direct effect*.

3   This view is among others supported by Stein (1981), Curtin (1993), and Weiler (1981; 1996; 1997). For a different view see Wyatt (1982).

4   'Culture' is in this context to be understood very broadly to include language, history, political and civic culture etc. A shared culture is decisive in relation to group identity, but the specific aspects of culture that people share can take different forms relating to the model of *nationhood* in question. For further discussion see Smith (1991) and Brubaker (1994).

5   Ireland likewise held a referendum in June 1992 on the question of ratification of the Maastricht Treaty, but here an overwhelming majority of 69 per cent voted in favour as opposed to 31 per cent voting against.

6   Thus Moxon-Browne cites Henig as follows: 'Europe's institutions will be legitimate insofar as individual citizens are prepared to accept decisions made by them when their own lives and livelihoods are affected and insofar as there is (consequently) a transfer of loyalties and expectations to those institutions ... It is desirable of course that the European institutions receive the accolade of legitimacy only if they are organized in accordance with certain democratic principles, but the critical conditioned for integration is legitimacy rather than democracy' (Henig, 1974; cited in Moxon-Browne, 1996: 77).

7   This period was another affirmation of Denmark as the 'odd man out' in a European context. In the 1986 referendum on the Single European Act, the Danish population voted 'yes' notwithstanding a majority in the Danish Parliament, that advocated a 'no'. In other words: the exact opposite situation of the 1992 referendum on Maastricht, where a majority in the parliament was in favour, while a majority of the population voted 'no'.

8   The authors writing on the lack of legitimacy include among others Weiler (1997); García (1992); Howe (1995); Moxon-Browne (1996); Laffan (1996).

9   For a thorough discussion of the so-called 'no-demos' thesis, see Weiler (1996 and 1997).

10   In the discussion of the substance of European citizenship authors such as Elizabeth Meehan (1993), Antje Wiener (1996) and Paul Howe (1995) do argue, that European citizenship makes a difference in it's own right. They see this as holding great promises for the development of a European identity. However, this is a contested view as apparent

in the writings of Hans Ulrich Jessurun d'Oliveira (1995), Edward Moxon-Browne (1992) and to a lesser extent David O'Keeffe (1994).

11   This part will rely on a number of sources as well as interviews conducted in Danish. Where direct quotation is used, the translation is my work, thus any inaccuracy that might occur is my responsibility only.

12   There have in all been 17 referendums in Denmark: three on constitutional changes, five on the electoral age, three on surrender of sovereignty, four demanded by a minority in the parliament, and two consultative referendums (Siune et al., 1994: 31–3). In addition, there was a referendum on the Amsterdam Treaty on 28 May 1998.

13   The numerical difference between the two percentages amounted to 46,269 votes.

14   However, when it came to the Danish request on having arguments and votes of each member state in the Council of Ministers be made public, the 'Edinburgh agreement' constitutes a significant negative response, as it is explicitly stated that 'negotiation on legislation in the Council must remain confidential' (Curtin and Ooik, 1994: 353).

15   The 'Edinburgh agreement' is made up of part B of the conclusions from the summit and is properly entitled 'Denmark and the Treaty on the European Union'. But since it is continuously referred to as the 'Edinburgh agreement' in the Danish debate this is also the appellation used here.

16   It is worth mentioning that the domestic problems did not have to do with the referendum of 1992. Instead, it was caused by the so-called 'Tamil case', which brought down the Conservative-Liberal government. It was followed by a Social-Democratic lead coalition government including the Social-Liberal Party, the Centre-Democrats and the Christian People's Party.

17   On the night on the second referendum, there were severe and violent clashes with firearms between the police and opponents of 'Maastricht' in the area of Nørrebro in central Copenhagen. Several people were hurt, though not severely. This is the only occasion in peacetime that the police has used firearms against a crowd, and, naturally, it led to a huge debate and a number of investigations in an attempt to explain how the situation could end up in such an extreme – and in a Danish context, basically unknown – situation.

18   *Folketing* (Danish *Folketinget*) is the name of the Danish Parliament.

19   This is enshrined in the view expressed by the government, stating that the most appropriate way of finding a solution was to 'put itself outside the door' (Svensson, 1994: 71).

20   This specific 'opt-out' has been the first to have political consequences, as the supra-national cooperation in this field is extended in the 'Amsterdam Treaty', where Denmark consequently cannot participate. However, the time is clearly not ripe for having a referendum on *any* of the opt-outs, and since it also is clear that it won't be politically possible to disapply any of the opt-outs *without* a referendum, Denmark still maintains the opt-out.

21   The wording in the decision is almost identical with the wording of the declaration from the intergovernmental conference leading to Maastricht cited above. This is just another manifestation of the hollowness of the opt-out.

22   For a discussion of the possibilities for expansion of European citizenship see Meehan (1993), García (1992) and Howe (1995).

23   The peculiar name of the June Movement has to do with its foundation after the first referendum on 2 June 1992.

24   Indeed, it often is. The Progress Party is an extreme right-wing party with an agenda made up of anti-tax and anti-immigration issues, and is not considered 'responsible' as a political coalition partner. The party has been represented in the *Folketing* since the 'earthquake'

election in 1973, but has never been in government. In 1996 it split in two as a consequence of internal, personal rivalries. One part of the party kept the original name, the other is now named *Danish People's Party*.

25 Karen Siune, Palle Svensson and Ole Tonsgaard (1994) have in a comprehensive study shown that the way the voters made a priority between economic gains of EC cooperation and preservation of political sovereignty could explain 85 per cent of the turn-out in 1992. In 1993, the figure had fallen about 10 percentage points, but it was still the most significant explanation for the choice of the voters (Siune et al., 1994: 132).

26 Note that the area of justice and home affairs, which makes up the last opt-out, is not included in the table.

27 As mentioned above the government changed from a conservative-liberal government to a social-democratic-centre government in late 1993. Uffe Ellemann-Jensen, former president for the Liberal Party, was the long-time foreign secretary of the conservative-liberal government.

28 The List of Unity comprises four small, socialist parties, namely: the Communist Party, the Communist Workers Party, the Socialist Workers Party, and the Left-Socialists. The Party is a strong opponent to the EU. Notwithstanding the fact that the Party was not in Parliament before 1994, it has been included here, as it represents a part of the population which rejected Maastricht both times.

29 The high-school movement started as part of the farmers self-education scheme in the late 19th century. The movement is carried by values signifying equality, education for all and public participation.

30 David O'Keeffe in a lecture on *European Citizenship and Fundamental Human Rights* delivered at the Faculty of Law, Cambridge University, 5 February 1997.

31 *Dannebrog* is the name of the Danish flag.

32 One might argue the discussion after the BSE crisis is an example of a second all-European debate.

References

Brubaker, W.R. (1994), 'Immigration, Citizenship, and the Nation-State in France and Germany: A Comparative Historical Analysis', in B. Turner and P. Hamilton (eds), *Citizenship: Critical Concepts*, Vol. II, Routledge, London, pp. 310–40.

Cesarani, D. and Fulbrook, M. (1996), *Citizenship, Nationality and Migration in Europe*, Routledge, London.

Clarke, P.B. (1994), *Citizenship*, Pluto Press, London.

Closa, C. (1992), 'The Concept of Citizenship in the Treaty on European Union', *Common Market Law Review*, 29, pp. 1137–69.

Closa, C. (1994), 'Citizenship of the Union and Nationality of Member States', in D. O'Keeffe and P. Twomey (eds), *Legal Issues of the Maastricht Treaty*, Chancery Law Publishers Ltd, Sussex, pp. 100–19.

Close, P. (1995), *Citizenship, Europe and Change*, Macmillan, London.

Coppel, J. and O'Neill, A. (1992), 'The European Court of Justice: Taking Rights Seriously?', *Common Market Law Review*, 29, pp. 669–92.

Craig, P, and de Búrca, G. (1995), *EC Law. Text, Cases, and Materials*, Clarendon Press, Oxford.

Curtin, D. and van Ooik, R. (1994), 'Denmark and the Edinburgh Summit: Maastricht without Tears', in D. O'Keeffe and P. Twomey (eds), *Legal Issues of the Maastricht Treaty*, Chancery Law Publishers Ltd, Sussex, pp. 349–65.

Fontaine, P. (1991), *A Citizen's Europe*, Office of Official Publications of the European Communities, Luxembourg.

García, S. (1992), 'Europe's Fragmented Identities and the frontiers of Citizenship', *RIJA Dicussion Papers 45*, Royal Institute of International Affairs, London.

García, S. (1993), *European Identity and the Search for Legitimacy*, Pinter Publishers, London.

Goddard, V.A., Llobera, J. and Shore, C. (eds), *The Anthropology of Europe. Identities and Boundaries in Conflict*, Berg Publishers Ltd, Oxford.

Goul Andersen, J. (1994), 'Danskerne og Europa, Skillelinier, motiver og politisk kultur' [The Danes and Europe: Divisions, Motives and Political Culture], *Arbejdspapir 1994/5*, Københavns Universitet, Institut for Statskundskab.

Goul Andersen, J. and Hoff, J. (1994), '"Reluctant Europeans" and the European Union. Citizenship and Democratic Deficit', *Arbejdspapir 1992/4*, Københavns Universitet, Institut for Statskundskab.

Haahr, H.H. (1992), 'Folkeafstemningen 2. Juni 1992. Om dansk ratifikation af Maastricht-traktaten. En analyse af udfaldet og dets baggrund' [The referendum of 2 June 1992. Regarding Danish Ratification of the Maastricht Treaty. An Analysis of the Outcome and its Reasons], *Arbejdspapir*, Institut for Statskundskab, Århus Universitet.

Habermas, J. (1992), 'Citizenship and National Identity: Some Reflections on the Future of Europe', *Praxis international*, Vol. 12, No. 1, pp. 1–19.

Heater, D. (1990), *Citizenship: The Civil Ideal in World History, Politics and Education*, Longman, London.

Howe, P. (1995), 'A Community of Europeans: The Requisite Underpinnings', *Journal of Common Market Studies*, Vol. 33, No. 1, pp. 27–46.

Knudsen, T. (1992), 'A Portrait of Danish State-culture: Why Denmark Needs Two National Anthems', in M. Keistrup (ed.), *European Integration and Denmark's Participation*, Politcal Studies Press, University of Copenhagen, pp. 262–96.

Laffan, B. (ed.) (1996), *Constitution-building in the European Union*, Brunswick Press, Institute of European Affairs, Dublin.

Lodge, J. (1994), 'Transparency and Democratic Legitimacy', *Journal of Common Market Studies*, Vol. 32, No. 3, pp. 343–68.

Marshall, T.H. (1950), *Citizenship and Social Class and Other Essays*, Cambridge University Press, Cambridge.

Meehan, E. (1993a), *Citizenship and the European Community*, Sage, London.

Meehan, E. (1993b), 'Citizenship and the European Community', *The Political Quarterly*, Vol. 64, No. 2, pp. 172–86.

Moxon-Browne, E. (1992), 'The Concept of European Community Citizenship and the Development of Political Union', paper prepared for presentation at the ECPR Joint Sessions at the University of Limerick 30 March–4 April 1992.

Nielsen, H.J. (1992), 'The Danish Voters and the Referendum in June 1992 on the Treaty of Maastricht', in M. Keistrup (ed.), *European Integration and Denmark's Participation*, Politcal Studies Press, University of Copenhagen, pp. 365–80.

Nielsen, H.J. (1994), 'Danmark og center-perifi-tesen' [Denmark and the Thesis of Centre-Periphery], *Arbejdspapir 1994/5*, Københavns Universitet, Institut for Statskundskab.

O'Keeffe, D. and Twomey, P. (eds), *Legal Issues of the Maastricht Treaty*, Chancery Law Publishers Ltd, Sussex, pp. 100–19.

Petersen, N. (1993), 'Denmark and the European Community 1985–1992, An Interpretation', paper presented for seminar on *Danish Foreign Policy 1967–1992*, Danish Institute of International Studies, 'Rolighed', Skodsborg, 7–8 October.

Petersen, N. (1993), 'Game, Set, and Match: Denmark and the European Union after Maastricht', *Workingpaper*, Department of Political Science, Århus University.

Rosas, A. and Antola, E. (eds), *A Citizens' Europe*, Sage Publications, London.

Rudden, B. and Wyatt, D. (eds) (1994), *Basic Community Laws*, 5th edn, Clarendon Press, Oxford.

Siune, K. (1992), 'The Danish Yes to Maastricht and Edinburgh. The EC Referendum of May 1993', *Skandinavian Political Studies*, Vol. 17, No. 1, pp. 69–82.

Siune, K. and Svensson, P. (1992), *Det blev et nej* [It was a No], Forlaget Politica, Arhus Universitet.

Siune, K., Svenson, P. and Tonsgaard, O. (1994), *Fra et nej til etja* [From a No to a Yes], Forlaget Politica, Århus Universitet.

Smith, A.D. (1991), *National Identity*, Penguin Books, Harmondsworth.

Smith, A.D. (1992), 'National Identity and the Idea of European Unity', *International Affairs*, Vol. 68, No. 1, January 1992, pp. 55–76.

Svensson, P. (1994), 'The Danish Yes to Maastricht and Edingburgh. The EC Referendum of May 1993', *Skandinavian Political Studies*, Vol. 17, No. 1, pp. 69–82.

Tassin, E. (1992), 'Europe: A Political Community?', in C. Mouffe (ed.), *Dimensions of Radical Democracy. Pluralism, Citizenship, Community*, Verso, London, pp. 169–92.

Thomsen, B.N. (ed.) (1993), *The Odd Man Out? Danmark og den Europceiske Integration 1948-1992* [Denmark and European Integration], Odense Universitetsforlag, Odense.

Weiler, J. (1996), 'European Neo-constitutionalism: In Search of Foundations for the European Constitutional Order', *Political Studies*, Vol. XLIV, Special Issue, pp. 517–33.

Weiler, J. (1997), 'Legitimacy and Democracy of Union Governance', in G. Edwards and A. Pijpers (eds), *The Politics of European Treaty Reform. The 1996 Intergovernmental Conference and Beyond*, Pinter, London, pp. 249–87.

Wiener, A. (1996), 'Constitution Making and Citizenship Practice – Bridging the Democracy Gap in the EU?', *SEI Working Paper No. 1*, Sussex European Institute.

Wiener, A. (1997a), 'Citizenship in a Non-state – The Developing Practice of "European" Citizenship', in J.P. Gardener (ed.), *Citizenship: The White Paper*, The British Institute for International and Comparative Law, London.

Wiener, A. (1997b), 'Promises and Resources – the Deveoping Practice of "European Citizenship"', in M. La Torre (ed.), *European Citizenship: An Institutional Challenge*, Kluwer International, London.

Wistrich, E. (1991), *After 1992. The United States of Europe*, 2nd edn, Routledge, London.

Worre, T. (1994), 'Fra nej til ja: Folkeafstemingerne om den europmiske unionstraktat 1992 og 1993' [From No to Yes: The Referendums on the Treaty on European Union 1992 and 1993], *Arbejdspapir 1994/5*, Københavns Universitet, Institut for Statskundskab.

Worre, T., Nielsen, H.J. and Goul Andersen, J. (1994), *Tre studier af Maastricht-afstemningerne* [Three Studies of the Referendums on Maastricht], *Arbejdspapir 1994/5*, Københavns Universitet, Institut for Statskundskab.

Interviews

Keld Albrechtsen, Member of Parliament for the *List of Unity* since 1994, spokesman on European Affairs since 1994. Conducted 12 June 1997.

Charlotte Antonsen, Member of Parliament since 1984 for the *Liberal Party*, spokeswoman on European Affairs since 1990. Conducted 26 May 1997.

Elisabeth Arnold, Member of Parliament for *the Social-Liberal Party* since 1988, spokeswoman on European Affairs. Conducted 6 June 1997.

Bent Brier, lawyer, spokesman for *the People's Movement against the EC*. Conducted 9 June 1997.

Drude Dahlerup, senior lecturer at the University of Århus, spokeswoman for the June Movement. Conducted 4 June 1997.

Peter Duetoft, Member of Parliament for the *Centre-Democrats* since 1988, second chairman of the Parliamentary Committee on the European Union since 1991. Conducted 27 May 1997.

Ove Fich, Member of Parliament for the *Social-Democratic Party* since 1990, chairman of the Parliamentary Committee on the European Union. Conducted 2 June 1997.

Henning Grove, Member of Parliament for the *Conservative People's Party* since 1977, Minister of Fishery 1982–86, chairman of the Parliamentary Committee on the European Union 1987–91. Conducted 11 June 1997.

Annette Just, Member of Parliament for the *Progress Party* since 1987, spokeswoman on European Affairs. Conducted 2 June 1997.

Flemming Kofod-Svendsen, former party leader of the *Christian People's Party* 1979–93, Member of Parliament 1984–94, Minister of Housing 1987–88, Minister of Housing and Nordic Affairs 1993–94, member of the Parliamentary Committee on European Affairs 1984–87, 1988–93. Conducted 28 May 1997.

Gert Petersen, former party leader of the *People's Socialist Party*, Member of Parliament since 1966. Conducted 11 June 1997.

Karen Siune, principal for Institute of Analysis of Research since 1997. Conducted 4 June 1997.

Official Publications

Commission: *Bulletin of the European Communities*, Supplement 1/76, 'Tindemans Report'.
Commission: *Bulletin of the European Communities*, Supplement 7/85, 'Adonnino Report'.
Commission: *Bulletin of the European Communities*, Supplement 7/86, 'Voting Rights in Local Elections for Community Nationals'.
Commission: *Bulletin of the European Communities*, No. 10, 1992.
Commission: COM (93) 702, 'Report on the Citizenship of the Union'.

Chapter 4

Who Governs the Europeans?

Dolores Taaffe

> Men love power ... Give all power to the many, they will oppress the few. Give all power to the few, they will oppress the many. Both therefore ought to have power that each may defend itself against the other (Alexander Hamilton, 1787).

The Maastricht Treaty was ratified with very large majorities in the legislatures of all the member states of the European Community (Bogdanor, 1996: 101). Initially no one questioned whether these majorities reflected the wishes of the electorates of the member states. Three countries put the question directly to the people, Denmark, France and Ireland. The results in the former two shook the European establishment to its foundations. Some Europeans had diverged quite seriously from their elected representatives and by expressing their displeasure, were responsible for the eruption of the people onto the stage of European integration.

Much has been written on the topic, who are the Europeans? My focus will be less who they are than on how the European people, or peoples, are governed, and on whether the form of government at European Union (EU) level is truly democratic. Democracy has been called a capacious concept (Greenfield, 1993: 127). It means different things to different people. Though in general it connotes the idea of popular sovereignty, from '*demos*' – people, and '*kratein*' – to rule, the word is used to describe political structures that have very little in common. It could be argued that democracy means a form of government in which, in contradistinction to monarchies and aristocracies, the people are the rulers. Bogdanor comments that 'while democracy is a form of government in which ultimate power lies with the people, in almost every modern democracy the role of the people is negative' (1997: 24). The character of democracy in any state will depend on the specific definition of democracy and the meaning of popular sovereignty in that society. At all levels definition and practice differ widely between procedural and participative democracy. In most Western political systems the power of the state is legitimated through the democratic process, in that government is supposedly based on the consent of the governed, who broadly support the values on which the state is founded.

This legitimacy has both a social aspect, in being rooted in popular consent, and a normative aspect in terms of the underlying values on which the consent is based (de Burca, 1996: 349). The core of the problem is, does this apply in the context of the EU?

After Maastricht attempts were made to bring the people closer to the European project, this became a priority in the lead up to the negotiations on the Amsterdam Treaty. Submissions made by various institutions and bodies to the Reflection Group[1] paid homage to the notion of a people's Europe. Grainne de Burca suggests that the concern was largely a response to the experience of the ratification process and to the general concern with openness and accountability which emerged during the Maastricht debate (1996: 355). In particular the submissions share a concern about the standing of the European project in the eyes of the European citizens. There was increased focus on who is governed in contrast to who governs and how. The Reflection Group suggested there was a need for public information because the people's opinion was necessary for carrying out the reforms of the Intergovernmental Conference (IGC). However, de Burca questions whether this is because the Group believed, as a matter of principle or democratic theory, that the citizens should be involved in negotiating the issues and policies to be debated at the IGC. It is more likely that the spectre of another referendum debacle motivated their concern. The sincerity of their intentions was tested soon enough. The chairman of the Reflection Group had announced his intention to conduct a poll through the Commission's *Eurobarometer* survey to discover 'what citizens expect' from the IGC (Agence Europe, 15 September 1995). This was to take place after the presentation of the first progress report. However, due to 'difficulties of funding' this limited measure of public consultation was dropped (Agence Europe, 27 September 1995).

The incremental nature of the development of the EU has made it difficult to identify its true nature with regard to democracy at any point in time. What we can be sure of is that it has never been controlled by the people, however defined. Moravcsik (1993) would argue that the lack of clarification when it comes to basic democratic principles in the EU may even have contributed to the initial success of integration. Flexibility may enhance effectiveness, and the EU's ability to deliver results may itself be seen as a major source of legitimacy, thereby engendering specific support. That ultimately it was not enough is demonstrated by the reaction to Maastricht, which showed that effectiveness is not a substitute for democratic control. Political support was considered by David Easton to be a crucial input for any political system (cited in Deschouwer, 1996: 264). If the level of support falls below a critical level, then the system may collapse. After Maastricht elites began to worry that the level of support for the EU was not as high as suggested by the various opinion polls.

The debate on democracy became an issue for reasons other than the Maastricht ratification process. Much of the discourse on the experience of contemporary democracy has focused on the emergence and consolidation of democracy in central and eastern Europe, indeed there has been a substantial rise in transition studies over the past decade. But democracy in established entities has also come under scrutiny. The fall of the former communist regimes gave new scope for what Furet called 'the familiar repertoire of liberal democracy' (1995: 80). This has led to a sense of complacency that this form of government has prevailed universally, and has provoked one commentator to proclaim the end of history (Fukuyama, 1989). Schmitter alerted us to the danger of complacency in the West in 1994. 'Modern democracy will have to face unprecedented challenges in the 1990s and beyond' (1994: 63). He argues that since 1989 the absence of a credible systemic alternative is bound to cause new strains, and that what remains now are internal standards for evaluation enshrined in a vast body of normative democratic theory, 'and in the expectations of millions of ordinary citizens' (ibid.). He asks what will happen when 'entrenched elite practices in such countries are measured against long subordinated ideals of equality, participation, accountability, responsiveness, and self realisation' (ibid.). The EC/EU is a relatively new political entity, yet it has existed long enough to generate a certain sense of elite entrenchment.[2] The quotation which opens this chapter calls for a balance in the distribution of power. The Amsterdam negotiations demonstrated that power is in the hands of the very few. Fifteen mainly middle-aged men gathered to make decisions that would affect the lives of 380,000,000 citizens. Even when we take into consideration the contribution of a collection of elected and non-elected actors, the Council of Ministers, the Commission, the European Parliament, member state parliaments, the Reflection Group, the Committee of the Regions, ECOSOC and many others, it still remains the case that the vast majority of citizens remain remote from the decision-making process.

The Making of a Democratic Polity

In the crucial early years of the Community the locking in of interests from business, labour and national administrative agencies took priority over the direct involvement of Europe's publics. Monnet's strategy of elite led gradualism was in contrast to Spinelli's assertion that 'in a leap for federation popular support would be found' (Wallace and Smith, 1995: 140). There were those who believed that there was a deep pool of support for integration. At the Hague Conference of 1948 Paul van Zceland insisted that governments could afford to be daring, as he expected that public opinion would follow them, if it were not, in fact, already ahead of them.[3] Spinelli fervently believed that 'there is a large reservoir of popular support for closer unity among the public at large' (Wallace and Smith, 1995: 141). Spinelli did attempt to plumb this well of support in his campaign for a European Constituent Assembly, and he succeeded in collecting 600,000 signatures in Italy. However there was little evidence elsewhere of a popular demand for unity. Those who supported the technocratic method, the most influential of whom was Monnet, believed that the issue of popular consent could be postponed. In his memoirs he wrote: 'I thought it wrong to consult the peoples of Europe about the nature of a community of which they had no practical experience'.[4] At the end of the day 'enlightened administration on behalf of uninformed publics, in co-operation with affected interests and subject to the approval of national governments, was the compromise struck in the Treaties of Rome' (Wallace and Smith, 1995:143). Pascal Lamy, Delors Chef de Cabinet described the Monnet method in the following terms: 'the people were not ready to agree to integration, so you had to get on without telling them too much about what was happening' (quoted in Laffan, 1996: 83).

This approach did bear fruit, but there was a price to pay. On the evidence of a *Eurobarometer* survey a worrying gap has opened between the responses of elites to European Union and the responses of the ordinary people. In 1996 the Eurobarometer carried out a wide ranging survey involving persons holding high positions.[5] There were five groups, elected politicians, high civil servants, business and labour leaders, the media, persons playing a leading role in the academic, cultural, religious life of their country. Response to the question whether membership of the EU was a 'good' or a 'bad' thing showed that 94 per cent of top decision-makers considered it a good thing, 2 per cent considered it a 'bad' thing, and 4 per cent 'neither good nor bad'. This is in sharp contrast with the general public where the comparable figures were 48 per cent considered membership a 'good' thing, 15 per cent a 'bad' thing, and 28 per cent 'neither good nor bad'. This seems to substantiate Laffan's fear that 'a European identity may be the preserve of Europe's elites for whom Europe is already a social space' (1996:99). Integration had indeed progressed, sustained by the prop known as permissive consensus. This allows for integration by elites as long as there is consensus between elites, or opposing elites are unable to mobilize sufficient public opinion.[6]

This raises the question of legitimacy, which is separate from the issue of democracy.[7] According to David Beetham there are three basic elements associated with legitimacy (1991:15), conformity to established rules, the rules can be justified by reference to beliefs shared both by rulers and subordinates and there is evidence of consent by the subordinates to the particular power relation. Support for the European project is reasonably high. We must, however, question the quality of the support, whether it is based on a firm foundation so as to facilitate the build up of the type of political support that Easton insists is necessary for any political system. Easton differentiated between diffuse support and specific support. Specific support is directly linked to political outputs, i.e. decisions and associated verbal statements (Deschouwer, 1996: 264, 265). Diffuse support is not connected directly to the concrete performance of the system, it is more a reservoir of goodwill that allows the citizen to take, at least for the time being, unpleasant as well as pleasant outputs (ibid.). Weiler claims that those who supported Maastricht were motivated in large measure by a 'what's in it for me' calculus – a shaky foundation for long term civic loyalty (1997: 150). Irish support for the process of integration has been consistently strong, and the Irish people gave a ringing endorsement to the Maastricht Treaty in the 1992 referendum.[8] However this was achieved within a carrot and stick framework. The promise of billions of pounds (the carrot) should the Treaty be passed, and the threat of the loss of benefits (the stick), should the Treaty be rejected.[9] Thus, in an exchange for material gain, the people and the Irish Parliament were in agreement. The poverty of this approach is that it does nothing to create a sense of genuine public interest, or to encourage affirmative community action in the pursuance of common goals, it relates more to specific support and does little to nurture diffuse support.

'Imagining' a Community

It is necessary to briefly profile those governed at Community level at this point. Democratic theory presupposes a *demos* and a polity, and it is this which throws up one of the first problems that we need to deal with in the exploration of democratic content in the EU. In the case of Europe we have difficulty in identifying the people, and we have to ask, can there be democracy without a transcendent vision of a *European* people? There is a further complication in that we have to confront the notion of peoples rather than people, *demoi* rather than *demos*.[10] The problem of *demos* or no *demos* was given its strongest expression by the German Constitutional Court in Karlsruhe. The Court defined the *demos*, the 'Volk, the nation in a national ethno-cultural sense' (Weiler 1995: 227). Only nations may have states, and as the EU is not a nation, it may not have a state. Thus it is difficult to conceptualize a *demos*. Without a *demos* there cannot be a democracy. The European Community is not a state and its institutions and political system will not correspond to that of a classic liberal democracy (Dinan, 1994: 292). It is clear that a national understanding of governance does not fit. Dinan recommends that, in view of the *sui generis* nature of the EU, we must look for 'novel and unconventional' methods of dealing with problems. Weiler challenges the view which insists that the only way to think of a *demos* is in 'volkish' terms and the only way to envisage the Union is in statal form (1995: 238). He argues that we should think in terms of a 'civic' *demos* as 'underlying foundations of a polycentric governance structure' (ibid.). The difficulty is further compounded by the fact that political communities are, as convincingly argued by Brigid Laffan, 'based not just on rational calculation but on sentiment, solidarity and a degree of political cohesion' (1996: 95). The need to create a people's Europe has nagged on the periphery of action and debate since the 1960s, and made huge advances in elite thought and rhetoric after the Maastricht Treaty, and it intensified in the lead up to the 1996 Intergovernmental Conference. It would seem that the major task of this IGC was to 'bring Europe closer to the people',[11] to make Europe 'the business of every citizen',[12] to 'enhance its credibility in the eyes of its citizens',[13] to 'ensure grassroots involvement in the integration process'.[14]

In the absence of a European consciousness is it possible for community builders to construct it? Neumann argues that the existence of regions comes after the emergence of region builders, political actors who 'imagine certain spatial and chronological identity for a region, and disseminate this imagined identity to others' (1994: 58). This approach resembles the notion of nation building, and imagined communities as described by Benedict Anderson (1983). Laffan argues that the policies that flowed after the Adonnino Committee (1985) were an attempt to gradually change people's consciousness of political realities, and the political domain to which they belong. This, she argues, is a deliberate attempt to manufacture and legitimize a European identity from the top down (1996: 96).[15] Laffan concludes that, just as nation states are *imagined communities*, official policy in the Union is to construct Europe as an *imagined community*. This seems to receive validation from the fact that the notion of citizenship is no longer cut off at national boundaries.[16] People will never know most of their fellow Europeans yet they are expected in their minds to create the 'image of their communion' – imagining the extended boundaries.[17] It is not clear that as of yet they have any real desire to do so as to date, the *Eurobarometer* surveys have shown national identity leading European identity. The best that can be expected accords with Reif's reading of Eurobarometer data which seems to indicate that while national identity has not given ground to a sense of European identity, it may develop as a weaker form of identity in a hierarchy or circle of identities (Reif, 1993).

Voting as a Mechanism of Participation and Control

This short examination of the issues surrounding the notion of a *demos* and identity has illustrated some of the problems in achieving democratic content. It is time to look at the mechanisms by which the people, or peoples, exercise influence under these unique conditions. Elections are a particularly important form of participation in a democracy, and the simplest and least costly in effort and individual resources. Crewe (1981: 216–17) argues that elections based on a full adult franchise encapsulate more directly than any other means of participation the two core principles of universality and equality. Every one, no matter what the social circumstances, will have an equal say – but how effective is that say? It can be so slight that the notion of a single vote among a million or more others in a large electorate has prompted Dahl to ask whether the simple act of voting could be justified as a rational action by the individual voter (1982: 13). Schumpeter claimed that the democratic method is merely an institutional arrangement for arriving at decisions in which individuals become decision-makers by means of a competitive struggle for the people's vote. Democracy does not mean, and cannot mean that the people actually rule in any obvious sense of the terms *people* and *rule* (1947: 284). Toffler points to what he calls the 'mechanical nature of this system' (1992: 15). People are allowed to choose between different candidates at fixed times, and then the 'democracy machine' is turned off (ibid.). Isaac is critical of a procedurally based definition of democracy as it leaves too much of the meaning of democracy behind: 'In the name of realism, the ideal of rule by the people became wholly metaphorical, meaning nothing more than the right of citizens occasionally to select candidates who appeared to offer them some of what they wanted from government' (1994: 164–5).

Rousseau was the first to point out that opportunities for, and the importance of, citizen participation decrease with every increase in the number of citizens. The population of the EU has increased steadily with each enlargement. This links in with the ongoing debate with respect to appropriate representation in the European Parliament, and to the problem of ensuring that the vote of every European is of equal weight. The European elections cannot be considered equal because the weight of votes differs considerably among member states: while one German MEP represents more than 800,000 German citizens, one MEP from Luxembourg represents 66,000 citizens. The Amsterdam Treaty did not deal directly with this problem, but it did set a ceiling of 700 MEPs in the event of further enlargement.[18] This will complicate the task of the enlargement IGC. Drastic changes which might significantly reduce representation would be keenly felt by small nations.

On a practical level, no one who votes in the European elections has a strong sense of influencing critical policy choice at the European level, and certainly not of 'confirming or rejecting European governance' (Weiler, 1995: 8). Eighteen per cent of European citizens believed they are influential with regard to EU institutions (*Eurobarometer* Survey 44, Spring, 1996). Interestingly the three countries who entered the Union in 1994 felt they have least influence with 14 per cent of Austrians, 11 per cent of Finns and 10 per cent Swedes believing they can exercise influence. Schmitter (1995: 7) emphasizes that individual citizens voting in free, fair, and competitive Euroelections cannot influence the composition of Euro-authorities, much less bring about a rotation of those in office.

Indicators of Parliamentary Effectiveness

Crucial also is the perceived effectiveness of the European Parliament within the institutional structure of the EU. Wessels and Diedrichs (1997: 2) employ three indicators to measure the effectiveness of the European Parliament: how it effects policy making, how it impacts on system development, and how it interacts with the citizens. The policy-making making function concerns the influence exerted by the European Parliament in the EU-policy cycle in its relationship with the Council and the Commission, i.e. its ability to participate in the preparation, making and implementation of decisions. The EP has increased its role here incrementally over the decades, especially with the introduction of Art. 189b TEC (co-decision). Its competence in this area has been further expanded in the Amsterdam Treaty. Crucially it does not have the right to initiate legislation. However, it has proved its determination to maximize the powers available to it. In 1995 it concluded 164 resolutions according to the consultation procedure, 38 based on cooperation, 61 based on the co-decision procedure and 17 on the assent procedure (Wessels and Diedrichs, 1997: 5). The TEU also involved the EP in the selection of the Commission President, and the appointment of the rest of the College (Art. 158 TEU). The last incoming Commissioners were individually grilled by MEPs. Jacques Santer won a slender approval in a consultative vote on his presidency. The Parliament objected to the way he had been 'dragooned into the job and presented to the Parliament for its rubber stamp' (*The Economist*, 23 July 1994). However, even the power of dismissing the Commission, which is one of the powers of the EP does not in any way reassure the people that their representatives are actually throwing a government out on their behalf. Weiler comments that there is no civic act of the European citizen where he or she can directly influence the outcome of any policy choice (1997: 152).

In the case of system development, the influence of the Parliament seems to be quite limited and uneven, despite the fact that the 1984 Draft Treaty on European Union inspired the proceedings and preparations leading to the conclusion of the Single European Act (Wessels, 1996: 6). The Reflection Group installed in Messina which prepared the ground for the IGC included two members of parliament. Due to French and British pressure, however no member of parliament participated at the conference itself, though a close association was to be ensured by the governments (Wessels and Diedrich, 1997: 6), and there were two observers from the EP at all the sessions.

As regards interaction with the public, the signs are not entirely encouraging. Even where it is possible for a citizen to contact an MEP it must be reiterated that the EP, and single MEPs have in many cases no direct impact on EU politics.[19] A stronger relationship might have been forged between Parliament and people in the 1980s. In 1984 the European Council dismissed the Parliament's Draft Treaty on European Union. The only resort open to the Parliament was to take its plans to the streets in the elections of that year (Urwin, 1991: 224). A good turnout would have enhanced the stature of the European Parliament and might have strengthened its hand in its relationship with the other institutions. However the election experience was disappointing, national issues predominated, thus denying the Parliament the opportunity of claiming that the turnout displayed large scale support for their stance. Turnout in EP elections has fallen in successive elections even as the powers of the Parliament have increased. In 1979 the average turnout was 62.5, it fell to 58.5 per cent in 1989, and to 56.5 per cent in 1994. Other factors, such as member states voting on different days, and using different electoral systems are not helpful, and voting normally occurs in June, which sees the start of the holiday season. Sinnott et al., in a book published in June 1998, recommends that voting for EP elections should take place over two days, with easier access to postal votes, and simpler registration procedures.[20]

The EP suffers from another malaise that affects parliamentary institutions generally. Andersen and Burns (1996: 244) argue that while parliamentary institutions and representatives remain accountable in everyday political culture as well as in normative theory, the complexity of the issues that confront governments continue to expand, leading to a gap between responsibility and capability. Bobbio (1987: 116) goes further to state that:

> collective decisions come from negotiation and agreements between unions and political parties rather than an assembly where voting operates ... These votes take place, in fact, so as to adhere to the constitutional principle of the modern representative state, which says that individuals and not groups are politically relevant ... but they end up possessing the purely formal value of ratifying decisions reached in other places by the process of negotiation.

Thus the role of elected representatives is reduced to rubber-stamping decisions reached elsewhere.

A redefinition of representative democracy's role or function seems to be called for, or else marginalization of parliaments will continue. The European Parliament suffers from the changing perceptions that the public may be developing of national parliaments. Television coverage of parliamentary debates in the Bundestag in Bonn, in Congress in Washington, in the British Parliament shows half empty chambers. The media seems to be paying less and less attention to parliaments (Geoffrey Wheatcroft, *Sunday Independent*, 12 April 1998). The leader of the main opposition party in Ireland, John Bruton, has had occasion to rebuke the Minister for Finance for failing to use the Dail as the appropriate venue for announcing that stamp duty for first time house buyers was to be abolished, and on answering questions on the issue at a press conference. Ministers answering questions outside the Dail 'makes the place look a little silly'.[21] Likewise in Britain, instead of announcing new measures in the Commons the Blair government has repeatedly announced them at press conferences or in off the record briefings (Geoffrey Wheatcroft, *Sunday Independent*, 12 April 1998). The EP is at a more serious disadvantage. It does not always get the attention it needs from the Press as journalists tend to concentrate on the organs, (the Commission, the Council of Ministers, and the European Council), which produce the hard decisions. Andersen and Burns (1996: 227) argue that the EU is an instance of post parliamentary governance, where the direct influence of the people through formal representative democracy has a marginal place.

A Role for the People in Decision-making?

On occasion some of the people have voted directly on European integration, in referendums. Despite favourable opinion polls, there has proved to be a gap between ruled and rulers. This highlights the inability of purely procedural democracy to detect growing divergence. The elected representatives may diverge quite seriously from the people they represent. The two Norwegian referendums on joining the Community, and the first Danish referendum on the Maastricht Treaty are examples of this. In Denmark the first referendum was lost despite nearly 75 per cent of the *Folketing* having supported ratification, and in the case of France 87 per cent of both houses voted in favour of the Maastricht Treaty, and 49 per cent of the people voted against it. In Britain where the government, with the support of the opposition, refused to hold a referendum on the issue, surveys indicated that defeat for Maastricht was inevitable if the people been asked for their opinion (Bogdanor, 1996: 103).

The referendum on the Amsterdam Treaty in Ireland, unaccompanied by the promise of billions of pounds, might have been expected to give a clearer picture of the extent of Irish support than hitherto, the carrot and stick method used by the government during the Maastricht referendum was a factor in the level of support at that time. There has been a great deal of anxiety expressed about the level of turnout of voters, and as to the outcome. Garret Fitzgerald wrote in the *Irish Times*: 'As things now stand I fear that a stand alone referendum – on the Amsterdam Treaty ... might see a turnout of less than 40 per cent' (Saturday 14 March, 1998). The Treaty contains no issue that could effectively concentrate the electorate's mind. Apathy and 'the yawn factor' were identified as the greatest problem facing the political parties on the referendum.[22] The decision to hold the Amsterdam referendum and the referendum on the Northern Ireland Peace Agreement on May 22 has been criticized by some of the media (*Irish Independent, The Times, Irish Times*) and the smaller political parties. 'The only reasons vouchsafed for this move included the cost saving, and the "philosophical approach" which says that one [referendum] is bringing us closer to Europe, and the other [referendum] is bringing the people on the island closer together' (Minister of State, Seamus Brennan as quoted in the *Sunday Independent* (26 April: 32). Not since 1918 has the whole island of Ireland participated in the same electoral exercise. In the Amsterdam referendum the people are helping to shape the future of the EU. A poll carried out by the Referendum Commission[23] showed that 11 per cent of the people knew there was to be a referendum on the Amsterdam Treaty, and 67 per cent of the people had not even heard of the Treaty (*Irish*

Times, 21 April 1998). A major study carried out by RTE/Landsdowne (25 April 1998) showed that 69 per cent of the electorate did not know how they were going to vote with 25 per cent intending to vote yes, and 6 per cent intending to vote no.[24] These findings reinforce the fears that a stand alone referendum on the issue would have proved to be a public relations disaster for the government, and Ireland, in the European context.

Referendums and Transnationalism

The 1994 referendums on EU membership produced three 'yes' results and one 'no' result. It was a very unusual occurrence, four referendums in four different countries on the same issue, EU membership, in a short time frame.

Fitzmaurice (1995: 227) claims that the referendums are examples of a growing degree of *transnationalism* in modern west European politics. The issues, styles and campaigns crisscrossed from one country to another. The order in which they were held was significant. It was believed in 1972 that a positive Danish result would have influenced the Norwegian vote had the Danish vote been held first. Fitzmaurice holds that, though there is no conclusive proof, yet there was at least some informal planning in the timing of the Norwegian referendum in 1994, thereby giving credence to the notion of transnationalism (ibid.). The Austrian referendum was first and was held on the same day as the European parliament elections. There was a strong 66.6 per cent 'yes' vote. It might be thought that the Austrian vote would not affect the Scandinavians, but coupled with the return of the SPO-OVP Grand Coalition at the Austrian General Election on October 9, the result did offer the Scandinavians some reassurance that they would be part of a strong social democratic bloc within the EU (ibid.). However Norway diverged from the other three and voted no.

Should it transpire that there was an element of nascent transnationalism in the referendums it should bode well for an evolution in this direction, and might help to give people a sense of shared control over the future shape of *their* Europe. Unfortunately there is unlikely to be an early repetition of this scenario. Only Denmark, Ireland and Portugal will hold referendums on the Amsterdam Treaty (Portugal will hold an advisory vote). Sweden, Finland and Austria have opted not to ask their people to take part directly in the decision-making process on this occasion. It is possible that joining the single currency may see more referendums, the Swedish government have promised either a referendum, or a general election before joining. Tony Blair also has promised a referendum in the UK. However there is unlikely to be a series of votes, which is the only way an element of transnationalism could be established. The proposed referendums on the Amsterdam Treaty will promote transnationalism only in so far that a positive outcome in Ireland might influence Danish voters. However Irish minds and hearts will be less concentrated on transnational issues or in deciding the future of the EU. They will be more interested in trying to resolve the past.

There is, of course another expression of transnationalism in the EU context. On occasion the farmers or workers of Europe together take to the streets in Brussels to express concern about their various problems. In March 1997 Belgian workers were joined by delegations from Spain, Portugal, Germany, Italy, Netherlands, France and Greece *(Irish Independent,* 17 March 1997). Protest is allowed, if not encouraged, but it serves no purpose when the citizens are corralled off at a safe distance from those they most want to influence.[25] This method admits the right of protest while ensuring business as usual for the elites. Crucial to the health of democracy is the perception on the part of the citizens of their political efficacy: do they believe that they can influence or shape government policy decisions? In its present state, no one who votes in the European elections has a strong sense of influencing critical policy choice at the European level, and certainly not of 'confirming or rejecting European governance' (Weiler, 1995: 8). This is borne out by the findings of the *Eurobarometer* Survey 44 (Spring, 1996) which shows that just 22 per cent of citizens believe that they have influence over their national governments, while 18 per cent believe they are influential with regard to EU institutions.

Suggested Solutions

Buried in the mass of rhetoric declaring a people's Europe, are some suggestions relating to the problem of democratic content of the Union. Many of the suggestions endorse at least an element of direct democracy. Frey and Bohnet suggest that as both federalism and direct democracy work well in large as well as small polities they could provide the way forward in the future of European Integration. They believe that confronting the democratic deficit is beyond the capacity of the 'huge and amorphous European Parliament' (1995: 228). Held, in his model of cosmopolitan democracy (1995: 358) favours the enhancement of political regionalization (EU and beyond) and advocates the use of transnational referendums as a method of keeping the citizens involved. We have already referred to referendums as methods of achieving transnationalism. It is necessary to also ask how effective they might be as a method of involving citizens. In *City of Eastlake v. Forest City Enterprises, Inc.*, the US Supreme Court held that a referendum was not a delegation of power from the representative institution to the people:

> Under our constitutional assumptions, all power derives from the people, who can delegate it to representative instruments which they create ... In establishing legislative bodies, the people can reserve to themselves power to deal directly with matters which might otherwise be assigned to the legislature.[26]

On the evidence of this ruling, referendums should be quite powerful tools in the hands of the people. Practical experience paints a different picture. Crucial to the status of the people in exercising control is whether or not referendums are binding. It is also necessary to consider the degree of regulation and intervention by governments. Attempts to influence a favourable outcome can be quite powerful. In order to determine the extent to which referendums serve the function of increasing popular control, they have been classified according to two criteria by Gordon Smith: controlled versus uncontrolled, and pro- versus anti-hegemonic referendums (Smith, 1976: 6). A referendum is controlled if the government can decide whether to hold it or not, when to hold it, and can decide on the wording. On the other hand if a referendum is the result of a popular initiative it is then uncontrolled. Virtually all international issue referendums are controlled, thus giving advantage to the government's wishes.[27] When governments use the referendum for purposes other than a mandatory constitutional requirement, they will do so only when they except to win.[28] The second criterion concerns the actual result of the referendum: a referendum is pro- or anti-hegemonic depending on whether its consequences are 'supportive or detrimental to a regime' (ibid.). The vast majority of EU issue referendums have been passed, with the exception of the Norwegian votes in 1972 and 1994, and the Danish referendum in 1992.

The idea of direct democracy has stealthily made its way into pronouncements from high political levels. At EU level there have been calls from the Austrian and Italian Governments for a European wide initiative process, where the signatures of 10 per cent of the electorate of at least three EU Member states would make a valid proposal for EC legislation forwarded to the European Parliament (Agence Europe, No. 6823, 02/10/1996). Weiler et al., in a working paper commissioned by the European Parliament, suggests introducing a form of direct democracy.[29] This arose from their concern with the citizen's inability to choose a European government. They proposed a

form of Legislative Ballot Initiative coinciding with elections to the EP.[30] This
would allow the introduction of legislative initiatives to be voted on by the
citizens and should remain in place until at least 'meaningful representative
democracy is established at EU level' (1997: 152). Results would be binding on
the Community institutions and on Member states. These initiatives would be
confined to the sphere of application of Community law (153). Weiler argues
that apart from enhancing symbolically and tangibly the voice of citizens, the
proposal would encourage the formation of true European Parties as well as
transnational mobilization of political forces.

It is a large step from consultation of citizens to power sharing with them.
Yet there is evidence that there has been a rise in direct democracy worldwide
(Gallagher and Uleri, 1996; Rourke et al., 1992; Butler and Ranney, 1994;
Luthardt, 1991–92). Representation may be the norm, but in many cases it
is tempered with forms of direct democracy. It is neither possible to identify
pure direct democracies, nor pure representative democracies. Even countries
where there is no provision for *national* referendums (e.g. USA, India and
Israel) one can trace elements of direct democracy, at *subnational* level, as in
many of the states in America, or in subordinate territories, as in India. The
direct election of the prime minister in Israel likewise contains an element of
direct democracy. Not only are citizens increasingly deciding domestic issues,
they also have begun to acquire an authoritative voice on international affairs
(Rourke et al, 1992: 202). The incidence of international issue referendums
has risen sharply in the past ten years. The latter include such issues as
membership of NATO, Spain; 1986, and Hungary; 1997, membership of the
EEA Switzerland; 1992, membership of the European Community; Ireland;
1972, 1986, 1992 and 1998, Denmark; 1972, 1992, 1998. Britain held their
only referendum to date on integration in 1975. France held a referendum
on the proposed enlargement of the EEC in 1972, and a referendum on the
Maastricht Treaty in 1992. In 1994 there were the four referendums on the
question of accession to the EU.

Conclusion

The institution of representation involves a substantial limitation of citizen
autonomy, setting bounds to citizen participation. At EU level this is
exacerbated by the prevailing institutional balance. Laws have been passed
that lacked a clear origin in the sovereignty of the people thereby 'creating
an imbalance in the development and exercise of power between popular

election and regulation by jurisprudence' (Furet, 1995: 89). This is where the initiative and referendums may be useful, to provide ongoing legitimation, and to reassure people of their continued and continuing sovereignty. Recent studies conclude that pressure for more referendums will be felt across Europe in the years ahead (Gallagher and Uleri, 1996: 250).

To create and sustain diffuse support for the EU empowerment of people must be nurtured, at local level, as in power delegated to local authorities, at national level, as in consultation and the use of the tools of semi-direct democracy, and at EU level by taking decisive measures to ensure that a citizen's Europe passes from the realms of myth to a concrete reality, and that the concept is nourished by the growing realization by citizens themselves of the rights, duties and *power* associated with participation.[31] It must also be said that governments cannot shoulder the responsibility alone, the challenge is aimed too at the citizens of the EU. If they do not respond we will be left with the paradox of an attempted democracy containing few participating citizens. The years ahead will present us all with a formidable undertaking, but no more formidable than that undertaken by the early pioneers of integration.

Notes

1 In June 1995 the formal task of drawing up the agenda for further treaty reform was given to this Group. It included one nominee from each of the Member State Governments, two nominees from the European Parliament, and the President of the European Commission.
2 The European Community (EC) and the European Union (EU) are used interchangeably throughout this chapter.
3 Patijn, 1970: 22.
4 Monnet, 1978: 93, 292–3, 295, 296, 321, 324, 383, 387.
5 *Top Decision-makers Survey. Summary Report*, Fieldwork: 19 February–20 May 1996 September 1996.
6 This consensus was described by *Eurobarometer* Autumn 1995 as being more permissive and benevolent than demanding, challenging, pushing and pulling.
7 Legitimacy can exist in a polity that is not governed democratically, the focus is on consent. An example is Germany under Hitler, where consent of the majority was given to the power relation. The Weimar republic, on the other hand, boasted democratic institutions and a constitution, but there was a shadow of doubt over its legitimacy.
8 In a 57.3 per cent turnout of eligible voters, 69.1 per cent voted yes.
9 In 1992, just days before the referendum on the Treaty on European Union, the Irish government made the unprecedented move of ordering the state television and radio network to give air time to a broadcast calling for support of the Treaty by the Taoiseach, Albert Reynolds. There were last minute fears that the campaign had not been as successful as had been expected. The government did not allow the opposition the opportunity to respond. It was an action more appropriate to a state of emergency.

10   Article A, Treaty on European Union: 'This Treaty marks a new stage in the process of creating an ever closer union among the peoples of Europe'. See also Preamble of The Treaty of Rome, and the Preamble of The Treaty on European Union.

11   Council Report, p. 6 and Committee of the Regions Report, pp. 35, 38.

12   Commission Report, preface, p. 1.

13   Parliament Resolution, 1.1.

14   ECOSOC Report, 1.2.

15   The Commission Reports make frequent reference to 'Europe's cultural heritage' and to 'spreading European messages across borders'. There is also an emphasis on symbols, a European flag, a European anthem, European passport, and European sporting occasions.

16   It must be emphasized that EU citizenship is conditional on holding the nationality of a member state. According to Article 8 EC Treaty (as amended by the Treaty on European Union), 'Citizenship of the Union is hereby established'. Among other rights, European citizens were granted the right to vote at municipal elections, and to vote in and stand as candidate for, the European elections when residing in a country where he/she is a non-national. The underlying dynamic in the establishment of European citizenship is described by Elisabeth Meehan as a new kind of citizenship that is 'neither national nor cosmopolitan but is multiple in enabling the various identities that we all possess to be expressed, and our rights and duties exercised through a complex configuration of common institutions (Meehan, 1993: 185).

17   This notion parallels Anderson's definition of the nation as an imagined community. Geilner sees nationalism 'not as the awakening of nations to selfconsciousness: it invents nations where they do not exist' (1964: 169). It cannot be said that it is possible to invent European consciousness, or European identity, and in any case nation building was a long process. There are unlikely to be short cuts.

18   Article 137 [189 new].

19   This holds true also for contacting other representatives, such as the Committee of the Regions, and the Economic and Social Committee, since their position in the power scale is even weaker than the EP.

20   Sinnott, R., Blondel, J. and Svensson, P. (1998) *People and Parliament in the European Union: Participation, Democracy and Legitimacy.*

21   *Dail Debate*, 23 April 1998, Vol. 489, n. 8.

22   John Downing's *About Europe* column, *Irish Independent Monday* and Kevin Moore, *Irish Independent*, 5 April 1998.

23   The commission, which was established as an independent statutory body under the Referendum Act 1998, is charged with overseeing the information campaign on the Amsterdam Treaty referendum. It must also facilitate balanced and fair debate.

24   Ireland's leading authority on polling attitudes to the EU, Dr Richard Sinnott remarked that he could not remember ever having seen such a high 'don't know' figure (*Irish Times*, 3 April).

25   Citizen frustration during the Amsterdam negotiations was contained by the threat of detention. Dutch police arrested about 120 protesters who were shouting outside hotels where European Leaders were staying. On Sunday night 15 June 340 people were arrested following demonstrations. Several hundred protesters marched for two months across Europe, and were joined by thousands of others. They clashed with riot police, order was restored before 'Europe's big boys flew in' (*The European*, 19–25 June 1997). Riot police were equally solicitous about the sleep of the leaders, and arrested the citizens who tried to make a loud din outside various hotels.

26 426 US 668, at 672 (1995).
27 One reason is that the initiative is used in so few countries.
28 Governments cannot always predict the outcome, and will occasionally still forge ahead with a referendum. The Spanish referendum on NATO in 1986 is a case in point, as all actors at the time admitted that the government were taking the risk that the referendum might be lost. Although the vote was to be consultative, the Spanish government promised not to go against the will of the people.
29 A form of direct democracy was also proposed by the EP in Doc_en\rr\311\311839. Rapporteur: Mr Philippe Herzog.
30 This proposal is one of many contained in a recent study commissioned by the European Parliament (Weiler, 1996).
31 A crucial issue is the growing apathy among electors. This to will have to be addressed if democracy is to continue to thrive.

References

Anderson, B. (1983), *Imagined Communities*, Verso, London.

Anderson, S. and Burns T.R. (1996), 'The European Union and the Erosion of Parliamentary Democracy: A Study of Post-parliamentary Governance', in S. Anderson and K.A. Eliassen (eds), *The European Union:How Democratic is it?*, Sage Publications, London.

Anderson, S. and Eliassen, K.A. (1996), *The European Union: How Democratic is it?*, Sage Publications, London.

Beetham, D. (1991), *The Legitimation of Power*, Macmillan, London.

Bobbio, N. (1987), *The Future of Democracy. A Defence of the Rules of the Game*, Polity, New York.

Bogdanor, V. (1994), 'Western Europe', in D. Butler and A. Ranney (eds), *Referendums around the World. The Growing Era of Direct Democracy*, Macmillan, London.

Bogdanor, V. (1996), 'The European Union, the Political Class and the People', in J. Hayward (ed.), *Elitism, Populism, and European Politics*, Oxford University Press, New York, pp. 101–20.

Bogdanor, V. (1997), *Power and the People*, Victor Gollanz, London.

Butler, D. and Ranney, A. (eds) (1994), *Referendums around the World. The Growing Era of Direct Democracy*, Macmillan, London.

Crewe, L. (1981), 'Electoral Participation', in D. Butler et al. (eds), *Democracy at the Polls: A Comparative Study of Competitive National Elections*, American Enterprise Institute for Public Policy Research, Washington, DC, pp. 216–23.

Deschouwer, K. (1996) Political parties and Democracy: A mutual murder? *European Journal of Political Research.* 29 (April) pp. 262-78.

Dinan, D. (1994), *Ever Closer Union*, Lynne Rienner London.

Gallagher, M. and Uleri, P. (1996), *The Referendum Experience in Europe*, Macmillan, London.

Greenfield L. (1993), 'Nationalism and Democracy: The Nature of the Relationship and the Cases of England, France, and Russia', in F.D. Weil (ed.), *Research on Democracy and Society*, Jai Press, Connecticut.

Hayward, J. (ed.) (1996), *Elitism, Populism, and European Politics*, Oxford University Press, New York.

Monnet, J. (1978), *Jean Monnet Memoirs*, Collins, London.
Neuman, W.R. (1986), *The Paradox of Mass Politics*, Harvard University Press, Cambridge, MA.
Patijn, P. (ed.) (1970), *Landmarks in European Unity. 22 Texts on European Integration*, Sijthoff, Leydem.
Reif, H. (1993), 'Cultural Convergence and Cultural Diversity as Factors in European Identity'. in S. García (ed.) (1993), *European Identity and the Search for Legitimacy*, Pinter, London, pp. 131–53.
Reisinger, W.R. (1997), 'Choices Facing The Builders of a Liberal Democracy', in R.D. Gray (ed.), *Democratic Theory and Post-Communist Change*, Prentice Hall, New Jersey, pp. 24–51.
Rourke, J.T., Hiskes, R.P and Zirakzadeh, C.E. (eds) (1992), *Direct Democracy and International Politics. Deciding International Issues through Referendums*, Lynne Reine, London.
Sartori, G. (1987), *The Theory of Democracy Revisited*, Chatham House, Chatham.
Schmitter, P.C. (1995), *Democracy in the Emerging Euro-polity: Temporary or Permanent Deficit?*, ms, Stanford, Centre for European Studies, Stanford University.
Schumpeter, J.A. (1947), *Capitalism, Socialism, and Democracy*, Harper and Row, New York.
Sinnott, R., Blondel, J. and Svensson, P. (1998), *People and Parliament in the European Union: Participation, Democracy and Legitimacy*, Oxford University Press, New York.
Urwin, D.W. (1991), *The Community of Europe. A History of European Integration since 1945*, Longman, Essex.
Weiler, J.H.H. et al. (1996), *Certain Rectangular Problems of European Integration*, European Parliament.

Journals

De Burca, G. (1996), 'The Quest for Legitimacy in the European Union', *Modern Law Review*, Vol. 59, No. 3, pp. 349–76.
Fitzmaurice, J. (1995), 'The 1994 Referenda on EU Membership in Austria and Scandinavia. A Comparative Analysis', *Electoral Studies*, Vol. 14, No. 2, pp. 226–32.
Frey, B.S. and Bohnet, I. (1995), 'Switzerland – a Paradigm for Europe?', *European Review*, Vol. 3, No. 4, pp. 287–94.
Furet, F. (1995), 'Europe after Utopianism'. *Journal of Democracy*, Vol. 6, No. 1, p. 80.
Isaac, J.C. (1994) 'Oases in the Desert: Hannah Arendt on Democratic Politics', *American Political Science Review*, Vol. 18, No. 1, pp. 156–68.
Laffan, B. (1996), 'The Politics of Identity and Political Order in Europe', *Journal of Common Market Studies*, Vol. 34, No. 1, pp. 81–102.
Luthardt, W. (1991–92), 'Direct Democracy in Western Europe: The Case of Switzerland', *Telos*, Vol. 90 (Winter), pp. 101–12.
Neumann, I. (1994), 'A Region Building Approach to Northern Europe', *Review of International Studies*, Vol. 20.
Papadopoulos, Y. (1995), 'Analysis of Functions and Dysfunctions of Direct Democracy', *Politics and Society*, Vol. 23, No. 4 (December).
Schmitter, P.C. (1994), 'Dangers and Dilemmas of Democracy', *Journal of Democracy*, Vol. 5, No. 2 (April).

Toffler, A. and Toffler, H. (1992), '21st-Century Democracy: An Idea Whose Time Has Come', *New Perspectives Quarterly*, Vol. 9 (Fall).

Wallace, W. and Smith, J. (1995), 'Democracy or Technocracy? European Integration and the Problem of Popular Consent', *Western European Politics*, pp. 137–57.

Weiler, J.H.H. (1995), 'European Democracy and its Critique', *West European Politics*, Vol. 18, No. 30, pp. 4–39.

Weiler, J.H.H. (1997), 'The European Union belongs to its Citizens', *European Law Review*, Vol. 22, No. 2, pp. 150–56.

Papers

Nentwich, M., 'Opportunity Structures for Citizens'? Participation: The Case of the European Union. *European Integration online papers*, Vol. 0, 1996, No. 1, http://eiop.ac.atleiop/texte/1 996-001.htm.

Wessels, W. and Diedrichs, U., 'A New Kind of Legitimacy for a New Kind of Parliament – The Evolution of the European Parliament', *European Integration online papers*, Vol. 1, 1997, No. 006, http://eiop. or at/eiop/texte/1997-006a.htm.

Chapter 5

Dealing with Diversity Regional Policy – A Possible Solution?

Bríd Quinn

The European Community,[1] since its formation, has been the repository of the dreams of both utilitarians and utopians. The issue of regional development is one on which utilitarian and utopian views concomitantly coincide and collide. Though originally established as an economic entity the European Community has continually aspired to political unity while endeavouring to preserve the diversity of its component parts. The process of European integration has had both static and dynamic effects on its constituent regions with some regions being more affected than others. One approach to dealing with the uneven impact of integration has been the Community's evolving regional policy, a policy which encompasses aspirations and actions aimed at reducing regional and social disparities. The rationale for Community regional policy has stemmed from normative, remedial, social, integrationist and economic motives. Among the changes wrought have been improvements in the economies and infrastructure of the Community's poorer regions, adjustments in the relationship between national and subnational actors within the member states and the forging of new relationships between these actors and Community institutions and officials. No specific theoretical framework or even a synthesis of theoretical perspectives has served to explain fully the disparity of regional development within and between the Community's member states.[2] Regional policy as it has evolved within the Community does not fit neatly into the intergovernmental, neo-functional or consociational ways of theorizing about the Community while the multilevel governance approach serves to describe the process but is not conducive to hypothesizing possible institutional outcomes. Yet, regional policy has served to redistribute resources, counter the negative aspects of integration, foster development, promote strategic planning and systematic procedures. encourage transnational and interinstitutional cooperation, expand the role of subnational authorities and embody solidarity between member states with such varying capacity and institutions. Bachtler and Turok assert that the structural and cohesion policies of the Community 'are among the most significant areas of EU action in many respects. They have a direct impact on the lives of millions of citizens and may help to make the concept of Europe more meaningful to ordinary people' (1997: 5). This chapter sets out to explore the conceptual and practical approaches to Community regional policy as they impinge on the 'ordinary people', the Europeans who make up the Community.

The diversity of regional disparities has long been a source of concern to European Community actors. Walsh (1991: 10) has thus encapsulated the unevenness:

> [t]he inner central regions cover 5 per cent of the surface area, include 22 per cent of the population, 25 per cent of the employment and account for 28 per cent of the GDP of the Community. By contrast the peripheral regions cover 56 per cent of the total surface area and account for 33 per cent of the total population. They provide only 27 per cent of the total employment and generate under 24 per cent of the total GDP.

The ideology of integration and recognition of regional realities have not been enough. Solutions ranging from subsidies to subsidiarity have been suggested but socioeconomic and political inequalities between the regions persist. The European Commission's *First Report on Economic and Social Cohesion* has summarized the disparities as follows:

> Over the 10 years 1983 to 1993, growth in GDP has varied markedly between regions. The difference in GDP per head between the 10 richest regions and the European average has widened while the gap between the 10 poorest and the average has narrowed at a slightly faster rate (1996a: 21).

National approaches to regional policy have also altered over the years and Bachtler and Michie (1993) suggest that the change has involved a reappraisal of the role of national governments, a devolution of policy responsibilities to the subnational level, an increase in the discretionary element and the growing importance and influence of Community regional policy. Within the European Community the regional debate has taken place on two platforms – the economic with convergence/divergence being the main issue and the political platform with the role of national, subnational and supranational levels of governance being the focus of debate. The dominant discourse on regional policy has been economic, albeit a changing discourse which has reflected the theoretical trends in economics – the emphasis on international trade theory in the early stages of European integration, then the acceptance of cumulative causation theories, the advocacy of regional growth centres and more recently the promotion of indigenous development and regional innovation strategies.

This chapter concerns itself with the human dimension of regional policy and the ever-changing relationship between the various actors involved in Community regional policy. The difficulties in delineating regions and conceptualizing development are outlined. The evolution of Community Regional policy is then traced with attention being drawn to the impact of this policy on the Europeans involved, namely the policy-makers, those charged with implementation of regional policy and the 'recipients' of the policy. Specific examples are drawn from the experiences of Ireland, a member state for whom Community regional policy has been particularly significant. In conclusion some issues which must be addressed in formulating a new strategy for regional policy in an enlarged Community are highlighted.

Depicting the Regions

A map of 'Europe of the regions' would vary considerably depending on the criteria chosen. The notion of unequal development at the core and periphery has frequently been used as an explanation for varying patterns of economic growth, but other factors are also significant, namely the political, institutional, social and industrial culture of the region. The term 'region' has been variously used to describe historical, cultural, economic or political entities, thus posing problems of nomenclature, not only for academic theorists but for economists, politicians, anthropologists and citizens. Some see this multiplicity of conceptualization as the essence of regional problems: 'Peripheral predicaments and politicization emerge out of the incongruity between cultural, economic and political roles that has existed on the continent as long as there have been states' (Rokkan and Urwin, 1983: 192).

Whereas the primary characteristic of political regions is their politico-administrative status, constitutional recognition and regional identity are not synonymous. Scotland exhibits a strong consciousness of separateness though it does not yet enjoy political autonomy. The Spanish regions display varying degrees of independence from Madrid resulting in an asymmetric regionalism but the financial and political empowerment bestowed by Community regional policy is of immense significance in regions such as Extremadura and Catalonia. Although the German *Länder* are constitutionally strong, there is evidence of powerful national sentiments with inter-regional cultural diversity being less evident in Germany than in Italy's more politically entwined regions. Thus, regional definition along political lines does not eliminate ambiguity. It is not only the political delineation of the region which poses problems but also their changing political roles with regions now serving both as actors and arenas in the process of regional policy, a phenomenon which has become more evident with each reform of the Community's regional policy process.

In economic terms, 'region' is an equally difficult concept to define, particularly for comparative purposes. Within the European Community one of Germany's constitutionally defined regions, Nord-Rhein Westphalia, contains 4.7 per cent of the Community's population and would be ranked tenth in the world's export economy rankings (Newman, 1996: 127). Ireland, on the other hand, accounts for only 1 per cent of the Community's population. Yet, both Nord-Rhein Westphalia and Ireland are perceived as regions within the Community and are treated accordingly. The Community has had to invent its own classification categories, the infamous NUTS (nomenclature of units for territorial statistics), and is creating a database of regional conditions but Balme (1997) warns about the impossibility of methodologically isolating regional entities according to empirical criteria and the danger of political stigmatization if such classification procedures are employed.

Two centuries ago Edmund Burke wrote of the difficulties of reconciling the regional and the universal, the particularist past with the cosmopolitan future. The dilemma of trying to slot culturally distinctive regions with particular ethnic identities into strictly politically defined areas has not still been resolved as the tensions in Spain would indicate. The 1993 'regional reconstruction' in Belgium grew from a form of cultural intransigence while the current desire for regional autonomy in Italy has roots in the socio-cultural North–South divide. So, even the notion of cultural homogeneity does not serve to delineate regional entities. Regions may also be perceived as social spaces with ever-changing patterns of interaction between those occupying the social space, patterns which include convergence of values but also value conflicts. These various historical, political, economic, social and cultural configurations illustrate the complexity of regional definition and reflect the widespread depiction of the region as both a concept and a construct within the process of European integration, wherein the region is both 'a forum of governance ... and a possible area for mobilisation' (Le Galés, 1998).

The Development Dilemma

Notwithstanding the difficulties of regional definition, great faith has been

placed in the notion of regional development as the solution to the problem of disparity, but scant attention has been paid to the nature of development. Too often development has been equated with economic growth in the regions, as exemplified by the performance indicators usually selected by the European Community, namely GDP and unemployment rates. Some 'developers' have attempted to adopt U Thant's maxim that development = economic growth + social change – but without analysing the type of growth necessary or the type of change which is desirable resulting in a situation where actors perceive 'development as the lexicon of palliatives'. A further flaw in such approaches is the tendency to assign a passive role to the target population and to impose development on them rather than assisting them to develop. Initial attempts at regional policy in the Community adopted such a prescriptive tone. More recently attention has been focused on development as a multidimensional process circumscribed by ecological possibility, social acceptability and economic gainfulness.[3] This approach sees development as a response to human rather than economic need and is based on enabling principles such as partnership and subsidiarity, principles enshrined in the Maastricht Treaty and the cumulative reforms of Structural Funding. Engaging in such development has enormous institutional, social, political and economic implications. Viewed as a multidimensional process development may have various starting points, may operate at different levels and will have different emphases determined by local circumstances. Accordingly, within the Community, the purposes and particular patterns of development will vary greatly from region to region and will be affected to varying degrees by other policies such as budgetary policy, social policy and single market policy as well as the Community's desire to promote justice and equity. Therefore, regional development within the Community is not just about regional policy but is concerned with other policies, relationships and strategies.

The Evolution of Regional Policy within the European Community

The Treaty of Rome sought to ensure 'harmonious development by reducing the differences existing between the various regions and the backwardness of the less favoured regions'. Until 1973 any attempts at regional policy were made in terms of derogation from particular policies such as competition policy, thus permitting member states to grant special aid to problem regions. The first enlargement put the problem of uneven regional development firmly on the Community's agenda. Ireland's membership negotiations included the writing in of a special protocol referring to the need to reduce regional imbalances. The Werner Report of 1970 highlighted the need for a Community regional policy to offset the effects of EMU. The Thomson Report of 1973[4] articulated the moral, environmental and economic case for a regional policy. The growing awareness of the need for a regional policy culminated in the establishment of the European Regional Development Fund (ERDF) in 1975. Criticisms of early attempts at regional development concerned the degree of national control over ERDF spending, the piecemeal approach (since individual projects were funded) and poor targeting (Wise and Gibb, 1993: 217). Changes in 1979 and 1985 brought about a movement towards funding programmes rather than individual projects. Major reforms were introduced in 1989 (spurred by the Single European Act and preparation for the Single Market) and in 1993, as a consequence of the Maastricht Treaty and there were also some adjustments to accommodate Sweden, Finland and Austria when they became members of the Community in 1995. These reforms achieved better coordination of the various Structural Funds – which include the ERDF, the European Social Fund (ESF) and the guidance section of the European Agricultural Guidance and Guarantee Fund. The reforms also included the establishment of a Cohesion Fund which would finance environmental and transport investment projects in member states with a per capita GDP of less than 90 per cent of the Community average. The other specific instrument of regional policy is the Community Initiative, of which there are thirteen in the current funding period ranging from initiatives underpinning technological development to employment and human resource initiatives such as Youthstart and NOW (New Opportunities for Women). Community Initiatives account for just over 9 per cent of the Structural Fund budget and a further 1 per cent is allocated to innovative measures. The Objectives of Structural Fund expenditure are clearly defined as:

- Objective 1: promoting the development and structural adjustment of the regions whose development is lagging behind;
- Objective 2: converting regions or areas seriously affected by industrial decline;
- Objective 3: combating long-term employment;
- Objective 4: increasing youth employment;
- Objective 5a: adjustment of agricultural structures;
- Objective 5b: facilitating the development and structural adjustment of rural areas;
- Objective 6: promoting the development and structural adjustment of regions with an extremely low population density.

The reforms upgraded the position of regional policy within the Community while the articulation of Objectives 1, 2, 5b and 6 gives a specific regional dimension to the Community's promotion of economic and social cohesion. Bachtler and Turok (1997: 357) are critical of the complexity of institutional arrangements implicit in the regional policy structure. They draw attention to the allocative procedures which involve:

> five main funding sources, administered by four different Directorates-General to four geographic objectives (1, 2, 5b and 6) and three horizontal objectives (3, 4 and 5a), producing a complex matrix of expenditure allocation.

This complexity has led to interconnected phases of multilevel design, implementation and evaluation within the regional policy process. By means of these elaborate mechanisms the regional policy of the Community strives to reduce disparities by increasing the capacity of poorer regions and by reducing their infrastructural deficiencies through the use of various financial, coordination and dissemination instruments. Community regional policy has also led to the establishment of Euro-regions, transnational initiatives and cross-border programmes which have brought about new forms of cooperation. There has also been an increase in the number of Regional Information Offices established in Brussels and a flourishing of transnational organizations such as the Assembly of European Regions, the Association of Regions of Traditional Industry and the Conference of Peripheral Maritime Regions. Since 1994 the Committee of the Regions has served a consultative function, a function which has been consolidated and reinforced by the Amsterdam Treaty. These bodies bring together regional and local actors and socialize them into what Loughlin has described as a European political class with a specific regionalist identity and vocation.

If its regional policy is the Community's means of dealing with disparity, the question may be posed – who are the Europeans involved in this policy and has the Community's regional policy strengthened their identity? Leonardi (1995: 215) asserts that regional policy has impacted on subnational government: 'The existence of cohesion as an explicit and widely shared goal of the Community has significantly changed the prospect for and the daily reality of the role and function of regional and local governments at the European level.' Community regional policy also affects and frequently circumscribes national policies. The introduction of the principles of programming, partnership, concentration and additionality in the reform of the Structural Funds as well as inclusion of the principle of subsidiarity in the Maastricht Treaty drew attention to the need for inclusiveness in the formulation and implementation of regional policy. These principles have impacted on the relationships between the various levels of authority and have drawn non-governmental actors into the regional policy arena. The regional policy process brings actors from European, national, regional and local authorities together for a mutual exchange of ideas and resources – financial and legislative from some and expertise, experience and knowledge resources from the others. Structural Funding thus succeeds in galvanizing national, regional and local actors into forming partnerships to identify needs and devise appropriate strategies within the framework of the Community's regional policy instruments, thereby affecting the 'daily reality' of Europeans, strengthening the position of subnational entities and modifying the power structures at all levels.

The Application of Community Regional Policy

This section focuses on the three groups of Europeans – policy makers, policy implementers and the 'recipients' of the policies – involved in the application of Community Regional policy. Special emphasis is given to Community regional policy as it affects Ireland since, as Hooghe (1996) asserts, Ireland is the clearest example of how EU cohesion programming has begun to energize subnational politics. The Community Support Framework agreed for the 1994–99 period means that Ireland will receive approximately 5.62 billion ECU (which when combined with public and private sector funding will mean a total investment of approximately 12.5 billion ECU). The 1989–93 tranche represented an annual allocation of 253 ECU per head of population while the 1994–99 Objective I allocation yields 262 ECU per head of population annually (Commission, 1996b: 151). These investments have been translated into tangible benefits such as improved transport (a total time-saving of 87.8 minutes on the four key road corridors) and communication infrastructure (a 14 per cent increase in the digitalization rate), increased opportunities for education and training, assistance with many aspects of business (3,926 new business start-ups)[5] as well cultural and heritage projects and local development initiatives. The National Economic and Social Council (1997: 249) draws attention to the qualitative effects.

> Ireland's involvement in EU regional policy has significant qualitative advantages. EU regional policy requires the preparation of development plans and multi-annual programmes. It has supported new approaches to local

development and, in general, has been an important stimulus to innovation in the design and implementation of policy.

Community regional policy has helped Ireland to overcome its post-colonial underdevelopment and transcend its peripherality while simultaneously strengthening its external and internal institutional links.

For policy makers, Community regional policy has acted as a catalyst for change. From the earlier outline of the evolution of Community regional policy, it is clear that there has been a metamorphosis in the philosophy of regional policy and regional development. Initially, the approach was top-down and prescriptive with a strong economic orientation. The adoption of consultative procedures and the involvement of regional actors in the policy process as well as the broadening of policy issues to include social and environmental concerns illustrate the change of approach by policy makers. In effect regional policy is one of the few areas where the involvement of subnational units of governance is an integral part of Community policy and the resultant regulations and implementation procedures, a system which succeeds despite the wide variation in member state structures and practices. Ireland's highly centralized state structure coupled with the designation of the entire country as a single region for Community Regional policy purposes had given the national government a key role in the implementation of Community Regional policy with most funding being disbursed by government departments. However, Community regional policy was one of the factors which led to the establishment of eight Regional Authorities in 1994. Among their primary functions is the review and monitoring of Community Assistance programmes in the regions. Although still weak and rather artificial bodies the Regional Authorities have the potential to become significant players. Since 1997 their chairpersons have been included in the Structural Fund Monitoring Committee. *Agenda 2000* places great stress on decentralized and simplified implementation, sentiments which were reinforced in the proposed regulations for the next round of Structural Funding, published in March 1998. Accordingly, the Department of Finance (the government department with overall responsibility for implementing the Community Support Framework) has requested each Regional Authority to prepare a submission outlining their views on priorities for the next National Plan and Regional Authorities, in turn, have begun consulting with public and voluntary bodies in the regions. This management of the consultation procedure marks a growth in status for the Regional Authorities and an institutionalization of a process which was merely symbolic during the drafting of the previous National Development Plan.

For those charged with implementing Community Regional policy at all levels – European, national and regional/local there has been a realignment of roles. At the European level this has meant a new set of relationships as well as a greater administrative burden because of the complexities of organizing and monitoring the plethora of programmes involved. Community regional policy has also served to strengthen the role of the Commission since, as a result of the various reforms of regional policy, the Commission has effectively become the 'process manager'. At national level there has been a reorganization of political activity as studies such as those carried out by Leonardi (1993) and Hanf and Soetendorp (1998) demonstrate. Europeanization has led to administrative and institutional adjustment in all member states. In Ireland acceptance of the principles of programming, partnership, concentration and additionality has changed the *modus operandi* of successive governments since 1988. The need to implement these principles has been one of the catalysts of change. Recent research (carried out on behalf of the European Commission) assessing the implementation of the Structural Funds concludes that in Ireland the 'Structural Fund programmes have for the first time introduced a radical decentralization of tasks to the local level' (Lang, forthcoming). The increasing importance accorded to the 'Third Level' on the European stage has also helped to strengthen the role of Ireland's subnational actors. The opening up of direct links between Irish local authorities and Brussels offered what Coyle has described as 'a lifeline for Irish local authorities' although criticism is warranted of the fact that the links are generally with administrators rather than the elected representatives on the authorities. In recent years local authorities have built up relationships with Commission officials, participated in training programmes in European affairs, widened their network of horizontal and vertical relationships and generally benefited from their involvement. Since 1992 the local authorities have a consultancy service available to them which provides information about EU affairs and is operated by the Institute of Public Administration. Thus, EU membership and particularly the Union's regional policy instruments have served to strengthen the subnational tier in Ireland. However, even in Ireland, regional policy has not proved a panacea for subnational actors. Rees (1996) and Coyle (1994) have found concern among local/regional officials in Ireland about the administrative and personal costs of cooperation in this area.

In Ireland the role of the 'recipients' has changed. The partnership approach had already become the norm in the negotiation of national wage agreements in Ireland and in recent years has become the cornerstone of local development activities. Indeed, the OECD has lauded the Irish model of partnership in Sabel's evaluation which suggests that 'the partnerships have provided models for widening participation in the processes of change within the economy and society. The partnerships act as conduits for local involvement in formulating strategies, channelling resources and implementing policies'(1996: 4). The 1988 reform of Structural Funding obliged member states to prepare national development plans incorporating multi-annual integrated programmes and based on consultation with the various partners involved in all aspects of development, thus further formalizing the consultative procedure and the partnership process. Involvement in initiatives facilitated by Community regional policy such as IRD Pilot Projects, area-based partnerships and model action programmes under the EC Poverty programme, has strengthened the identity of many of local actors. The extent of involvement is illustrated by the LEADER programme, for example, which provides an opportunity to innovate and test alternative approaches to rural development. The entire catchment area of this Community Initiative accounts for over 60 per cent of the national population and the geographical area involved is estimated at about 99 per cent of the land area of Ireland (Kearney, 1997). Such manifestations of Community regional policy serve not only as a source of funding but also act as a means of empowerment and a channel through which to influence policy and harness the capacity of local communities.

Conclusions

Leonardi (1993) claims that during the last 40 years, economic and social cohesion has taken place in the European Community. He shows that of 80 regions monitored the gap between the single most developed and the single least developed region fell from the 1970 level of 5.0/1 to 3.5/1 in 1990. In addition to positive economic effects there has been a growth in the identity, confidence and the recognition of regions. Relationships between the actors involved in regional policy have changed, networks have been established, territorial politics have been adjusted and a progressive understanding of the nature of development has emerged as well as an increase in cooperative work practices between public, private and voluntary actors. Community regional policy has acted both as a catalyst and a laboratory for such change and has facilitated the application of subsidiarity while at the same time overlaying a uniform framework on kaleidoscopic national and regional contexts. The regional policy dynamics and policy processes have led to a kind of political photosynthesis with European Community institutions penetrating the politics and society of member states and the national, local and regional structures of the member states becoming an integral part of the institutions and procedures of the European Community. Yet, many social, political and economic disparities continue. Neither do all commentators see regional policy in a positive light. Economists such as Hanson are sceptical about the efficacy of regional policies as a means of reducing disparities, while some eminent political scientists cast doubts on the credo of regionalism – one even argues that '[r]egionalism as a political doctrine verges on the absurd, failing to distinguish between the contrary values of national separatism or irredentism, on the one hand, and the general decentralization of state authority on the other' (Coombes, 1991: 134). Such debate on the efficacy of regional policy as a means of dealing with diversity is indeed healthy and helpful.

The context of Community regional policy is likely to undergo profound change in the near future – enlargement of the Union will have serious implications for the making and implementation of regional policy as will the achievement of economic and monetary union. The publication of *Agenda 2000* and the mid-term evaluation of the current round of Structural Funding combined with the ongoing discussions on reform of regional policy instruments have highlighted the need to adapt the current model of policy formulation, implementation and evaluation. There is a need to rationalize and simplify the range of policy instruments. The scope and timing of measures needs to be tightened and the operational complexity needs to be reduced. The financing of regional policy remains a major issue since the limits imposed by the budgetary ceiling and the question of co-financing have still to be resolved. Evaluation procedures also need to be streamlined and the purposes and procedures for evaluation need to be clarified so that the effectiveness of Community regional policy in dealing with diversity can be assessed. These issues need to be addressed if regional policy is to continue to reflect the aspirations expressed by the former President of the European Parliament: 'Europe should not be about anonymous bureaucracies and supranational power games. It is above all about the quality of life and aspirations of the individuals who live in our regions, cities towns and villages' (Klepsch, 1993).

Notes

1   The term European Community is deliberately used throughout the chapter.
2   See, for example, the works of Albrechts, Amin, Christiansen, Hooghe, Keating, Marks, Rhodes and Sharpe.
3   See for example, Kearney (1994), Scott (1995), Walsh (1995) and Grimes (1992).
4   Supplement 8/73.

5   Figures in this section are taken from the Structural Funds Information Unit's Press
     Release.

References

Albrechts, L. (ed.) (1989), *Regional Policy at the Crossroads: European Perspectives*, Jessica
    Kingsley Publishers, London.
Amin, A. and Tomaney, J. (eds) (1995), *Beyond the Myth of the European Union*, Routledge,
    London.
Bachtler, J. and Michie R. (1993), 'The Restructuring of Regional Policy in the European
    Community', *Regional Studies*, Vol. 27, No. 8, pp. 719–25.
Bachtler, J. and Turok, I. (eds) (1997), *The Coherence of EU Regional Policy*, Jessica Kingsley
    Publishers, London.
Balme, R. (1998), 'Regional Policy and European Governance', in M. Keating and J. Loughlin
    (eds) (1997), *The Political Economy of Regionalism*, Frank Cass, London.
Commission of the European Communities (1996a), *First Report on Economic and
    Social Cohesion*, Office for the Official Publications of the European Communities,
    Luxembourg.
Commission of the European Communities (1996b), *The Structural Funds in 1996*,
    Eighth Annual Report, Office for Official Publications of the European Communities,
    Luxembourg.
Coombes, D. (1991), 'Europe and the Regions', in B. Crick (ed.), *National Identities: The
    Constitution of the United Kingdom*, Blackwell, Oxford.
Coyle, C. (1994), 'Irish Local Administration in the National and European Policy Process',
    Research in Urban Policy, Vol. 5.
Crick, B. (ed.), *National Identities: the Constitution of the United Kingdom*, Blackwell,
    Oxford.
Dehousse, R. and Christiansen, T. (1996), *What Model for the Committee of the Regions?*,
    European University Institute, Florence.
European Parliament (1995), *The Impact of National Public Expenditure on the Regional
    Disparities Within Europe* (External Study W-14), Directorate General for Research,
    Luxembourg.
EU Structural Funds Information Unit (1997), 'EU Structural Funds for Ireland: A Continuing
    Success Story', Press Release, 29 July, Department of Finance, Dublin.
Fitzpatrick Associates (1997), *Mid-term Evaluation: Regional Impact of the Community Support
    Framework for Ireland 1994–1999*, Fitzpatrick Associates, Dublin.
Goulet, D. (1992), '"Development" ... or "Liberation?"', in C. Wilber and K. Jameson (eds), *The
    Political Economy of Development and Underdevelopment*, McGraw-Hill, New York.
Grimes, S. (1992), 'Beyond Economics, Redefining Development', *Administration*, Vol. 40,
    No. 2, pp. 125–33.
Hanf, K. and Soetendorp, B. (1998), *Adapting to European Integration, Small States and the
    EU*, Longman, London.
Hooghe, L. (ed.) (1996), *Cohesion Policy and European Integration: Building Multi-level
    Governance*, Oxford University Press, Oxford.

Hooghe, L. and Marks, G. (1995), 'Channels of Subnational Representation in the European Union', in R. Dehousse and T. Christiansen (eds), *What Model for the Committee of the Regions?*, European University Institute, Florence.

Holmes, M. and Rees, N. (1995), 'Regions within a Region: The Paradox of the Republic of Ireland', in B. Jones and M. Keating (eds) (1995), *The European Union and the Regions*, Clarendon Press, Oxford.

Jeffery, C. (ed.) (1997), *The Regional Dimension of the European Union, Towards a Third Level in Europe?*, Frank Cass, London.

Jones, B. and Keating, M. (eds) (1995), *The European Union and the Regions*, Clarendon Press, Oxford

Kearney, B. (1997), *Mid-term Evaluation of the EU LEADER Initiative in Ireland*, Environmental Productions, Dublin.

Keating, M. and Loughlin, J. (eds) (1997), *The Political Economy of Regionalism*, Frank Cass, London.

Klepsch, E. (1993), Sunderland Lecture, quoted in Newman, M. (1996), *Democracy, Sovereignty and the European Union*, Hurst and Company, London.

Le Galés, P. and Lequesne, C. (eds) (1998), *Regions in Europe*, Routledge, London.

Leonardi, R. (1993), 'Cohesion in the European Community: Illusion or Reality?', *West European Politics*, Vol. 16, No. 4 (October), pp. 492–517.

National Economic and Social Council (1997), *European Union: Integration and Enlargement*, NESC Paper No. 101, NESC, Dublin.

Newman, M. (1996), *Democracy, Sovereignty and the European Union*, Hurst and Company, London.

O'Donnell, R. (1993), *Ireland and Europe: Challenges for a New Century*, ESRI Policy Research Series Paper No. 17, ESRI, Dublin.

OECD (1996), *Ireland: Local Partnerships and Social Innovation*, OECD, Paris.

Rees, N. (1996), 'Inter-regional Cooperation: An Effective Means towards Sustained Economic Development?', paper presented to the Conference *Inter-regional Co-operation for Regional Development*, Limerick, September.

Sharpe, L.J. (ed.) (1993), *The Rise of Meso Government in Europe*, Sage, London.

Scott, J. (1995), *Development Dilemmas in the European Community*, Open University Press, Buckingham.

Walsh, J. (1995), 'Local Development Theory and Practice: Recent Experiences in Ireland', paper presented to the seminar, *Sustainable Regional and Local Development*, Maynooth, July.

Wilber, C. and Jameson, K. (eds), *The Political Economy of Development and Underdevelopment*, McGraw-Hill, New York.

Wise, M. and Gibb, R. (1993), *Single Market to Social Europe*, Longman, Harlow.

Chapter 6

Pecuniary Identity and European Integration

Nickolas Reinhardt

At their Brussels Summit meeting in May 1998, the heads of state and government of the European Union (EU) endorsed the decision to create an economic and monetary union (EMU) among 11 member states by 1 January 1999. In the process, the currencies of the participating member states will be replaced by one single European legal tender.

This chapter discusses the political and psychological consequences of switching from the national to a single European currency. It is argued that money is more than a tradable commodity. Money is an integral part of each country's national and state identity. As regards the European integration process, two conflicting conclusions can be drawn from this observation. On the one hand, the existing national 'pecuniary identities' can constitute a powerful obstacle to monetary union in the transition towards EMU. On the other hand, once introduced, the single currency has the potential of developing into a central symbol of a new European citizenship and identity. This chapter will discuss these two countervailing effects and lay out conditions under which the European currency could become a focal point for a common European identity.

As Handler warns us, the term 'identity' is in itself ambiguous, open to constant construction, deconstruction and reconstruction (Handler, 1994: 27). Identity, much like the terms of 'culture', 'nation' or 'state' on which it is based, never stands by itself, but is used within the context of a particular political discourse. It is constructed of numerous symbols which give meaning to abstract and intangible political processes, such as common historic experiences or shared values (Edelman, 1974[1964]: 6–8). Currencies serve as one such symbol. Based on the name, history, appearance and public acceptance of the national currency, each country has developed its own monetary symbolism or 'pecuniary identity'. To prove the validity of this argument, this chapter will study the German and British debates on EMU. In both countries, public opinion remains overtly sceptical of European monetary integration. The loss of identity features prominently as a motive for this opposition to monetary union. Other reasons include the fear that EMU will lead to high unemployment and lower living standards (European Commission, 1996).

As the debates in Germany and the United Kingdom reveal, each country has developed its own distinct pecuniary identity. In Germany the currency is closely associated with postwar economic recovery and price stability. In the United Kingdom, in contrast, national control over monetary affairs is inseparably linked to the constitutional principle of 'parliamentary sovereignty'. As a result, different prospects for joining European monetary union arise for both countries. While Germany's pecuniary identity is more likely to give way to EMU if certain economic conditions are met, in Britain the situation is more protracted. Here the new single currency potentially challenges the constitutional foundations of the British state. The significance of currencies as symbols of national and state identity can therefore be only understood if applied to a specific national discourse. The diverse nature of the existing national 'pecuniary identities' has to be borne in mind when discussing the likelihood of a common European 'pecuniary identity' emerging.

The chapter is structured as follows: four different but inter-related arguments will be put forward to show why currencies can be powerful images of national or state identity. These are contrasted with an extreme position explicitly rejecting such a role for money. The chapter goes on to compare the German and British discourses on EMU by asking how the particular national 'pecuniary identity' has affected the process of European monetary integration. The chapter closes with some comments on whether Europe will develop its own 'pecuniary identity' and, if so, whether this new feeling of belonging will facilitate further moves towards European integration.

Currencies as Tradable Commodities

Before laying down different arguments supporting the claim that money fulfils political and social functions which make it a symbol of identity, this chapter will state the extreme position which explicitly rejects such a role. This derives from the economic functions of money.

Most importantly, money serves as a *numéraire* or 'unit of account' for economic transactions. The relative prices of all goods and services can be expressed as a value of this one commodity. This does not have to be a currency in the conventional sense, nor does it have to be issued by a central institution. In postwar Germany, for example, cigarettes became a widely accepted *numéraire*.

Money, secondly, is a medium of payment. Direct barter transactions depend on a coincidence of wants between the buyer and seller. This can be avoided if money is introduced as an intermediary form of payment. The process of buying and selling can be conducted at different times and with various agents (Brunner and Meltzer, 1971). According to Tobin, the benefits of money rise with the number of people using it. Consequently, a currency area should be as large as possible (Tobin, 1961). Following Tobin's argument, national currency boundaries have more economic disadvantages than benefits.

Finally, money makes it possible to defer payments and store wealth. This last function is based on the assumption that money retains its value and credibility through time. Storable commodities, such as gold, meet this condition.

An overview over the economic functions of money does not readily lead to the conclusion that money could be an important symbol of state or national identity. In fact, it appears that the circulation of money need neither be restricted to national or state boundaries, nor that money has to be issued centrally by political institutions. The increasing volatility of the capital markets seems to indicate that money has become detached from its political entities (Fraenkel and Johnson, 1976). There are also numerous historic examples where currencies fulfilled their economic role outside distinct national or state boundaries. This was especially the case when the value of money was determined by its content in metal (the gold and silver coins).

From this Hayek et al. conclude that there is no logical economic justification for the state's control over money (Hayek, 1937, 1976; Salin, 1985). They call for a 'denationalization of money' and propose to entrust private banks with issuing their own money. These currencies should then freely compete against one another on the money markets. The more stable currencies would gradually replace the less stable ones; ensuring credibility and price stability for all the market participants. An historic precedent for this currency competition existed in Scotland where three chartered banks issued their own money in the eighteenth century (Vaubel, 1984). The concept re-emerged during the EMU negotiations and was officially submitted by the British government to the intergovernmental conference on monetary union in 1989 (Basevi et al., 1975; HM Treasury, 1989; Major, 1990).

As Hayek himself acknowledges, it is unlikely that competition between currencies will take place on a large scale or under anything but extreme circumstances, such as hyper-inflation or economic and political upheaval. He makes the long historic tradition or 'myth' of state control over money responsible for this:

[The state prerogative over money] can only be explained by a myth becoming so firmly established that it did not even occur to the professional students of these matters (for a long time including the present writer) even to question it (Hayek, 1976: 27).

Currencies as Symbols of Identity

This section will in turn look at the different roots of these historical 'myths'. Four different but interrelated themes are put forward which support the argument that currencies are symbols of identity and convey particular images. The first two of these themes are closely related to the state, while the other two return to the broader concept of national identity.

In his book entitled *Theories of Nationalism* Anthony D. Smith distinguishes between the notion of state identity (reflected in the state's symbols of authority and the demarcation of territorial borders) and national identity (as expressed in a common cultural, linguistic, religious or historical heritage of people) (Smith, 1971: 186). As national conflicts all too clearly demonstrate, these two forms of identity seldom coincide.

With his reference to the 'Janus-faced nature' of money, Kenneth Dyson makes a similar distinction. He stresses that a currency not only fulfils the above-mentioned economic functions necessary for running a modern economy but similarly serves as a symbol of political and cultural identity (Dyson, 1994: 3). The two terms 'politics' and 'culture' (as used by Dyson) are synonyms for 'state' and 'nation' (as defined by Smith). A currency is closely associated with a state's political and legal authority. Moreover, it also reflects and is indeed a result of the common economic history and shared values of society. In the words of Schumpeter, money expresses everything that 'people want, do, suffer and are' (Schumpeter, 1970: 1). As life is determined by economic activity, money becomes an inseparable element of the people's historical heritage.

The State's Prerogative over Money

Wherever a state becomes independent one of the first actions it takes is to issue its own currency. When, in 1583, Bodin listed eight constituting acts of sovereignty, he mentioned the state's prerogative over money as one of the first (Bodin, 1980[1583]: ch. 10). The right to control the circulation of money is given the same status as the state's authority over foreign and defence policy.

Today, there are few cases where a currency area and the territorial borders of a state do not coincide. In most countries the national currency is legal tender. This means that all market participants are obliged by law to accept this national currency as a form of payment.

Since the value of money is no longer fixed to a commodity such as gold, it is the state's authority which renders it credible. It is also the means by which all taxes are paid. The success of a government's monetary policy is measured by the rate of inflation and the external value of the national currency. In the period prior to the EMS crisis of 1992/93, governments invested much of their political reputation into maintaining exchange rates. Devaluation is generally perceived to be a political failure.

Within a state, competences for monetary affairs can be transferred to autonomous or private bodies. In Germany the Deutsche Bundesbank was granted statutory independence in 1957. In Britain the Bank of England remained a private institution until its nationalization in 1948. In 1997 its status changed again when it gained operational independence. While the internal distribution of powers in monetary affairs can cause political conflicts (Marsh, 1992; Roberts and Kynaston, 1995), it does not challenge the state's ultimate responsibility for the national currency. The right of states to conduct their own independent monetary policy is specifically acknowledged by multilateral agreements on monetary cooperation (Mann, 1992).

The state's sole authority over monetary affairs is reaffirmed by the symbols and inscriptions used on the notes and coins. The psychological and political significance of the currency's appearance becomes apparent in multi-ethnic societies. Helbich's case study on Canada's introduction of bank notes in both English and French in 1937 shows how the issue of language and appearance of the currency was tied to the broader debate on the cultural and political foundations of the Canadian state (Helbich, 1995). The significance of the name and symbols of a currency was also apparent during the British debate on decimalization. It was decided to retain pound sterling as the name for the British currency in 1971 because of the 'global reputation' and 'prestige' it enjoyed (Moore, 1973: 36).

The State's Economic and Monetary Sovereignty

The state's monopoly to issue and control the flow of money is closely tied to the question of the state's sovereignty over its own economic and monetary policy. In postwar Europe, there has been a broad consensus that monetary policy should play a crucial role in securing the smooth functioning of the market economy (Euckcn, 1990[1952]: 256). Since then, much of the economic debate has centred around the question how this could best be achieved. Economists in the Keynesian tradition argue that money should facilitate the state's efforts to stabilize the economy and fight unemployment. 'Monetarists', such as Milton Friedman, favour a stable money supply (Screpanti and Zamagni, 1993: 295–339). The progressive liberalization of capital markets has already raised doubts about a state's ability to pursue an independent monetary policy. On joining EMU, the state forfeits this option altogether. Monetary policy is then conduced centrally for the union as a whole.

Monetary union also requires joint decision-making in economic and fiscal policies – hence the reference to an *economic* and *monetary* union. The exact degree of economic policy coordination and harmonization has been the subject of intense debate ever since the European Community first studied the feasibility of monetary integration in 1970. The Werner Report proposed a joint management of budgetary policies, a common approach to social and income policies, fiscal harmonization and a close cooperation in matters of structural and regional affairs. For the purpose a 'European centre of economic decision-making' was to be established. The Report did not elaborate on this last point but clearly supported a supranational and democratically accountable institution (Werner et al., 1970).

At Maastricht, attention focused on stringent budgetary rules for the EMU member states. Although this approach was minimalist in contrast to the earlier proposals, the Maastricht Treaty provisions do nonetheless infringe on traditional rights of national parliaments to decide over the budget. Addressing the House of Commons on 1 March 1995, the then British Prime Minister John Major concluded that the changes brought about by EMU in fiscal and monetary affairs would be 'the most sweeping this house has ever seen' (Hansard, col. 1068). More than most issues the currency lies at the heart of the constitutional arrangements of a state and touches on core elements of its economic sovereignty.

Moreover, the parallel negotiations on EMU and political union at Maastricht demonstrate that for many participants monetary union is not a means in itself but can serve as a motor for further integration. Many authors claim that monetary union will necessarily lead to a collective decision-making on fiscal policies, tax harmonization, an enlarged EU budget and a convergence of social and income policies (Biehi, 1991; Busch, 1994; Eichengreen, 1990). According to the German central bank, EMU will transform the European Union into an 'indissoluble community of solidarity' (Deutsche Bundesbank; 1990: 41). Such an expansion of EU competences would strengthen Europe's supranational institutions with which a new single currency could be readily identified (von Harder, 1996: 373–83).

The Currency as a Medium of Social Interaction

Based on its functions as a 'unit of account' and a medium of payment, money can be described as a means of social interaction or a form of communication (Dowd and Greenaway, 1993: 1180). The economic benefits of a currency increase with the number of people using it. The larger the population sharing the same money, the greater are its network-related benefits and the higher the costs of switching to other forms of payment; especially if the national currency is also the legally binding tender. The economists Dowd and Greenaway call this the 'network externalities' of money. These 'network externalities' explain why even in times of high inflation most market participants continue to use their national currency. Dowd and Greenaway (1993: 1188–9) conclude that the:

> choice of language is similar in many respects to the choice of currency ... The utility of a language to the user depends, in part, on how many others also use it, and we observe the same economies of standardisation in that area as we do in the choice of currency. We also observe similar switching costs problems, and the value-trade-off between the gains of using a common language and the costs of switching over to it.

The proposed concept of currencies as a means of social interaction ties into the 'transactionalist' explanation of nation-building and European integration proposed by Karl W. Deutsch et al. They argue that it is the communication between people (in this case facilitated by the single currency) which shapes their identity. The regular interaction of people promotes the development of common ideas, values and shared historical experiences (Deutsch, 1957, 1966[1953]). The economic functions of money do thereby actually reinforce the currency's importance as a symbol of identity. They also explain why people might find it difficult to part with their well-established terms of economic reference and get accustomed to a new currency.

The Currency as a History of Relationships

Closely linked to the issue of communication is the final point which has to be raised in the context of currencies as symbols of identity. It has already been established that a shared national heritage need not only be based on linguistics, religion and culture but that it can similarly derive from a predominant collective interpretation of history and shared values or beliefs (Bertramsen et al., 1991: 49–65; Gillis, 1994).

A currency is closely associated with the past economic experiences of a nation. It similarly reflects the level of underlying consensus within a society for specific economic objectives, such as price stability, growth or unemployment. As such, the currency is a product of the socialization process within a country. This also finds its reflection in the formal and informal institutional arrangements of the state (Bertramsen et al., 1991: 25–32; North, 1990: 36–53). In Germany, for example, the consensus on price stability has rendered the independent Deutsche Bundesbank a high degree of political influence and credibility.

To underline this last argument of currencies as symbols of national identity, it has to be discussed within the context of a specific political discourse of a country. In the next section, this will be done in turn for Germany and the United Kingdom. It will also be shown how the national 'pecuniary identity' serves as an obstacle to European monetary integration.

Germany: D-mark Nationalism?

After German partition in 1945 as a result of the Second World War, the D-mark initially emerged as a symbol of West German state identity. With reunification the currency then developed into a symbol of national identification.

The West German currency reform of 1948 was initially viewed with suspicion. As the former President of the Reichs Bank Schacht points out, there were concerns that the currency reform would cement the partition of Germany and eliminate 'one of the strongest links remaining with the German empire' (Schacht, 1971: 13). There was also much contention within West Germany itself about its future monetary policy orientation (Hentschel, 1988; Tietmeyer, 1996a).

By the late 1950s, the stable D-mark had become closely associated with the country's postwar economic miracle (Roeper and Weimer, 1996: 24–37, Giersch et al., 1994[1992]: 16–44). The independence of the Deutsche Bundesbank and its primary objective of 'price stability' (enshrined in the statute of the Bundesbank of 1957) rendered the currency additional credibility. In its deflationary policy the central bank can strongly rely on German public support. The detrimental effects of two hyper-inflations within the lifetime of one generation (1922–23, 1945–48) have shaped the 'collective historical memory' of the German people up to the present day. The strong belief in the virtues of price stability cannot only be explained by the negative historical experiences of hyper-inflation, but also by the positive effects which this policy has had for German postwar reconstruction. The stability of the currency has encouraged people to save substantial parts of their income and as a consequence promoted high levels of inward investment.

The currency is not only closely linked to economic progress but also to the political stability of the West German state. The economic and monetary performance of the country in the postwar era gave legitimacy to the re-established parliamentary democracy in Bonn and reaffirmed the success of Germany's model of economic organization – the social market economy.

Already within the Bretton Woods system the D-mark was subject to some appreciation. With the disintegration of this global monetary regime in the early 1970s, the external value of the German currency surged even faster. Between 1960 and mid-1995 the value of the D-mark increased sixfold against pound sterling. This development can partly be explained by the very nature of the previous monetary arrangements which for a long time had left the D-mark undervalued. Nevertheless, the growing demand for the currency was a reflection of West Germany's global economic power and the international reputation which the D-mark enjoyed.

Following the National-Socialist dictatorship under Adolf Hitler any expression of overt German nationalism became extremely rare both in the Federal Republic and the Democratic Republic of Germany. In this context, the D-mark lent validity to the growing West German state identity. This changed with reunification. The currency no longer serves as an exclusive manifestation of West German state authority but has been exported to and similarly endorsed by the population in the Eastern part of the country. In doing so, the currency became a symbol of national pride.

There were strong expectations in Eastern Germany that monetary union between the two German states would, within a short period of time, lead to a similar economic prosperity in the East as had been achieved in West Germany (Geiger, 1998; Knischewski, 1996). This has since caused considerable disillusionment in the former GDR. During reunification in 1989/90 the narrow focus on economic and monetary issues met with heavy criticism. Fears were raised that Germany was about to engage in 'D-mark nationalism', if not 'D-mark chauvinism', at the expense of the country's internal and external political stability. According to the philosopher Jurgen Habermas, the preoccupation with the D-mark and economics during the reunification process could in time threaten Germany's internal political consensus, by preventing a public debate on the constitutional foundations of the German state (Habermas, 1990a, 1990b; also Williams, Bishop and Wight, 1996). His concerns were shared by Ralf Dahrendorf whose assessment is rather apocalyptic:

> German democracy remains unstable precisely because it is so closely linked to material prosperity. Even the liberated Eastern Germans were looking, it seems, for loot as much as liberty. A sense of institutions is missing, and when economic fortunes take a turn for the worse, one must fear for the constitution of liberty (Dahrendorf, 1990: 84–5).

The former German Chancellor and founding father of the EMS, Helmut Schmidt, was more worried about the international consequences of German nationalism in monetary affairs. He concluded that if Germany was not prepared to integrate the D-mark into a European framework, this would fuel doubts about the country's international commitment and reliability and thereby endanger its long-term security interests (Schmidt, 1990a, 1995).

Economic and monetary considerations have transformed the D-mark into a potent factor of German domestic and international politics (Dyson, 1994: 6). German reunification further reinforced the importance of the currency as a symbol of identity. At the same time, the creation of a unified German state also accelerated the negotiations on EMU which led to the signing of the Maastricht Treaty in December 1991 (Schönfelder and Thiel, 1994: 69). In this Treaty the German government conceded what has emerged as one of – if not the most – important expression of German nationalism.

German 'Pecuniary Identity' and Monetary Integration

Despite an underlying (but recently slightly declining) general public consensus on European integration, opinion polls conducted in Germany reaffirm public opposition to monetary union (European Commission, 1998; Rattinger, 1994). More than half the population prefer to retain the D-mark. As many as 80 per cent of those questioned in Germany are convinced that the European currency will not be as stable as the German Mark. 84 per cent are 'proud' or 'very proud' of their currency (Gibowski, 1996; von Wilamowitz-Moellendorf, 1996). These findings support the claim that the currency is an important symbol of German national identity. This said, the German general public does not seem as concerned about a loss of identity resulting from EMU as the citizens of the United Kingdom, Denmark, Sweden, Austria or Finland – see Figure 6.1.

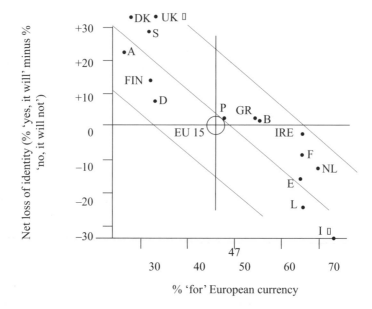

**Figure 6.1   The relationship between the support for a European
                currency and concerns about a loss of identity**

Source: Eurobarometer No. 44 (European Commission, 1996).

This discrepancy is at first startling. It can nonetheless be explained by the
specific nature of Germany's 'pecuniary identity'. Corresponding to the
generally more positive attitudes towards European integration and political
union (two in three citizens support EU membership) (European Commission,
1998), the loss of national sovereignty over the country's economic policy
is no major issue in Germany – see Figure 6.2. Public opposition to EMU is
first and foremost founded on concerns about the possible stability of a single
European currency. More than half of those presently opposing EMU have
indicated that they would change their opinion and support the project if the
German government was able to guarantee the stability of a future European
currency (Gibowski, 1996; von Wilamowitz-Moellendorf, 1996).

The German government was initially hesitant about French and Italian
proposals for European Economic and Monetary Union. There are two reasons
which explain the revision of Chancellor Helmut Kohl's policy on EMU by
mid-1988. On the one hand, he did not want Germany to be perceived as the
country blocking moves towards European integration. For him, EMU was
an important step towards his long-term objective of political union. On the

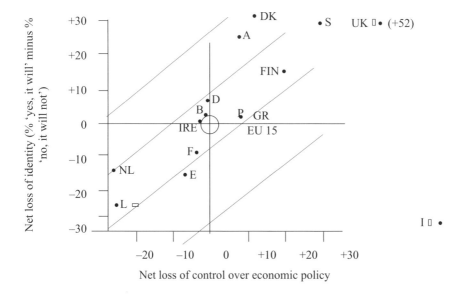

Figure 6.2   Are fears about a loss of identity and a loss of economy control related in people's minds?

Source: *Eurobarometer* No. 44 (European Commission, 1996).

other hand, Helmut Kohl wanted to take a lead at the negotiations and exert a shaping influence on the process. This would allow him to disperse domestic doubts about the future stability of the single currency and ensure public support for the project (Harmsen and Reinhardt, 1998).

To demonstrate the government's commitment to the principle of price stability, Germany insisted that the European Central Bank should be as independent as the Deutsche Bundesbank. Kohl's government also set out a number of economic preconditions (the so-called 'convergence criteria') which EU member states were expected to fulfil before being eligible to join a single currency. Finally, Germany sought to introduce binding public deficit rules and automatic sanctions against those states not complying with these rules. The EU partners accepted all but the last German condition during the negotiations.

When economic conditions deteriorated in the European Union in 1995, the German public demanded the stringent adherence to the agreed convergence criteria. In response the German Finance Minister revived earlier proposals of a legally binding sanctions mechanism (the 'Stability and Growth Pact' as it became known) to give the government's claims for monetary stability extra validity. Germany also insisted that the European Central Bank should be located in Frankfurt to symbolize the continuation of monetary prudence under the new regime. Equally, it rejected proposals to name the single European currency 'ECU'. Instead, it wished to make a fresh start by selecting a name for the new currency which was free of any historical connotations – the 'Euro'.

Members of the Social Democratic Party, the main parliamentary opposition party in Germany's lower chamber, the Bundestag, openly challenged the prevailing political consensus on European integration during their election campaign in Baden-Wurttemberg from January to March 1996. They proposed that monetary union should be postponed by a number of years. In doing so they hoped to benefit from the obvious scepticism in the German general public. Plans to postpone EMU were also raised by Bavaria's Christian Social Union, Helmut Kohl's Christian Democratic sister party (Paterson, 1996; Stoiber, 1997). Against prior expectations, the Social Democrats lost a substantive share of their vote (Reinhardt, 1997a).

This episode demonstrates that despite its identification with the D-mark as a symbol of identity, the German public is generally supportive of European integration and has resigned itself to the idea of monetary union. In 1996, 52 per cent of those questioned believed that EMU would be introduced as scheduled while only 27 per cent did not expect it to go ahead (Gibowski, 1996). Support for EMU has since further increased. In autumn 1997, 40 per cent supported the project and 45 per cent opposed it (European Commission, 1998). While differences will continue to exist between the political parties on the political and economic implications of monetary union, it is unlikely the introduction of the single currency will itself be subject to party competition; especially since the Deutsche Bundesbank has publicly endorsed the project in April 1998.

Summing up, Germany's 'pecuniary identity' did clearly shape its bargaining position at the negotiations to the Maastricht Treaty. The government entered the process with a set of non-negotiable conditions which aimed to secure the stability of the new currency and mobilize the needed public support for its introduction in Germany. While sometimes criticized by its European partners for its 'hegemonic' influence (Dyson and Featherstone, 1996: 337–9), the German government's success in enshrining these conditions in the Maastricht Treaty and in the subsequent Council Resolutions, weakened the impact of the national 'pecuniary identity' as an obstacle to the EMU project.

The Sovereignty of the Pound

Following the Anglo-Saxon tradition, the distinction between state and national identity remains blurred in the United Kingdom. Consisting of at least four culturally distinct entities (England, Scotland, Wales and Northern Ireland), British identity is based on the concept of citizenship rather than on that of a common cultural heritage. Aware of these differences, Meinecke refers to the United Kingdom as a 'state nation' ('*Staatsnation*') but not as a 'cultural nation' ('*Kulturnation*'). In 'state nations' the citizens are primarily bound together by their loyalty to the state and its constitution. As examples he mentions, next to the United Kingdom, Switzerland and the USA (Meinecke, 1969[1907]; see also Kearney, 1991). British attitudes towards the national currency are consequently shaped by political and constitutional rather than economic and monetary considerations. This makes the debate on monetary union more protracted in the United Kingdom than in Germany.

Until the 1920s the convertibility of the pound sterling into gold encapsulated the strength and stability of the British economy. The currency witnessed the country's opening to free trade and its rise as an imperial power. Even today the pound remains the fourth largest global reserve currency. The City of London is the largest financial centre in Europe and one of the largest in the world. Nonetheless, 'there is no more potent symbol of Britain's [relative] postwar decline than sterling' (Stephens, 1996: xi). As was pointed out earlier, the pound lost five-sixths of its external value against the D-mark between 1960 and mid-1995. Since then it has slightly recovered but is still at one-fourth of its 1960 value.

British policy-makers have remained ambivalent about these developments. On the one hand, there is a desire to maintain the pound's international role. On the other hand, the decline of the pound is a logical reflection of the diminishing weight of Britain's economy. As a result, decision-making has been driven by two different, mutually exclusive, philosophies. In line with the prevailing liberal market beliefs, the government often treated the currency as another tradable commodity. 'Benign neglect' characterizes these phases in British monetary policy-making. At other times, the currency featured as the utmost symbol of national pride. In these periods the stabilization of the exchange rate received absolute priority (Dimsdale, 1991). As Stephens concludes:

> Politics and the pound have proved an unpredictable explosive mixture. At different moments, the government has sought to sustain sterling's exchange rate, to ignore it, and to devalue it. Sometimes the pound has been given an

exalted role in economic management; at other times it has been treated as no more than one indicator among many. Occasionally, the policy has been one of complete indifference. These approaches have been repaid at different times with economic upheaval and political convulsion. And, as ideology has altered with pragmatism, sterling has continued to depreciate (Stephens, 1996: xi).

In general, the overall performance of the currency does not help to explain the strong domestic attachment to the pound. Whenever a prime minister has tried to establish such a link by equating rising exchange rates with growing British competitiveness or devaluations with national humiliation, he had to pay a high political price. Both Harold Wilson and James Callaghan lost considerable credibility over their monetary policy after the 1967 devaluation and Britain's submission to the International Monetary Fund (IMF) in 1976. Similarly, John Major's insistence on preserving the high parity rate of sterling in the European Exchange Rate Mechanism (ERM) and the country's subsequent ejection from the system in 1992 severely weakened his leadership of the Conservative Party and fuelled the party's opposition to the Maastricht Treaty (Stephens, 1996: 226–60; Thompson, 1996: 181–217).

The German case-study demonstrates, that 'monetary identity' often depends on the stability of the currency. Based on Figure 6.1 (above) the same phenomenon can be observed in Finland, Austria and partly in Denmark where 'pecuniary identity' and currency stability coincide. The United Kingdom does not fit into this rule.

Decimalization in 1971 and the circulation of various pound coins and notes throughout the United Kingdom (England–Wales, Scotland and Northern Ireland each issue their own bank notes) raise similar questions about the relevance of Sterling as a symbol of identity. It is interesting to point out that only the English–Welsh but not the Scottish and Northern Irish bank notes actually depict the Queen's profile. The significance of the currency as a symbol of identity is therefore neither rooted in the economic and monetary performance of the country, nor in the depiction of particular emblems on the currency.

British 'pecuniary identity' can only be understood within the context of the predominant political discourse in Britain, often referred to as the Whig interpretation of British history (Butterfield, 1963[1931]), According to this interpretation, British identity has evolved in conjunction with the state's constitutional values and norms which centre around the doctrine of 'parliamentary sovereignty' (Wallace, 1986). Dicey describes this doctrine as follows:

> The principle of Parliamentary sovereignty is nothing more nor less than this … namely, that Parliament … has, under the English constitution, the right to make or unmake any law whatever; and, further, that no person or body is recognised by the law of England as having a right to override or set aside the legislation of Parliament (Dicey, quoted in Page, 1996: 32).

The currency lies at the very heart of the British state and constitutional arrangements in as much as it expresses the country's ability to pursue its own monetary, economic and fiscal policy. Under the Maastricht Treaty provisions, significant competence in these matters will have to either be transferred to an independent European authority or severely curtailed by existing treaty obligations, such as the public deficit rules. EMU thereby fundamentally challenges the British doctrine of the indivisible power of parliament and, hence, the very existence of the British state.

Speaking on behalf of many members of the Conservative Party, but also of the other political parties, the former prime minister Margaret Thatcher stated: 'A nation without a currency is no nation at all' (Katz, 1995). EMU 'would be a fundamental and crucial loss of sovereignty and would mark a decisive step towards Britain's submergence in a European superstate' (Margaret Thatcher, quoted in Stephens, 1996: 309). Although it is debatable what future the United Kingdom would have outside the European Union, her comments allude to the fact how closely the issues of monetary integration, parliamentary sovereignty and political union are intertwined. it is this linkage which transforms pound sterling into a powerful symbol of British identity.

British 'Pecuniary Identity' and Monetary Integration

Public support for European integration has been lower in the United Kingdom than in Germany. This is also reflected in British attitudes towards monetary union. In autumn 1997, 59 per cent of the British population opposed EMU (European Commission, 1998). Both the loss of identity and that of control over national economic and monetary policy feature as prominent motives in determining the British people's attitudes – see Figures 6.1 and 6.2.

The close correlation of opinions on these two questions of identity and economic policy making underlines the argument that it is the issue of sovereignty which determines public opinion on EMU in the United Kingdom. This is especially apparent within the British political elite.

Most of the research on British party attitudes towards Europe has recently been conducted on the British Conservative Party. While the cleavage on Europe and monetary union is more pronounced within this party, similar distinctions can be made within the Labour Party (Baker et al., 1996a, 1996b). Before the May 1997 general election, roughly one third of the British Conservative parliamentary party opposed monetary union (Sowemimo, 1996: 85). During the election campaign this number increased slightly (Reinhardt, 1997b). Given the slim parliamentary majority of John Major's government in the House of Commons since the ratification of the Maastricht Treaty in 1993, EMU did at times threaten the political survival of the government. As a result, British politics focused on the question whether to join monetary union, rather than on how it could best be achieved.

Initially, the British government proposed an alternative approach to EMU. Rather than substituting existing national currencies by a new single legal tender, it took up Hayek's model of parallel currencies and proposed that national currencies should compete against each other on the European money markets (HM Treasury, 1989; Major 1990). When other EU countries rejected the idea, Britain focused all its attention on securing an 'opt-out' from the final stages of EMU. This right was enshrined in a Protocol to the Maastricht Treaty. It codifies Britain's ambivalence to further transfers of sovereignty to the European Union (Harmsen and Reinhardt, 1998).

Comparing the political debate in Germany and the United Kingdom it appears that in the case of Germany the general acceptance of further European integration actually helps to promote acceptance of monetary union. In the United Kingdom, it is this very same linkage between EMU and political union which weakens political support for the project.

Nonetheless, there are signs that the political discourse is changing in the United Kingdom. The Whig interpretation of British history and the supremacy of parliament are increasingly challenged in the context of European integration, regionalization and global interdependence. The alternative discourse is led by the Liberal Democrats and sections of the British Labour Party. Since Labour's election victory in May 1997, this alternative discourse has had a shaping influence on British politics. Acknowledging Britain's altered economic and political position in the world, in October 1997 the Chancellor of the Exchequer Gordon Brown announced that the government no longer rejects monetary union on constitutional grounds but makes its decision of membership dependent on economic considerations (Hansard, col. 2045). While this, in itself, does not alter Britain's position on EMU in the short run, it severs the existing link between the currency and the notion of parliamentary and national sovereignty.

Conclusion: A 'Pecuniary Identity' for Europe?

The two case-studies of Germany and the United Kingdom examined in this chapter demonstrate that countries have developed distinct 'pecuniary identities'. These different traditions will have to be accommodated if monetary integration is to succeed. The preoccupation of some countries (Germany, Austria, and to a lesser extent Finland) with economic and monetary considerations, especially with that of price stability, has led to controversies over how monetary union should best be achieved. It does not challenge the project of European economic and monetary union itself. Other countries (the United Kingdom, Sweden and Denmark) are more concerned about the extent to which political and constitutional powers will have to be rendered to the EU. They are consequently more hesitant about EMU (Tietmeyer, 1996b).

Two groups of countries do not feature in this chapter because they either do not feel threatened by a loss of identity from monetary union or actually expect to regain some of their sovereignty through EMU – see Figures 6.1 and 6.2. Into the first group one can put Italy and Spain. In these two countries the national currency is associated with economic instability, rather than stability.

Consequently, monetary union is seen as a means to overcome the historic inflation record, while at the same time retaining an influence over the European integration process. In the second group comprising France, Belgium, the Netherlands and Ireland the single European currency provides an opportunity to regain some control over their own monetary fortunes. Given Germany's dominant role as the anchor of the European Monetary System in the 1980s and 1990s, each of these countries has, in the past, had to follow the monetary policy of the Deutsche Bundesbank without being able to influence its decisions. In a monetary union, these countries will have a vote in the European Central Bank. For Ireland, monetary union also provides an opportunity to assert its growing economic confidence, while the Netherlands and Belgium view it as another step towards the creation of Political Union. 'Pecuniary identity' does not therefore always impose obstacles on European monetary integration, but can also serve as a catalyst to the process. It is not surprising that the stimulus for EMU came from France and Italy.

What remains to be asked is whether a single European currency will also promote a common citizenship and identity in the European Union once a monetary union has been introduced. The significance of the single currency as symbol for a European citizenship and identity and as a manifestation of European unity had always been recognized (Kruse, 1980: 27; Urwin, 1991: 154). In the 1950s the French official Jacques Rueff claimed that 'l'Europe se fera par la monnaie ou elle ne se fera pas' (Gros and Thygesen, 1992: 3). The Werner Report of 1970 which was the first study on the feasibility of monetary union stated that:

> [EMU] may be accompanied by the maintenance of national monetary symbols or the establishment of a sole Community currency. From the technical point of view the choice between these two solutions may seem immaterial, but considerations of a psychological and political nature militate in favour of the adoption of a sole currency which would confirm the irreversibility of the venture (Werner et al., 1970).

Although no direct reference was made to monetary union and a single currency when the European Monetary System (EMS) was set up in 1979, its two founders the German Chancellor Helmut Schmidt and the French President Valery Giscard d'Estaing nonetheless expressed their hope that the new European Currency Unit (ECU) would eventually evolve into a common European tender (Ludlow, 1982; Schmidt, 1990b: 230). When asked in 1987 to identify the key issues of discussion for the Maastricht Treaty negotiations on EMU, the Delors Committee once more stressed the psychological and political significance of introducing a single currency:

> The adoption of a single currency, while not strictly necessary for the creation of a monetary union, might be seen – for economic as well as psychological and political reasons – as a natural and desirable further development of the monetary union. … The replacement of national currencies by a single currency should therefore take place as soon as possible after the locking of parities (Delors et al., 1989: para. 23).

Based on the concept of 'network externalities' proposed by Dowd and Greenaway, the common currency has the potential of becoming a far more concrete symbol of identity than the flag, anthem or other European emblems. As a medium of communication it will become an inseparable part of each European citizen's life, although its significance in this respect might somewhat decline as electronic means of payment become more widespread (Dowd and Greenaway, 1993).

The role of money as a symbol of identity will also be facilitated by the design of the bank notes and coins. The features selected share a common meaning in all EU member states; representing the different historical epochs of Europe. Nevertheless, the governments could not agree on a homogenous appearance of the currency which would help to foster a common identity.

They decided to retain a designated space on the bank notes and coins for national symbols; in itself an indication how hard it is for countries to part with their own 'pecuniary identities'.

The likelihood that a European 'pecuniary identity' will emerge depends first and foremost on the internal and external stability of the new currency. Only if the currency earns public trust and fulfils its central economic function as a means of storing wealth can it potentially emerge into a symbol of European identity. During the 1948 currency reform in Germany, the D-mark replaced a discredited and inflationary currency. This immediately rendered the new money credibility. Despite this, it still took nearly twenty years before the D-mark became a powerful image of West German identity. With EMU, citizens have to part with stable national currencies. To earn its credibility, the single currency has to be therefore as reliable as the D-mark and most other European currencies.

Moreover, in Germany, the launch of the D-mark was accompanied by a prolonged period of economic stability and recovery. In contrast, the introduction of the Euro occurs against the backdrop of high unemployment, difficult structural reforms and economic uncertainty in the European Union. Economists have long disagreed whether EMU will facilitate a European economic revival. Without engaging in this debate, it can be concluded that a currency's public acceptance will improve in conditions of economic growth and prosperity.

If the common currency proves to be a success, the United Kingdom will join the project at a later stage, adopting the same pragmatic approach as previously with regard to European integration. In this case, as before, the 'myth' of 'parliamentary sovereignty' (Wilks, 1996: 163) will give way to political and economic pressures. Labour's election victory of May 1997 is likely to reinforce this shift in the British political discourse away from the traditional Whig interpretation of the country's history.

There is no historic precedence where a monetary union preceded political union by more than a few years. Rather, as in the United States of America or the German Empire (1871–1918), it followed the political integration process (Theurl, 1992). The reason for this lies in the link between the currency and the authority of the state. In the EU there are no political institutions, such as a European government, with which a currency could be readily identified. Similarly, it remains to be seen in how far we are already witnessing a convergence of economic values and objectives (the Deutsche Bundesbank speaks of a 'community of stability' (Schlesinger, 1991)) between the European member states, or in how far these shared economic values will emerge as a result of a common monetary policy and the coordination of economic policies. While the single currency can be a powerful manifestation of a European identity, it cannot in itself create such an identity. It can only assist such a process where common political institutions already provide the basis for a European citizenship and identity. In this case national and state images will be transferred onto the new European currency – the Euro.

References

Baker, D., Gamble, A. and Ludlam, S. (1996a), 'Whips or Scorpions? The Maastricht Vote and the Conservative Party', *Parliamentary Affairs*, Vol. 46, No. 2, pp. 147–66.

Baker, D., Gamble, A., Ludlam, S. and Seawright, D. (1996b), 'Labour and Europe. A Survey of MPs and MEPs', *Political Quarterly*, Vol. 76, No. 3, pp. 353–70.

Basevi, G. et al. (1975), 'The All Saints' Day Manifesto', *The Economist*, 1 November.

Bertramsen, R.B, Frølund Thomsen, J.P. and Torfing, J. (1991), *State, Economy and Society*, Unwin Hyman, London.

Biehl, D. (1991), 'The Financial Constitution of the European Community: Its Deficiencies and a Proposal for Reform', in P. King and A. Bosco (eds), *A Constitution for Europe. A Comparative Study of Federal Constitutions and Plans for a United States of Europe*, Lothian Foundation Press, London.

Bodin, J. (1980 [1583]), *Six Bookes of Commonweale*, Ayer, London.

Brunner, K. and Meltzer, A.H. (1971), 'The Uses of Money: Money in the Theory of an Exchange Economy', *American Economic Review*, Vol. 61, pp. 784–805.

Busch, K. (1994), *Europäische Integration und Tarifpolitik. Lohnpolitische Konsequenzen der Wirtschafts- und Wahrungsunion*, Hans Böckler Forschung, Bund-Verlag, Köln.

Butterfield, H. (1963 [1931]), *The Whig Interpretation of History*, Bell and Sons, London.

Dahrendorf, R. (1990), *Reflections on the Revolution in Europe*, Chatto and Windus, London.

Delors, I. et al. [Delors Committee] (1989), *Report by the Committee for the Study of Economic and Monetary Union*, Office for Official Publications of the European Communities, Luxembourg.

Deutsch, K.W. (ed.) (1957), *Political Community and the North Atlantic Area*, Greenwood, New York.

Deutsch, K.W. (1966 [1953]), *Nationalism and Social Communication. An Inquiry into the Foundations of Nationality*, MIT Press, Cambridge, MA.

Deutsche Bundesbank (1990), *Monatsbericht der Deutschen Bundesbank – Oktober*, Frankfurt am Main.

Dimsdale, N.H. (1991), *The British Economy since 1945*, Oxford University Press, Oxford, pp. 89–140.

Dowd, K. and Greenaway, D. (1993), 'Currency Competition, Network Externalities and Switching Costs: Towards an Alternative View of Optimum Currency Areas', *The Economic Journal*, Vol. 193, pp. 1180–89.

Dyson, K. (1994), *Elusive Union. The Process of Economic and Monetary Union in Europe*, Longmans, London.

Dyson, K. and Featherstone, K. (1996), 'EMU and Economic Governance in Germany', *German Politics*, Vol. 5, No. 3, pp. 325–55.

Edelman, M. (1974 [1964]), *The Symbolic Uses of Politics*, University of Illinois Press, Urbana.

Eichengreen, B. (1990), 'Is Europe an Optimal Currency Area', Discussion Paper No. 478, Centre for Economic Political Research, London.

Eucken, W. (1990 [1952]), *Grundzüge der Wirtschaftspolitik*, Leske und Budrich, Opladen.

European Commission (1996), *European Citizens and the Euro, Eurobarometer* press release, Brussels.

European Commission (1998), *Eurobarometer*, Vol. 48, Office for Official Publications of the European Communities, Luxembourg.

Fraenkel, J. and Johnson, H. (eds) (1976), *The Monetary Approach to the Balance of Payments*, Toronto.

Geiger, T. (1998), 'Believing in the Miracle Cure: The Economic Transition Process in Germany and East-Central Europe', in K. Larres (ed), *Germany since Unification. The Domestic and External Consequences*, Macmillan, London, pp. 174–202.

Gibowski, W.G. (1996), *Meinungen und Einstellungen der Deutschen zu Europa*, Redemanuskript für die Deutsch-Britische Journalistentagung in Weimar, 24 October.

Giersch, H., Paqué, K.-H. and Schmieding, H. (1994 [1992]), *The Fading Miracle. Four Decades of Market Economy in Germany*, Cambridge University Press, Cambridge.

Gillis, J.R. (1994), 'Memory and Identity: The History of a Relationship', in J.R. Gillis (ed.), *Commemorations. The Politics of National Identity*, Princeton University Press, Princeton, pp. 3–24.

Gros, D. and Thygesen, N. (1992), *European Monetary Integration*, Longmans, London.

Habermas, J. (1990a), 'Der DM-Nationalismus', *Die Zeit*, 30 March.

Habermas, J. (1990b), *Die nachholende Revolution*, Suhrkamp Verlag, Frankfurt am Main, pp. 205–24.

Handler, R. (1994), 'Is "Identity" a Useful Cross-cultural Concept?', in J.R. Gillis (ed.), *Commemorations. The Politics of National Identity*, Princeton University Press, Princeton, pp. 27–40.

Harder von, B. (1996), *Die Interdependenz zwischen Wahrungsunion und Politischer Union in der Europäischen Union des Maastrichter Vertrages*, Peter Lang, Frankfurt am Main.

Harmsen, R. and Reinhardt, N. (1998), 'Negotiating the IGC's: Maastricht and Amsterdam', in E. Meehan and K. Larres (eds), *Uneasy Partners: British-German Relations and European Integration since 1945*, Oxford University Press, Oxford.

Hayek, F.A. (1937), *Monetary Nationalism and International Stability*, Longmans, Green and Co., London.

Hayek, F.A., (1976), *Denationalisation of Money. An Analysis of the Theory and Practice of Concurrent Currencies*, Institute of Economic Affairs, London.

Helbich, W. (1995), 'Die "Armen Verwandten". Die späte Einfuhrung der zweisprachigen Banknoten in Kanada, 1936–37', *Historische Mitteilungen*, Vol. 8, No. l, pp. 106–39.

Hentschel, V. (1988), 'Die Entstehung des Bundesbankgesetzes 1949–1957', *Zeitschrift für Bankgeschichte*, Nos 1 and 2, pp. 3–31, pp. 79–114.

HM Treasury (1989), *An Evolutionary Approach to Economic and Monetary Union*, November, London.

Katz, W. (1995), 'Nervös und neurotisch', *Die Zeit*, 5 May.

Kearney, H. (1991), 'Four Nations or One?', *The Political Quarterly*, Special Edition: *National Identities. The Constitution of the United Kingdom*, pp. 1–6.

Knischewski, G. (1996), 'Postwar National Identity in Germany', in B. Jenkins and S.A. Sofos (eds), *Nation and Identity in Contemporary Europe*, Routledge, London, pp. 125–54.

Kruse, D.C. (1980), *Monetary Integration in Western Europe: EMU, EMS and Beyond*, Butterworth, London.

Ludlow, P. (1982), *The Making of the European Monetary System. A Case Study of the Politics of the European Community*, Butterworth, London.

Major, J. (1990), 'Major's Plan for Monetary Union', *Financial Times*, 21 June.

Mann, F.A. (1992 [1938]), *The Legal Aspects of Money: With Special Reference to Comparative Private and Public International Law*, Oxford University Press, Oxford.

Marsh, D. (1992), *The Bundesbank: The Bank That Rules Europe*, Heinemann, London.

Meinecke, F. (1969 [1907]), *Weitbürgertum und Nationalstaat. Studien zur Genesis des deutschen Nationalstaates*, R. Oldenbourg, München.

Moore, N.E.A. (1973), *The Decimalisation of Britain's Currency*, HMSO, London.

North, D. (1990), *Institutions, Institutional Change and Economic Performance*, Cambridge University Press, Cambridge.

Page, A. (1996), 'The Constitutional Background', in P. Giddings and G. Drewry (eds), *Westminster and Europe. The Impact of the European Union on the Westminster Parliament*, Macmillan, London, pp. 31–48.

Paterson, W.E. (1996), 'The German Christian Democrats', in J. Gaffney (ed.), *Political Parties and European Integration*, Routledge, London.

Rattinger, H. (1994), 'Public Attitudes to European Integration in Germany after Maastricht. Inventory and Typology', *Journal of Common Market Studies*, Vol. 32, No. 4, pp. 525–40.

Reinhardt, N. (1997a), 'A Turning Point in the German EMU Debate. The Baden-Württemberg Regional Election of 24th March 1996', *German Politics*, Vol. 6, No. 1, pp. 77–99.

Reinhardt, N. (1997b), 'The "Goldsmith Effect". The Referendum Party and the British EMU debate', in B. Tonra and N. Rees (eds), *Aspects of Europe*, Conference Proceedings, The Irish Association for Contemporary European Studies, Dublin, pp. 160–92.

Roberts, R. and Kynaston, D. (1995), *The Bank of England. Money, Power and Influence 1694–1994*, Clarendon Press, Oxford.

Roeper, H. and Weimer, W. (1996), *Die D-mark. Eine deutsche Wirtschaftsgeschichte*, Societäts Verlag, Frankfurt am Main.

Salin, P. (ed.) (1984), *Currency Competition and Monetary Union*, Martinus Nijhoff Publishers, The Hague.

Schacht, H. (1971), *Die Politik der Deutschen Bundesbank*, München.

Schlesinger, H. (1991), 'Eine europäische Währung muß genauso stabil sein wie die D-mark', *Handelsblatt*, 31 December.

Schmidt, H. (1990a), 'Eine Währung für Europa', *Die Zeit*, 23 June.

Schmidt, H. (1990b), *Die Deutschen und ihre Nachbarn – Menschen und Mächte II.*, Siedler, Berlin.

Schmidt, H. (1995), 'Deutsches Störfeuer gegen Europa', *Die Zeit*, 29 September.

Schonfelder, W. and Thiel, E. (1994), *Ein Markt – Eine Währung. Die Verhandlungen zur Wirtschafts- und Wahrungsunion*, Nomos Verlagsgesellschaft, Baden-Baden.

Schumpeter, J.A. (1970), *Das Wesen des Geldes*, Gottingen.

Screpanti, E. and Zamagni, S. (1993), *An Outline of the History of Economic Thought*, Clarendon Press, Oxford.

Smith, A.D. (1971), *Theories of Nationalism*, Duckworth, London.

Sowemimo, M. (1996), 'The Conservative Party and European Integration 1988–1995', *Party Politics*, Vol. 2, No. 1, pp. 77–97.

Stephens, P. (1996), *Politics and the Pound. The Conservatives' Struggle with Sterling*, Macmillan, London.

Stoiber, E. (1997), 'Defender of a Decimal Point. Interview with Peter Norman', *Financial Times*, 7 July.

Theurl, T. (1992), *Eine gemeinsame Währung für Europa. 12 Lehren aus der Geschichte*, Österreichischer Studien-Verlag, Insbruck.

Thompson, H. (1996), *The British Conservative Government and the European Exchange Rate Mechanism. 1979–1994,* Pinter, London.

Tietmeyer, H. (1996a), 'Währung und Wirtschaftsordnung', *Auszüge aus den Presseartikeln*, Deutsche Bundesbank, Frankfurt am Main, 15 January.

Tietmeyer, H. (l996b), 'Der Beitrag der Währungspolitik zur Europäischen Integration', *Auszüge aus den Presseartikein*, Deutsche Bundesbank, Frankfurt am Main, 17 June.

Tobin, J. (1961), 'Money, Capital and Other Stores of Value', *Review of Economic Studies*, Vol. 51, pp. 26–37.

Urwin, D.W. (1991), *The Community of Europe. A History of European Integration since 1945*, Longmans, London.

Vaubel, R. (1984), 'Private Competitive Note Issue in Monetary History', in P. Salin (ed.), *Currency Competition and Monetary Union*, Martinus Nijhoff Publishers, The Hague, pp. 59–73.

Wallace, W. (1986), 'What Price Independence? Sovereignty and Independence in British Politics', *International Affairs*, Vol. 62, No. 3, pp. 367–89.

Werner, P. et al. [Werner Committee] (1970), 'Report to the Council and the Commission on the Realisation by Stages of Economic and Monetary Union in the Community', *Bulletin of the European Communities* (Supplement), No. 11.

Wilamowitz-Moellendorf von, U. (1996), 'Die Europäische Währungsunion in der öffentlichen Meinung', *Working Paper*, Konrad-Adenauer-Stiftung, Sankt Augustin.

Wilks, S. (1996), 'Britain and Europe: An Awkward Partner or an Awkward State?', *Politics*, Vol. 16, No. 3, pp. 159–65.

Williams, H., Bishop, C. and Wight, C. (1996), 'German (Re)Unification: Habermas and his Critics', *German Politics*, Vol. 5, No. 2, pp. 214–39.

Chapter 7

Muslims in the New Europe

Barrie Wharton

Over the last 30 years, the rise of Islam or more correctly, the Islamist movement as a political force across the Muslim world is a phenomenon which has been greeted with fear and trepidation by both European governments and academics.[1] In fact, the term Islamist movement is itself a misnomer as it tends to suggest that the Islamist movement, according to its interpretation in Europe, is a united entity with an expansionist character which knows no borders and a highly-developed programme of societal transformation which threatens the values, mores and, indeed, the sheer existence of European civilization. On the contrary, the Islamist movement is itself a deeply fragmented body, composed of a kaleidoscopic myriad of deeply divergent and often radically opposed groups, currents and trends whose methods, aims and objectives differ not only from country to country across the Islamic world but indeed within the respective states themselves.

In Europe, this preoccupation with Islam and the perceived threat posed by Islamist resurgence has increased significantly over the last two decades and since the fall of the Berlin Wall in 1989 and the end of the Cold War, this preoccupation has become intensified and far more visible as Islam has graduated to fill the threat vacuum left behind by the disappearance of the old Soviet enemy.[2] For a generation in Europe which had grown up in the shadow of a perceived Soviet desire for world dominance enshrouded by the threat of nuclear oblivion, the sudden and unexpected disintegration and disappearance of the Soviet empire left Europe in a state of confusion and uncertainty but the emergence of the perceived Islamic threat has in many ways, changed the shade of Europe's common enemy from Soviet red to the green hue of Islam and the existence of this enemy is an often ignored but undoubtedly important one in the fostering of social and political cohesion in the new Europe.

Over the last decade, the impact of the emergence of the Islamic threat has been undoubtedly accentuated by the need for a common enemy to cushion the effects and aid the accommodation of the great changes which the Maastricht Treaty has set in motion across the European societal landscape. In an era of unprecedented flux and change with commentators forecasting the end of history and the birth of a brave new world of integrated political and economic blocs,[3] Europe has found itself at a decidedly uncertain crossroads and the question of European identity and its future have been catapulted to the forefront of social and political agendas across the continent. The wheels of European integration have remained firmly in motion but for growing numbers of Europeans, the pace and extent of the changes have been excessive and ever-increasing harmonization and similarities at the level of monetary policy, transport and communications have been met in many cases, by conversely increasing cultural fragmentation and social dislocation. This emerging multi-tiered societal panorama in the new Europe is an urgent and pressing problem for its architects and attempts at the creation or inculcation of a common European cultural identity have been hitherto characterized by their lack of success or penetration.

One could therefore argue that one of the main impetuses driving and one of the main bases underpinning the concept of European unity is in fact the existence of an external threat. Legatees of a heritage of over 12 centuries of distrust and miscomprehension between the two parties, Muslims have become the most obvious and most easily identifiable candidates to fill this threat vacuum. The presence of increasing numbers of Muslims in European societies is a further development which has augmented considerably this idea of an Islamic threat in the new Europe. In particular, the visible increase in socio-political activity and demands for representation amongst second-generation European Muslims have provoked anxiety and disquiet throughout Europe whilst placing a spotlight on the question of the role that Muslims will play in the new Europe. However, in raising this issue, Muslims in Europe have also reactivated a complementary and one could argue, more fundamental debate as their situation highlights the still vague and ill-defined nature of the new emerging Europe from a sociocultural point of view and the need for this question to be properly and comprehensively addressed.

The relationship between Islam and Europe currently is and traditionally has been a relationship which has been principally based on a dual foundation of conflict and distrust.[4] The Judaeo-Christian foundations of modern European society and the historical evolution of Europe's borders are based principally on Europe's opposition to Islam and its geographical and cultural exclusion of the Islamic 'other' from the myriad bases of European identity and civilization. Indeed, the marriage of myth and historical experience which underpins the foundations of much of modern Europe is based on the struggle against the Islamic threat and events such as the Ottoman siege of Vienna in 1453 and the Spanish *Reconquista* have played a profound if often underestimated role in the formation of diverse national psyches and perception of identity across the European societal landscape.[5] The establishment and growth of the European Union and the march towards European integration has done little to suppress these national myths or dilute the idea of the importance of the identification and exclusion of the Islamic 'other'. On the contrary, national myths and prejudices have been transplanted to a supranational level and as increasing European integration has eroded former sources of national sociocultural identity, national myths and prejudices with regard to Islam have become aggravated, a development which has been fuelled by a variety of other sources including the increasing political activity and social mobilization of Muslims in European society and the perceived incompatibility of their desires and demands with the sociocultural programme of secular values which the new Europe embodies and the paradoxical Judaeo-Christian heritage which underpins them.

In the modern era, the study of the position of Muslims in European society has been an academic subject which has been chiefly characterized by its neglect and the corresponding dearth of relevant data.[6] However, alongside the emergence of the aforementioned perceived Islamist 'threat', there are also several other factors at work which have brought the question of the role of the Muslim community in the new Europe to the top of the socio-political agenda. Uncertainty surrounding the precise nature of European citizenship has clearly been one as it has focused increased attention on minorities such as Muslims and more than often, on the perceived incompatibility of these minorities with the ideals of the partisans of European integration. In the Muslim case, this new interest in their position has also come about at a time when Muslim communities within Europe are expanding due to increased immigration and simultaneously becoming more active politically as second and third-generation Muslim communities who have now consolidated their socioeconomic and legal positions in European society are showing an increased desire for a political voice. The disintegration of the former Yugoslavia is another contributory factor which has heightened contemporary interest in the role of Islam in the new Europe as the sectarian nature of the conflict in the Balkans has candidly revealed the present-day importance and relevance of an indigenous Muslim presence in Europe which had almost been forgotten.

Given the complementary and related nature of these varying factors, it is therefore no surprise from the beginning of this decade onwards to see a revival of interest amongst Western European academics in the position of Muslims in the new Europe and during this period, some excellent studies have been produced such as Nielsen's *Muslims in Western Europe*[7] alongside the work of Anwar and Niblock.[8] However, the rapidly changing face of the new Europe and the evolving nature of the Muslim community within it render the issue an extremely difficult one to address and it is undoubtedly a question which requires a multi-layered analysis as its study within neat geographical or chronological parameters will only be able to offer misleading results which may not be merely erroneous but also more importantly, of significant danger. The study of the position of Muslims in Europe and their future role in European society therefore requires a framework which not only investigates socio-political factors but moreover, one which also examines the cultural present and future of Muslims in European society for it will be the ability of the European cultural sponge to absorb Muslim communities which will determine their real future on the European societal landscape.[9] The saturation level of this sponge remains unknown and in the case of Muslims in Europe, it depends on a variety of factors ranging from rising unemployment in Europe coupled with increased Muslim immigration to Muslim communities' resistance to absorption and cultural integration and the implications that this presents for the future of European unity.

A serious deficiency in many contemporary studies on the role of Muslim communities in the new Europe is the tendency to generalize and use an overly simplified approach in the definitions applied both to the Muslim community in Europe and to Europe itself. Firstly, this usage of the term 'Muslim community' creates the erroneous concept of a homogeneous European Muslim community when the reality is in fact, a deeply fragmented and heterogeneous entity which contains a kaleidoscopic myriad of diverse and often conflicting groups, trends and currents of thought which differ not only from country to country across European society but indeed within individual countries themselves. It is therefore far more correct to speak of Muslim communities in Europe and to stress rather than play down their plurality and diverse nature. Likewise, the treatment of European society as a single entity is another definition which poses serious problems with regard to the situation of Muslim communities within this entity. The uncertain and malleable nature of European identity is a feature which must be recognized and acknowledged alongside the highly particular and individual traits of the respective constituent societies within the European framework and how this has affected the role of Muslim communities within them.[10] More importantly, in any discourse on the role of Muslim communities in Europe, one must also acknowledge the fundamental cleavage between the role of Muslim communities in Eastern Europe and their respective position in Western Europe. Both of these developments have enjoyed vastly different historical and political trajectories and whereas this essay will concentrate on the role of Muslim communities in Western Europe, it would be wrong to deny or not to mention the indigenous Muslim presence in parts of Eastern Europe which has been a social, political and cultural reality for centuries and is undoubtedly of vital importance in any contemporary debate regarding the present or future role of Muslims in the context of an expanding European society and political infrastructure.[11]

In the immediate postwar period, the position of Muslim communities in European society was not a pressing concern for the fathers of the European integration movement. The lack of focus or concentration on this position seemed at the time to be a logical one as Europe faced many more immediate challenges and the actual Muslim presence in Western European society was a weak and politically unimportant one. Therefore, until the 1970s, the relationship between Europe and the Islamic world continued to focus on the position of Muslim communities in the former European colonies and on political upheaval in the Middle East with problems of cultural integration and comprehension between the two bodies being seen as a distinctly external concern by both parties.

However, throughout the 1950s and 1960s, large numbers of Muslim immigrants had entered European society with the expansion of labour migration fuelled by Europe's economic recovery. These new Muslim communities were chiefly characterized by their relative silence in the socio-political and cultural arenas and their role in society was seen both by themselves and their respective host societies as a fundamentally economic one which was temporary in nature.

The mid-1970s were thus to be a watershed in the relationship between Western European society and its new Muslim communities as in response to the economic recession which had begun in 1972, Western European governments introduced radical changes in their hitherto relaxed immigration laws. These changes transformed the position of Muslim communities in Western Europe as they ended further labour immigration, a change which removed the purely economic character which had previously characterized the position of Muslim communities. However, the new laws allowed family unification, a policy which would have much greater repercussions for European society as a whole as it brought the hitherto economic communities in from the edge of European society as they were now brought into contact with the sociocultural mechanisms of their respective host societies.

Muslim communities were now no longer composed of migrant workers with an economically-defined, temporary status in Western European society.

On the contrary, Muslim communities were now made up of families and as wives and children arrived throughout the 1970s, these new communities began to adapt a much more permanent character which was marked by increasing involvement in the fields of education, housing and health.[12] Sociocultural concerns in these fields led to a growing demand for political expression on the part of Muslim communities and the simultaneous emergence of the 'second-generation' Muslims who had been born and educated in Western Europe exacerbated this demand as this group articulated the desires of a new Muslim community which saw itself as a permanent feature in a new Western European society and which was no longer willing to accept the temporary and economically-determined status which had been the lot of their predecessors.

From the early 1980s onwards, a marked rise in political activity could be noted on the part of Muslim communities in Western Europe. This rise was particularly evident in France and Great Britain where Muslim communities were already well established and where rights of citizenship were easiest to obtain. External factors were also of vital importance in the politicization of Muslim communities in Europe. The oil crisis of the mid-1970s had been perceived by some Western Europeans as an example of the Muslim world's belligerent attitude towards the West as the rise in oil prices had literally held Western Europe to ransom and had sent shockwaves throughout Western European economies. However, it was the Islamic Revolution of 1979 in Iran which really polarized European public opinion with regard to Islam.[13] The media coverage of and governmental reaction to the Islamic Revolution in Iran fuelled the idea that Islam was a radical and militant force which was incompatible with the aims and aspirations of Western Europe and whose presence in Western European society constituted a potential threat and a serious obstacle to further European integration.

Muslim communities reacted to this erroneous stereotyping of Islam in a reactionary and markedly negative manner by adapting an increasingly isolationist position with regard to political expression and societal engagement. Growing unemployment in Europe coupled with the realization that Muslim communities were now a permanent fixture on the Western European societal landscape aggravated the polarization between the two parties and as both sides adapted increasingly entrenched positions, there was a marked radicalization of their respective postures. This radicalization was characterized on the Western European side by the rise in support for right-wing parties and an increase in racist sentiment which led at times to almost anti-Islamic hysteria. Meanwhile, Muslim communities responded to these attacks by acting in a defensive manner which perceived the secular values underpinning Western European society as a threat to their identity and existence.

This theme of social and cultural dislocation is a fundamental one in the trajectory of the relationship between Muslim communities in Western Europe and Western European society over the last two decades. In the shifting cultural quicksand, this first generation of permanent immigrants found itself under attack and culturally at sea in what was perceived as the unwelcoming and alien harbour of Western Europe. It is therefore no surprise that they turned to Islam, their natural source of identity and belonging, as a safe haven and their increased emphasis on and assertion of this religio-cultural identity can be clearly seen in events such as the *Foulard* affair in late 1980s France and the Salman Rushdie crisis.[14]

This growing politicization of Muslim communities in Europe has come at a time of great and unparalleled political change across the continent and this has accentuated the importance of the demands of the Muslim communities as it has focused attention on the extent of plurality and tolerance which really exist within the new Europe.

Muslim communities' exclusion from the commonality of a Western European experience is undoubtedly an important question which must be examined before any project of religious or cultural integration or assimilation can be discussed. The entire concept of the commonality of a Western European experience and the role that religion plays in it is a highly divisive one. However, despite the myriad historical differences, it is valid to speak of a number of fundamental pillars which support a certain Western European sense of identity and which are by their very nature, exclusive rather than inclusive.

The secular principle underpinning Western European society is easily identifiable and has its historical roots in the Enlightenment and the French export of the 1789 Revolution. Concepts of socio-political organization and obligations, common myths, linguistic ties and racial bonds are all factors which feed in varying degrees into the Western European psyche and although its existence is often veiled or hidden, the role of a Judaeo-Christian unifying identity is still an important factor today as it has been implicitly absorbed into the national identities of the respective Western European states and has played an active if highly paradoxical role in the 'secularization' of contemporary Europe which is perceived by many Muslims as simply a thinly-veiled disguise for an anti-Islamic crusade.

The question of the incompatibility between the religio-cultural beliefs and the socio-political organization of Muslim communities with the secular values and Judaeo-Christian heritage of Western European society is therefore a crucial one. The notion of Islam as a seamless garment where the respective realms of politics and religion are inseparable is a fundamental tenet of the Islamic faith and it is true that you cannot divide a seamless garment without tearing it apart and destroying it.[15] However, in practice, Islam has historically been a pragmatic and accommodating religion and sociocultural system which enjoyed its original success and expansion through cultural synthesis and assimilation of existing socio-political conventions and practices. This presentation of Islam is radically different to its current perception in much of Western European society but as Khaldi points out, one of the most interesting features of the Islamic Revolution in Iran was its complete historical novelty and indeed, in the almost two decades which have passed since the Revolution, its export abroad has enjoyed very little success.[16]

Therefore, there exists very little historical evidence for the theory that Islam and henceforth, Muslim communities could not be accommodated within or integrated into a Western European societal landscape. On the contrary, there are many similarities between the ideas of citizenship and socio-political organization held by both parties and the roots of the concept of the Islamic 'other' are more likely to be found in cultural differences which may indeed have very little to do with Islam or religion at all.

This cultural polarization of Western Europe and the Muslim communities is a very interesting phenomenon and indeed, close examination reveals that religion is often merely a secondary factor in the conflict although it is often highly visible as a legitimizing banner or an identifiable enemy for the respective parties involved. Analysis of the political agitation and social expression of Muslim communities show a group which perceives itself as under siege and their reaction is the case of a cultural minority under attack searching for a rallying beacon rather than a unified body defending Islamic practices or principles. The same is true of much of Western European opposition to the increased Islamic presence in Western European society as its leaders represent the concerns of a growing number of Europeans who are suffering from similar problems of identity as globalization and the rapid drive towards European integration have eroded traditional reference points and symbolic identity pillars in many Western European societies while their replacements have often been agents of sociocultural exclusion rather than inclusion.

The fundamental concept concerning the present and future of Muslim communities in Western Europe is therefore a question of cultural absorbancy and the capacity of both parties to accommodate sociocultural change. The current crisis in cultural identity which can be identified in both camps only aids miscomprehension and widens the gulf between both sides. This has given rise to a climate of ignorance and fear in Western European society with regard to Islam and a climate of ignorance and fear within the Muslim communities with regard to the values and mechanisms of Western European society.

A clear example of this climate within Muslim communities was the book-burning which accompanied the Salman Rushdie affair in Great Britain which showed the complete incomprehension of many members of the Muslim community of the significance of book-burning in European history and its association with some of the continent's darkest periods such as the Spanish Inquisition and the rise of Nazi Germany. Meanwhile, Western Europeans' ignorance and fear of Islam is well documented in the European media and in the activities of many of its elected representatives. The EU's backing of the undemocratic 1992 *coup d'etat* in Algeria and its continued support of the increasingly delegitimized regime is a further manifestation of this fear and distrust of Islam and its message has been interpreted by Muslim communities in a distinctly negative manner which has only served to accelerate the polarization process.

Such arguments obviously cast serious doubt over the ability of Europe to function as a multicultural pluralist society and raise fundamental questions about the future of European integration. The situation of Muslim communities would tend to suggest that its existence as the alien 'other' is vital to the marrying of national identities in Europe in the face of a common enemy.[17] Most of these national identities are in fact based on quite uncertain and vague premises many of which are historically inaccurate. However, the successful inculcation in the national repository of memory and the continuing influence of the founding myths of these national cultures or projects have converted them into contemporary realities which are much more important and relevant today than their historical accuracy. The majority of these myths are founded and depend on an alien or foreign element for their existence and as mentioned at the beginning of this chapter, Muslim communities have been the prime historical candidates to fill this threat vacuum and legitimize the myth.

One could therefore argue that as Europe attempts to stretch itself beyond the limited commonality bonds of nation states, it is relying not only on external threats for internal cohesion but indeed, on perceived internal threats. This raises the disturbing scenario of an emergent Europe which needs conflict and distrust in order to achieve a degree of cultural cohesion and sense of social togetherness. The increase in cultural resistance amongst Western European nations to the integration in society of Muslim communities is a clear indicator of the rise in support for the latter scenario and although harmonious interaction between Muslim communities and their host nations and the quest for a consensus based on social and cultural cohesion are noble ideals and appear the logical road to follow, the reality is that contemporary European society is in fact taking a radically divergent path.

A good example of the interaction between Muslim communities and Western European societies is the French case. The French case is a particularly interesting one to analyse due to a number of factors. Firstly, Muslim communities in France are among the oldest and most-established in Western Europe. Secondly, much of the secular ideology and thought which dominates much of Western Europe's discourse with Islam emanated from France and French national culture. Finally, the numerical strength of Muslim communities in France and France's long association with Islam through its colonies have rendered both Muslim communities in France and the French as fundamental reference points for the development of the relationship between host nations and Muslim communities in other Western European states.

The relationship between France and Islam has always been an enigmatic one. Napoleon's embrace of Islam upon his arrival in Egypt coexists uneasily alongside France's reputation as the cradle of secularism. This paradoxical relationship between the two parties has continued throughout the contemporary era. In 1979, it was an Air France plane which brought Ayatollah Khomeini from exile in Paris to a triumphant return in Tehran whereas it was also in a French court in 1998 that an 84-year-old Muslim philosopher was threatened with imprisonment for the expression of his religious beliefs.[18]

The first primary factor of importance in the analysis of Muslim communities in France is the heterogeneity of these groups, a factor which is common to Muslim communities throughout Western Europe. This heterogeneous nature of Muslim communities in France and indeed, throughout Western Europe is a factor which is often neglected. This neglect is understandable given Western Europe's aforementioned need of a homogeneous Muslim threat but the reality of the 'Muslim community' is in fact, a fragmented, heterogeneous entity which is composed of a kaleidoscopic myriad of varying currents, trends and groups whose respective platforms and objectives are often radically different or even opposed.[19]

This heterogeneity has been a serious factor in the dilution and weakening of the political voice of Muslims in French society and it is no surprise therefore to find the representation of French Muslims in public life to be significantly less in proportion than what would be expected given their actual numerical strength. On the contrary, French society which is traditionally characterized by its diversity of opinion has been relatively homogeneous in its insistence that Muslim communities must be assimilated within the established norms and rules of secular French society and there is strong resistance across French society to the recognition of Muslim communities as a different or unique entity as public opinion and government policy strongly oppose such recognition under the premise that it would lead to the 'Lebanization' of France.

The French posture towards its Muslim communities is not however merely a case of French society protecting its secular heritage. Power relations also play a fundamental role and the fact that Muslim immigration in France is largely colonial-based has been vital and coupled with the socioeconomic weakness of the immigrants, power relations have been evident throughout the trajectory of the relationship between France and its Muslim immigrants in the contemporary era.

This colonizer/subject dichotomy has not only been important in the formulation of French policies and public opinion with regard to Muslim immigrants. Moreover, it has played a decisive role in the shaping of Muslim self-awareness in France and in the immigrants' perception of the role in the societal space which has been assigned for them in France. This has led to the development of a Muslim identity in France which is socio-political rather than religious and in many ways, this identity is an externally-imposed one rather than the result of any strong religious convictions.

Therefore, it is possible to speak of the Muslim community in France as a stigmatized one created by the exclusionary mechanisms of French society. This idea of stigmatization is vitally important for the fragmented 'Muslim community' as it brings into the 'community' non-practising Muslims and acts as a fundamental element of cohesion in the socio-political platform of the 'community'. The principal forces behind this isolation and stigmatization of Muslim communities in France are the discourse of traditionally inward-looking French nationalism coupled with the political activities of the *Nouvelle Droite* and *Front National* movements. In fact, it would not be impertinent to suggest that French nationalists, in the course of their perceived defence of their culture and society, have actually been the main impetus behind the re-Islamization of Muslim communities in France, a theme which strikes a common resonance with the actions of diverse right-wing groups throughout Western Europe.[20] This re-Islamization in the political imaginary of Muslim communities in France in the socio-political sense has had very real consequences for French society and the polarized situation it has created has been aggravated by external political developments in North Africa and an entrenchment of postures on both sides.

The chronological politicization of Muslim communities in France closely follows the aforementioned Western European model. Until 1974, the question of Muslims in France was mainly a temporal one which depended on the prevalent economic conditions and trends in labour migration. Muslims were 'guests' and France was a 'host' nation but the 1974 decision to halt all new immigration was a watershed as Muslim families united and the decision to remain in France now became a permanent one with the associated socio-political ramifications and demands that families now presented.

The first signs of a nascent politicization of Muslim communities came in the late 1970s with demands for the provision of prayer rooms and the recognition of Ramadan obligations in factories such as Renault.[21] These demands achieved considerable success and France seemed to be enjoying a multicultural honeymoon based on consensus and social harmony but in the wake of the 1979 Islamic Revolution in Iran, anti-Islamic hysteria would result in a backlash against Muslim communities which was reflected politically in the rise in support for parties of the far right. The Muslim communities reacted by adapting an increasingly entrenched and militant stance which was clearly visible in the strikes in the car industry which ravaged France from 1980 to 1983 and which became tainted with a distinct hue of Islamist militancy.

In this socio-political context of hostility and distrust, both parties began to adapt increasingly polarized positions. An absence of dialogue throughout the 1980s allowed radical elements on both sides to prosper and by the end of the 1980s, one can speak of a clear and defined division between Muslim communities in France and mainstream French society in their respective views of socio-political and cultural identity. On both sides, a climate of condemnation rather than comprehension was evident and the *Foulard* or Headscarf affair of 1989 was to be a visible manifestation of this deep fissure in French society which had been allowed to grow by both parties and it would become a defining episode in the relationship between Muslim communities and their host societies not only in France but indeed, throughout Western Europe as a whole.

The *Foulard* affair had its origins in the exclusion of three Muslim girls from French state schools for the wearing of Islamic headscarves or *hijab*. However, the affair soon became a catalyst for the examination of the position of Muslim communities in Western Europe and their relationship with the societies in which they lived. The *Foulard* affair dealt a severe blow to the mythical ideal of a multicultural Europe as it candidly revealed that French secularism was in fact still based on the ethos and practices of the Roman Catholic Church and that French society which was apparently based on principles of tolerance and equality was willing to compromise these principles where Muslim communities were concerned.

The affair revealed the non-extension in France of tolerance in the public imaginary to Islam and the hegemony of a Francocentric concept of the ordering of society which might allow assimilation but rejected integration. The ramifications of the *Foulard* affair resounded throughout Western Europe and it helped to define more clearly the escalating conflict and burgeoning divisions between Muslim communities and Western European society into a set of identifiable polarizations; tradition versus modernity, minority versus majority, oppressed versus oppressor, them versus us.

The *Foulard* affair was undoubtedly a watershed in the relationship between France and its Muslim communities and since then, there has been little progress made in repairing the divisions that it revealed. The outbreak of the Algerian conflict in 1992 has been a further source of division and the French government's unflinching support of the secular regime in Algiers and its clampdown on FIS (*Front Islamique du Salut*) supporters in France[22] has further fuelled the idea amongst Muslims in France that they are perceived by mainstream society as at best outsiders or at worst enemies of the nation. Furthermore, a strong link, nurtured by the media, has been cultivated in the French social imaginary between Islam and terrorism and this has increasingly led to a negative stereotyping of Muslim communities[23] and their further exclusion from mainstream French society. On the Muslim side, this exclusion has only served to galvanize and radicalize the socio-political Muslim community and on both sides, hard-liners rather than moderates have been the dominant voices in the discourse as was clearly exemplified in the recent hysteria which surrounded the trial of Roger Garaudy.[24]

The relationship between Muslim communities in France and the French state and society has been a high profile one over the last two decades and events in France have tended to influence relationships between Muslim communities and their host societies elsewhere in Western Europe. However, the relationship between Muslim communities and other Western European societies has also depended on national particularities alongside the diverse origins of the respective Muslim communities involved and generalizations about the position of Muslim communities in Europe and the attitude of Western European society towards them must acknowledge the inherent heterogeneity of both parties.

The position of Muslim communities in Great Britain with regard to their relationship with British society is another important one in the Western European equation and it presents some interesting variations on the French model. Firstly, Muslim communities in Britain are composed in the majority of Muslims of Asian origin[25] and secondly, Muslims in Great Britain have been far more successful than their French counterparts in having their demands recognized and met in the public sphere.

Muslim communities in Great Britain first came to prominence as in the rest of Western Europe in the late 1970s after family unification in the mid-1970s transformed them into a permanent fixture on the British societal landscape. The main difference between British Muslims and their French counterparts was the socioeconomic status of British Muslims which was markedly higher and which enabled them to organize themselves much more effectively in a socio-political manner. British Muslims were also stigmatized but they managed to harness this stigmatization for their own benefit and remain active in the public sphere.

The first real campaign of British Muslims was on the *halal* or food permitted by Islamic law issue which began in the early 1980s with Muslim calls for the provision of *halal* food in schools, prisons, hospitals and other public institutions.[26] Despite opposition from a variety of groups including right-wing nationalists and animal rights activists, Muslim communities fought an effective and successful campaign and *halal* food soon became a standard procedure in all British public institutions.

Spurred on by this victory, the socio-political voice of Muslim communities in Great Britain moved its campaign to the field of education and the Honeyford Affair of 1984–85 would represent a further victory for British Muslims with an implicit recognition and acceptance of their demands by the British state.[27] The Salman Rushdie affair would consolidate this importance of the Muslim voice in Great Britain and in contrast to the re-Islamization of the beleaguered Muslim communities in France, right-wing commentators began to call for a de-Islamization of British society in the early 1990s.[28]

The success of Muslim communities in Britain is due to a number of important factors which distinguish the attitudes of British Muslims from their French counterparts. Firstly, British Muslims tend to see themselves as a distinct group and have made very little attempt to integrate into mainstream British society. This cynicism has been a preemptive strike against attempts at assimilation and it is British Muslims who have been the fiercest opponents of multiculturalism.[29] This cultural resistance of British Muslims has been held responsible for the ghettoization of British society and Kalim Siddiqui's Muslim Parliament is often cited as an example of this.[30] Secondly, British Muslims have been able to maintain this isolationist stance through their socioeconomic power which allows them to circumvent the imposed demands of British mainstream society. Thirdly, British Muslims have managed to exploit the increasingly fragmented fabric of modern British society and as a relatively powerful socioeconomic minority, they have managed to reap the benefits of a divided Britain.[31]

The posture of Muslim communities in Britain has not been a popular one in British mainstream society and especially since the outbreak of the conflict over Salman Rushdie in late 1988, they have become increasingly perceived in a negative fashion. However, the posture of Muslim communities in Great Britain is understandable as a defence mechanism within a society which is perceived by them as a bastion of token multiculturalism where control still rests with a secular elite underpinned by Christian traditions. External events such as the Gulf War and the involvement of the British Armed Forces have not helped this negative image of Islam in Britain and during the last decade, there has been a noticeable retreat on the part of Muslim communities into an increasingly isolationist stance akin to their French counterparts, a development which does not augur well for the future of a British society based on mutual understanding and consensus.

The role of Muslim communities in Germany has evolved similarly along British lines. The origins of Muslim communities in Germany were also purely economic and their status as *Gastarbeiter* or 'guest workers' in the public imaginary and indeed in political discourse bears witness to this.[32] However, Muslim communities in Germany which are mainly Turkish in origin have become increasingly important numerically due to family unification policies in the 1970s and continued labour migration to Germany over the last two decades in order to serve the needs of German industrial expansion.

While they have not been as successful economically as their British counterparts, Muslim communities in Germany have been very active in the socio-political arena and Islam has played a key role in defining the cultural self-perception and identity of the immigrants in a German society which is often perceived as an overly homogeneous one which is intent on assimilation rather than integration or multiculturalism.

The economic demands placed on Germany by the reunification process have had a profound effect on the lives of Muslim communities in Germany and the host society's perception towards them. As unemployment becomes a growing problem with the need to absorb the East German labour force, social unrest has increased with xenophobic attacks against Muslims with the increasing realization on the part of both Muslims and German society that they are no longer guest workers but on the contrary, permanent fixtures on the German societal landscape whose fortunes are now inextricably intertwined with those of the new Germany.

This realization has provoked a growing polarization of divisions and dismay on both sides with Muslim communities turning increasingly to Islam as a psychological crutch in an unwelcoming society and second-generation Muslims have sought to use Islam as an indigenous source of socio-political expression in what they perceive as a societal system which is alien and unresponsive to their needs. On the German side, there has been a marked growth in support for and the activities of the far right and only the national historical context and German constitutional provisions have prevented this growth unlike France, from becoming registered in the form of parliamentary representation and access to political power.

Elsewhere across Western Europe, Muslim communities have been growing steadily but due to their still relatively small size, the debate over their future role has remained up until now relatively muted. However, Muslim communities in the liberal heartlands of the Netherlands[33] and Belgium[34] are becoming socially and politically, a much more important group whereas increasing Muslim immigration to Sweden[35] and Denmark[36] since the beginning of the 1980s has led to growing social unease over their role in the respective host societies and has provoked a profound self-examination on behalf of these societies of their hitherto accepted standards of tolerance and religious freedom.

In Southern Europe, the increase in Muslim immigration has been seen to reignite old historical prejudices as has been the case in Spain[37] and Greece[38] and the rapid growth of Muslim communities in Italy has seen Islam become Italy's second religion and the visible extension of Muslim influence in the very heart of Roman Catholicism is a fascinating development with the reaction of Italian society still a tentative and unsure one.[39] One of the most interesting areas for future study will surely be virgin territories such as Ireland and Portugal whose reaction to Muslim immigration and demands on their societies will reveal much about the existence or viability of a new 'European' approach.

Meanwhile, Muslim communities in Eastern Europe are increasingly becoming key players in the Western European dynamic through immigration to the West as political or economic refugees. As outlined at the beginning of this chapter, Muslim communities in the Balkans and to a lesser extent, Central Europe have enjoyed or indeed, in many ways, endured an entirely different historical and political trajectory than their Western European counterparts and treatment of their role in contemporary European society merits a separate study and methodological framework. However, the importance of the existence of these indigenous communities on the borders of Western Europe and the influence this has had on Western European policies and attitudes towards Islam cannot be underestimated and this influence can only grow in the future as immigration from these countries to Western European remains a contemporary phenomenon.[40]

While continuing to stress the heterogeneous nature of Muslim communities in Europe and indeed, the national particularities of their respective societies, it is possible to draw several general conclusions on the role of Muslim communities in contemporary Western European society and offer some suggestions as to how this role is likely to evolve in the future.

Firstly, one can state that there is a growing awareness throughout Western Europe of the importance of Muslim communities and the challenges posed by their problematic cultural absorbancy or integration capacity as the architecture of a new socio-political and cultural Europe continues to unravel. This growing awareness and concern is a theme for debate amongst both Muslims and their respective host societies and is due to a number of complementary factors. Principally, second-generation Muslims have been increasingly more vocal and active in their use of Islam as a means of socio-political expression and as an affirmation of their separate identity. This has led to a marked rise in the societal 'visibility' of the Muslim community through media coverage of events such as the Foulard affair or the Salman Rushdie controversy and this in turn has led Western European society as a whole to focus increased attention on Muslim communities and their demands and dynamics as an internal European concern rather than an external phenomenon.

One can also state that prevailing economic conditions command a powerful influence over the respective fortunes of Muslim communities in Western Europe and thus closely affect both the reaction of the host society towards Muslim communities and the corresponding response of the Muslim communities. This factor has been seen to be at work during times of economic recession and unemployment in Western Europe when the non-indigenous nature of respective Muslim communities and their perceived 'intrusionary' status was found to have been emphasized and exaggerated in a negative fashion.

Socioeconomic status is another key element in the relationship between Muslim communities in Europe and their host societies. Therefore, in countries such as Great Britain where Muslim communities have found themselves located higher up the socioeconomic strata than their continental counterparts, the position of the communities has been markedly stronger and far more effective in the socio-political arena. Socioeconomic status also plays a fundamental role in determining the posture of sectors of Western

European society towards Muslim communities and it is in the areas of lower socioeconomic status where the highest degree of intolerance towards Muslim communities is to be found and much of the xenophobic and anti-Islamic sentiment stems from these sectors of Western European society which form the traditional bulwark of national cultures and identity bases which are perceived as clashing with the stereotyped Muslim enemy.[41]

One interesting finding is that there is very little differentiation across Western Europe with regard to the attitude towards the role of Muslim communities on the part of both the Protestant churches and the Roman Catholic Church. This strengthens the idea that the apparent conflict between Muslim communities and Western European society may be taking place in the sociocultural rather than religious domain and one could suggest that the sectarian aspect of the conflict is in fact overexaggerated.

It is also important to note that access to an avenue of political expression and success in this arena has remained the domain of Muslim communities in societies such as Great Britain and France where citizenship was relatively easy to obtain for immigrants. Thus, exclusion from citizenship rights and access to the reins of political power has seriously weakened the voice of Muslim communities in countries such as Germany where these rights were more difficult to obtain.

A final salient point is that the relationship between Muslim communities in Europe and their host societies depends to a great degree on the respective confidence in its identity which is enjoyed by both parties. Resistance to cultural integration or absorption has been found to run almost parallel to the level in which the respective entity can be said to be undergoing a crisis of identity.

This factor is probably the most important as Europe and its Muslim communities stand on the verge of a new millennium and the future relationship between both parties will undoubtedly hinge on it. As Europe faces up to a serious identity crisis with the erosion of the nation-state and its replacement by a new European identity which is finding an unwelcome and decidedly frosty reception in many sectors of European society, Muslim communities may well feel the backlash of this growing tide of cultural dislocation and sentiment of social exclusion. Meanwhile, second- and third-generation Muslims will have to face similar challenges and their perceived status as unwelcome guests of foreign nations can only serve to radicalize their socio-political posture as they serve to establish some type of firm foothold in this emerging socio-political wilderness of cultural chaos and detachment.

The aforementioned questions of identity and cultural inclusion are fundamental issues which the new Europe needs to address and the underestimation of their potential impact is a perilously dangerous exercise. The refusal to recognize these symptoms of a spreading societal cancer has already led to the growth of the contemporary Islamist movement and its consequent radicalization across the Muslim world and it would not be foolish to suggest that a continued polarization of respective positions could lead to a similar scenario in Western Europe and the strength of the fragile European societal fabric should not be overestimated.

However, in the immediate future, it is unlikely that the role of Muslim communities in Western Europe will provide a catalyst for societal disintegration but it is time for both sides to engage in meaningful dialogue which will help to lessen the distance between the two parties. Such a dialogue is necessary for both sides but it must be a compromise where the cultural coherence and security of Western Europe is respected but Muslim communities are allowed to integrate on mutually acceptable terms which allow their proper evolution and development as social and cultural partners. Whether such a dialogue will be initiated and if it will succeed along the terms indicated are questions which still remain unanswered but the challenge and opportunity of dialogue is currently there for both parties and it may well be pertinent to address it before the whole question of dialogue with escalating polarization becomes classified in the terms of a problem.

Notes

1   See for example Halliday (1996). See also Roy (1994) and Roberson (1994).
2   See Fuller and Lesser (1995). See also for examples of newspaper coverage Adams (1994), Hirst (1995) and Higueras (1994).
3   See Fukuyama (1992) and his preceding article (1989). See also Huntington (1993).
4   See Wharton (1996), p. 54.
5   The anecdotal tale of the emergence of the croissant or crescent after the Siege of Vienna as a symbol of victory against the Muslim invaders may seem a humorous one but the influence of the 'crusader' mentality in the social imaginary of many Western Europeans should not be underestimated. In Spain, El Cid remains a revered and much-loved national hero and the existence of a multitude of Spanish towns with names such as Matamoros (Killers of the Moors) bears living witness to a history of conflict. Even the modern Spanish language is a vehicle for these sentiments and historical myths with a popular insult in Spanish being the expression, *ser un moro* which is translated as having a terrible cheek in English but literally means to be of Moorish descent.
6   This dearth of data or material on the internal positions of Muslims in Western Europe is paradoxically marked by an abundance of literature emanating from the West on the position of Muslims in the Islamic world reinforcing the idea of otherness and externality which dominates the perception of Muslims in the West. The seminal work of this school is Said (1978).

7   See Nielsen (1992).
8   See Nonneman, Niblock and Szajkowski (1996) and Anwar (1992).
9   For a good theoretical discussion of this issue, see Tibi (1990). See also Abu-Lughod (1963).
10 See for example Dehousse (1996). See also Tarrow (1994) and Jordan (1996).
11 See for example Szajkowski, Niblock and Nonneman (1996).
12 See Vertovec (1996).
13 For a good general account, see Bakhash (1985). See also Abrahamian (1982).
14 See Ruthven (1990). See also Asad (1990). For more background on the *Foulard* affair, see Siblot (1992).
15 For further discussion of this matter, see al-Sayyid (1981). From a more Islamist perspective, see al-Ghannoushi (1993).
16 See Khaldi (1992).
17 See note 5. A multitude of similar myths regarding the Muslim 'community' as an 'enemy' still exist across the European societal landscape and during fieldwork carried out by the author in Spain and Italy, their influence was found to be still considerable and significantly underestimated by national governments and supranational institutions.
18 Roger Garaudy is an 84-year-old French philosopher who was formerly a Communist but has now converted to Islam. He was recently tried in the French courts as his book, *Les Mythes Fondateurs de la Politique Israelienne* had questioned certain aspects of the Jewish Holocaust of World War Two. See Fisk (1998).
19 See Kepel (1987). See also Etienne (1990).
20 See Silverman (1992). For a more general treatment, see Ford (1992) and Harris (1994).
21 See House (1996), p. 226.
22 See Diwan and Mohamedi (1995).
23 A classic example of this is the report in the popular French weekly *Le Point* of 28 August 1993 (No. 1093). The front cover of the magazine led with the headline, 'Islam: 4 million Muslims in France' above the photograph of a Muslim in a *gallibiya* in front of a mosque. Only in the fine print of the actual article is it discussed how many of these Muslims are actually practising or whether this figure is exaggerated but it is the emotive headline which undoubtedly exerts most influence.
24 See Fisk (1998).
25 See Peach (1990).
26 See Vertovec (1996), pp. 170–71.
27 For a good analysis of this controversy, see Halstead (1988).
28 See Ruthven (1990). See also Bowen (1992) and Modood (1990) for a discussion on the aftermath of the Rushdie affair.
29 A good example of British Muslims' rejection of multiculturalism is the marked scarcity of their presence in comparison with other minorities in respective spheres of British popular culture such as the national sport, soccer and popular music (the No. 1 single at the time of writing, by the Pakistani band Cornershop is the first ever by a British Muslim group and the very name of the group reinforces the minority stereotype which exists in British society regarding its Muslim communities). On the contrary, the French national soccer team is largely made up of immigrants and French Muslims are well represented. Indeed, its current star player, Zinedine Zidane, is of Algerian descent whilst French Muslims have also been vibrant actors in the world of popular music. Sincere thanks is offered to Sorcha and Empire Music, O'Connell Street, Limerick for their helpful advice and research on music.

30   Well-known examples have been his championing of the Ayatollah Khomeini's fatwa
     against Salman Rushdie and his speech supporting civil disobedience where British law
     was found to be un-Islamic which he gave at the opening of the Muslim Parliament in
     January 1992.
31   For further discussion, see Asad (1990).
32   See Karakasoülu and Nonneman (1996).
33   See Landman (1992). See also Shahid and Van Koningsveld (1992).
34   See Dassetto and Bastenier (1984).
35   See Sander (1996).
36   See Hjarnø (1993). See also Hjarnø (1996).
37   See López-García (1993). See also Abumalham (1993). In fieldwork carried out by the
     author amongst Muslim immigrants of Moroccan and Algerian origin in Spain, many
     spoke of the latent hostility towards Islam which is fuelled by the power of the historical
     prejudices which exist in Spanish society and how assimilation or integration could only
     be at best superficial under these circumstances.
38   See Christidis (1996). The problems associated with Muslim communities in Greece are
     accentuated by the strained relationship between Turkey and Greece and the presence
     of an indigenous Muslim minority in Western Thrace which is regarded by Athens as
     being pro-Turk. A continuing influx of Muslim refugees from Albania has been a further
     problematic factor in the contemporary debate over the role of Muslim communities in
     Greece.
39   See Allievi (1993). In fieldwork carried out by the author of this chapter in Southern
     Italy, growing Albanian immigration was found to be having a significant effect on the
     perception of Islam in Southern Italy and in the context of the rise of the Lega Nord, Islam
     was seen by immigrants as a fundamental element of socio-political and cultural rather
     than religious identity.
40   This is particularly true in the Italian case and it was a recurring theme throughout the
     author's research there. For further discussion, see Szajkowski, Niblock and Nonneman
     (1996), pp. 27–51.
41   For further discussion of this question, see Harris (1994).

References

Abrahamian, E. (1982), *Iran Between Two Revolutions*, Princeton University Press,
     Princeton.
Abu-Lughod, I. (1963), *Arab Rediscovery of Europe: A Study in Cultural Encounters*, Princeton
     University Press, Princeton.
Abumalham, M. (ed.) (1993), *Actas del Simposio Internacional: Comunidades Islámicas en
     España y en la Comunidad Europea*, Ed. Trotta (Universidad Complutense de Madrid),
     Madrid.
Adams, J. (1994), 'CIA Fears Islamic Takeover of Egypt', *The Sunday Times*, 24 April, p. 24.
al-Ghannoushi, R. (1993), *Al-Hurriyar al-'Amah fi al-Islam* (*The Freedom of the Islamic
     Nation*), Centre for the Study of Arab Unity, Beirut.
Allievi, S. (1993), *Il Ritorno dell Islam. I Musulmani in Italia*, Edizioni Lavoro, Rome.
al-Sayyid, M.K. (1981), 'A Civil Society in Egypt?', *Middle East Journal*, Vol. 47, No. 2,
     pp. 228–47.

Anwar, M. (1992), 'Muslims in Western Europe', in J. Nielsen (ed.), *Religion and Citizenship in Europe and the Arab World*, Grey Seal Books, London, pp. 71–94.

Asad, T. (1990), 'Multiculturalism and British Identity in the Wake of the Rushdie Affair', *Politics and Society*, Vol. 18, pp. 455–80.

Bakhash, S. (1985), *The Reign of the Ayatollahs; Iran and the Islamic Revolution*, I.B. Tauris, London.

Bowen, D.G. (ed.) (1992), *The Satanic Verses: Bradford Responds*, Bradford and Ilkley College, Bradford.

Christidis, Y. (1996), 'The Muslim Minority in Greece', in G. Nonneman, T. Niblock and B. Szajkowski (eds), *Muslim Communities in the New Europe*, Ithaca Press, London, pp. 153–66.

Dassetto, F. and Bastenier, A. (eds) (1984), *L'Islam transplanté. Vie et organisation des minorités musulmanes de Belgique*, EVO, Brussels.

Dehousse, R. (1996), *Integration ou désintégration? Cinq thèses sur l'incidence de l'intégration européene sur les structures étatiques*, Working Papers No. 96/4, European University Institute (Robert Schuman Centre), San Domenico.

Diwan, R. and Mohamedi, F. (1995), 'Paris, Washington, Algiers', *Middle East Report*, Vol. 25, No. 1, p. 27.

Etienne, B. (ed.) (1990), *L'Islam en France*, Editions du CNRS, Paris.

Fisk, R. (1998), 'Rewriting History Appeals to Arabs in Denial', *Independent on Sunday*, 1 February, p. 14.

Ford, G. (1992), *Fascist Europe: The Rise of Racism and Xenophobia*, Pluto Press, London.

Fuller, G.E. and Lesser, I.O. (eds) (1995), *A Sense of Siege: The Geopolitics of Islam and the West*, Westview Press, Boulder and Oxford.

Fukuyama, F. (1989), 'The End of History?', *The National Interest*, Summer, No. 16, pp. 3–18.

Fukuyama, F. (1992), *The End of History and the Last Man*, Hamish Hamilton, New York.

Halliday, F. (1996), *Islam and the Myth of Confrontation; Religion and Politics in the Middle East*, I.B. Tauris, London.

Halstead, M. (1988), *Education, Justice and Cultural Diversity: An Examination of the Honeyford Affair 1984–1985*, Falmer Press, London.

Harris, G. (1994), *The Dark Side of Europe: The Extreme Right Today*, Edinburgh University Press, Edinburgh.

Higueras, G. (1994), 'Marruecos niega cualquier vínculo entre el asalto a un hotel de Marraquech y el terrorismo islámico', *El País* (Spain), August, p. 3.

Hirst, D. (1995), 'As Night Falls the Terror Begins', *The Guardian*, 15 November, pp. 1–2.

Hjarnø, J. (1993), 'Causes of the Increase in Xenophobia in Denmark', *Migration – A European Journal of International Migration and Ethnic Relations*, Vol. 18, No. 2, pp. 41–63.

Hjarnø, J. (1996), 'Muslims in Denmark', in Nonneman, Niblock and Szajkowski, 1996, op. cit., pp. 291–302.

House, Jim (1996), 'Muslim Communities in France', in Nonneman, Niblock and Szajkowski, 1996, op. cit.

Huntington, S.P. (1993), 'The Clash of Civilizations ?', *Foreign Affairs*, Vol. 72, No. 3, pp. 22–49.

Jordan, B. (1996), *A New Social Contract? European Social Citizenship: Why a New Social Contract Will (Probably) Not Happen*, Working Papers No. 96/47, European University Institute (Robert Schuman Centre), San Domenico.

Karakasoülu,Y. and Nonneman, G. (1996), 'Muslims in Germany; With Special Reference to the Turkish-Islamic Community', in Nonneman, Niblock and Szajkowski, 1996, op. cit., pp. 241–67.

Kepel, G. (1987), *Les Banlieues de l'Islam: Naissance d'une réligion en France*, Seuil, Paris.

Khaldi, T. (1992), 'Religion and Citizenship in Islam', in J. Nielsen (ed.), *Religion and Citizenship in Europe and the Arab World*, Grey Seal Books, London, pp. 25–30.

Landman, N. (1992), 'Van Mat tot Minaret', *De institutionalisering van de Islam in Nederland*, VU Uitgeverij, Amsterdam.

López-García, B. (ed.) (1993), *Inmigración Magrebí en España: el retorno de los moriscos*, Mapfre, Madrid.

Modood, T. (1990), 'British Asian Muslims and the Rushdie Affair', *The Political Quarterly*, No. 61, pp. 143–60.

Nielsen, J. (1992), *Muslims in Western Europe*, Edinburgh University Press, Edinburgh.

Nonneman, G., Niblock, T. and Szajkowski, B. (1996), *Muslim Communities in the New Europe*, Ithaca Press, London.

Peach, C. (1990), 'The Muslim Population of Great Britain', *Ethnic and Racial Studies*, Vol. 13, pp. 414–19.

Roberson, B.A. (1994), 'Islam and Europe: an Enigma or a Myth?', *The Middle East Journal*, Vol. 48, No. 2, pp. 288–308.

Roy, O. (1994), *Political Islam*, I.B. Tauris, London.

Ruthven, M. (1990), *A Satanic Affair: Salmon Rushdie and the Wrath of Islam*, Hogarth Press, London.

Said, E.W. (1978), *Orientalism*, Pantheon, New York.

Sander, A. (1996), 'The Status of Muslim Communities in Sweden', in Nonneman, Niblock and Szajkowski, 1996, op. cit., pp. 269–89.

Shahid, W. and Van Koningsveld, P. (eds) (1992), *Islam in Dutch Society: Current Developments and Future Prospects*, Kok Pharos, Kampen.

Siblot, P. (1992), 'Ah! Qu'en termes voilés ces-choses-là sont mises', *Mots*, No. 30, March, pp. 5–17.

Silverman, M. (1992), *Deconstructing the Nation: Immigration, Racism and Citizenship in Modern France*, Routledge, London.

Szajkowski, B., Niblock, T. and Nonneman, G. (1996) 'Islam and Ethnicity in Eastern Europe', in Nonneman, Niblock and Szajkowski, 1996, op. cit., pp. 27–51.

Tarrow, S. (1994), *Social Movements in Europe: Movement Society or Europeanization of Conflict*, Working Papers No. 94/8, European University Institute (Robert Schuman Centre), San Domenico.

Tibi, B. (1990), *Islam and the Cultural Accommodation of Social Change*, Westview Press, Boulder, CO.

Vertovec, S. (1996), 'Muslims, the State, and the Public Sphere in Britain', in Nonneman, Niblock and Szajkowski, 1996, op. cit., pp. 167–86.

Wharton, B. (1996), 'The Contemporary Islamist Movement in Egypt and its Effect on the Relationship between Egypt and the European Union', in M. Cox (ed.), *National Committee for the Study of International Affairs-Proceedings of the Graduate Seminar in International Relations*, Royal Irish Academy, Dublin.

Chapter 8

Nationalism and Unionism in Northern Ireland in the 1990s

Lissi Daber

Since the mid-1980s, and especially since the election of Mary Robinson, Ireland has undergone fundamental social and cultural changes mirrored in new Irish writing, in new Irish attitudes and concepts of self and nation, and, not least, in friendly and confident relations with the close neighbour and 'other', the United Kingdom.

What is of special significance here is that political and emotional ties to Northern Ireland have diminished dramatically, and neither state has any economic or territorial interest in claiming Northern Ireland for itself, and states this openly, to the dismay of traditional loyalism and republicanism in the North. Although attitudes to Northern Ireland are not based on parallel reasons and experiences, British and Irish interests have never been so close this century. Today both states are simultaneously willing to cooperate to reach a disinterested settlement, showing a rare common readiness to create long-term stability in Northern Ireland by locking the Northern Irish parties into a peace settlement of their own choice, and not dictated by special British or Irish interests. So if the old interpretation of the Northern Irish conflict as the final battle-field between unsolved Irish and British animosities held good, might we not expect a speedy end to the conflict resulting from changed perceptions of the two external actors? Just as Northern Ireland might be expected to benefit from its geographical position as mediator, or 'cultural corridor' (Longley, 1990) between Ireland and Great Britain. Unfortunately, this does not yet seem to be the case. The reality of Northern Ireland, in spite of considerable improvements as regards old Catholic grievances about discrimination and second-class citizenship, is an increase in polarization of attitudes and residential segregation, and a strengthening of political fundamentalist positions, as seen for example at the Forum elections of 1996 and the general election of May 1997. Nationalists and unionists share feelings of mistrust and uncertainty about Britain's motivations and intentions today. At times of increased tension, for example during the marching seasons of the last two summers, claims and accusations take on distinct sectarian overtones, and institutions such as the Royal Ulster Constabulary appear to operate on sectarian principles, and not as a neutral police body. This is a situation that is difficult to begin to change. However, the Peace Agreement of 10 April 1998, and the strong 71 per cent 'yes' vote on the agreement on the 22 May may be just such a beginning: it constitutes a framework for political cooperation between the parties in the North and between Northern Ireland and the Irish Republic which may, in the long term, put the relationship between the people in the North on a different footing, and bring about a sense of shared identity and place. Police records show that there has been a steady increase in loyalist marches in the past ten years, so that they now number well over 3,000 annual marches. The figures also show a vast imbalance between the number of marches and parades held by the two communities. Loyalist marches outnumber republican ones by 9:1 (Jarman, 1997). The marching season now spans the period from Easter to early autumn, and has become a very contentious issue and manifestation of division and power:

> We have no common nationality to rediscover, and the two mother countries we look to regard us as aliens. The lesson of last week was that if we can't learn to tolerate our differences, and find some way of accommodating our conflicting aspirations, we'll destroy ourselves, either in an all-out conflagration or a slow death (White, 1996).

The result of the past 30 years has been the establishment and the perpetuation of a culture of violence: where violence has altered social norms and behaviour, and where solutions to social problems are not necessarily taken through negotiations and compromise, as is clear from the continuation of 'policing' and punishment beatings by paramilitaries, even in times of ceasefire, not to mention the – more or less overt – acceptance of the use of violence to achieve political ends. This affects everybody, not just active participants in or supporters of violence:

> The culture of violence is also manifested passively. Those who oppose it even by the act of opposition, are also subject to it. Hence many people react to the culture of violence by seeking either to deny or escape it through emigration, or internal migration (as, for example, the middle-classes' gravitation to suburbs when inner cities become too violent), or mentally turning off. In Northern Ireland, for example, there was a measurable decline in the willingness of people to watch the local television during the height of the Troubles. These denials are also part of the culture of violence (Darby, 1997).

For a culture of violence to begin to move towards a culture of sharing or of coexistence and mutual acceptance, not to speak of a common culture, entails much more than just the absence of violence. A shared project, feelings of enough common ground, and agreed changes and common goals, are necessary prerequisites for a shift away from the safety of old-established and sectarian attitudes, and strong and, unfortunately, frequently reinforced feelings of mistrust and fear. Till now, there has been a resistance to change, based on sectarianism, partiality, and pervasive distrust. So the cultural divide in Northern Ireland is very real and has its own dynamic. On the whole, community relations in the 1990s appeared to be worsening in spite of an enormous amount of good intentions and hard work on the part of individuals and organizations:

> This worsening, according to a man greatly respected as a negotiator between Orangemen and Catholic residents, is because when the bombings and shootings were common, the majority on 'both sides' transferred all culpability to the paramilitaries: if only they would stop, this would be a great wee place. And then they did stop. And the silent majority became vocal. And the voices were discordant (O'Farrell, 1997: 154).

In Northern Ireland there was considerable distrust of the political process itself, partly because of wasted opportunities following the first IRA ceasefire in 1994 and earlier, and because of the very different priorities and solutions of the two communities for a lasting settlement. According to the 1997 Queen's University/Rowntree Survey Report it would appear that the British and Irish governments who set up the Stormont talks, 'and the politicians elected to take part, were not focusing on the issues that are of the greatest importance to their respective communities' (Irwin, 1998: 3). So much divides people in Northern Ireland that as confidence building or trust building measures, talks ought perhaps to concentrate at first on issues that receive high priorities for both sides, such as a Bill of Rights that guarantees equality for all and protects each community's culture, and a right to choose integrated education. It would seem that much preliminary ground-work had to be in place, before the big issues as regards constitutional belonging and political structure could be tackled. There were, after all, mutually exclusive aspirations here and very little middle-ground in Northern Irish politics, just as there is no floating vote on the constitutional question. So the revision of the Irish constitution from staking 'a claim' on Northern Ireland to one of 'future aspiration of unity in the event of consent' significantly changed the question and most contentious issue. The Northern Irish parties taking part in the recent very difficult but, fortunately, successfully concluded talks were in a curious double bind. On the one hand, they could not afford to be seen to be unwilling to negotiate, on the other hand there was a fear of the political peace process itself, that negotiation might lead to unacceptable compromise, such as forcing nationalists to accept partition, just as some hard-core unionists will not accept any Dublin role in a future settlement. Sinn Fein was constitutionally restricted from taking its seats in any partitionist body (Adams, 1998) till the Dublin Ard Fheis voted overwhelmingly to end abstentionism a few weeks ago and thus paved the way for inclusion of Sinn Fein in a future government of Northern Ireland. This is not giving politics to the terrorists, as some commentators have feared, but rather removing or redefining 'the cause' from the terrorists. It is, of course, admirable that Tony Blair and Mo Mowlam acknowledge Britain's responsibility and involve themselves positively in Northern Ireland, but there were mindsets to be reckoned with, and old attitudes may defeat solutions. The various parties had a veto of sorts over the outcome – the DUP by boycotting the talks and mounting a massive 'no' campaign, and Sinn Fein could have been forced to refuse to take their seats in a newly elected Northern Irish Assembly. After all, abstentionism was an old republican tradition. If mainstream republicanism and loyalism are not active parts of any future agreement or settlement, it will not bring lasting peace. The mutually exclusive political and constitutional aspirations for the future and very different interpretations of the past help to explain why national identity in Northern Ireland is formed just as much on the basis of what it *is not*, as on what *it is*, where identity *is* difference, and must always be formed in close contact with what is considered 'the other'. The social categorization process in Northern Ireland is a division of people by people for historical and economic reasons, and has taken on strong cultural and ethnic overtones, because it offers a definition of 'us' and a characterization of 'them' as mutually exclusive categories with strong group demands and loyalties passed down through the generations. Thus, Ken Maginnis of the Ulster Unionist Party in a recent Ulster Television interview criticized young unionists for being bigoted extremists with attitudes like 'only people who hate Taigs [Catholics] should represent unionists' (Maginnis, 1996). The two groups in Northern Ireland are today sometimes euphemistically referred to as 'two traditions' (the new politically correct expression), but much more than tradition is at stake, though tradition is frequently invoked as justification for action, as both sides stress and celebrate different myths, symbols, and values, sometimes to the point of cultivating or inventing difference. Just as they are very aware of which myths, symbols, and values to ascribe to the out-group/the other side. A sophisticated system of 'telling' has evolved in Northern Ireland, by which – through cues like first name, address, family background, accent, and school attended – you easily place people in their respective groups, and a whole set of values and attitudes are automatically ascribed to them. John O'Farrell calls this 'the partition no amount of talking can unite': 'Politically, the partition of Ireland has been a dismal failure; culturally it has succeeded beyond the wildest dreams of its instigators' (O'Farrell, 1997: 151).

If we consider nationalism a cultural construct, then national identity must ultimately be defined in cultural terms, but in a Northern Irish context, nationalist and nationalism denote Catholics and Irish Catholicism. The Irish use of the term 'nationalist' goes back to the mid- and late nineteenth century fight for home rule, and of course entailed anti-British and, ultimately, anti-Protestant attitudes, particularly in Ulster after the Ulster unionists at the time of partition got worried about their future position and managed to secure for themselves a large slice of Ireland, and were allowed to do so by the British. In the ensuing Orange State a majority community ruled: the law was theirs, the Stormont Parliament and most political institutions were theirs, the minority could effectively be ignored, and to begin with chose to be ignored politically, as they did not accept partition. So where a century and a half earlier, Ulster Protestants had been among the loudest campaigners against British rule, and had seen themselves as Ulster Irish liberal nationalists, they now disassociated themselves from everything Irish and nationalist, and stressed their British and Protestant identity. As a result, a polarized sectarian society emerged in the North, where the state played the key role in structuring sectarian relations, and made no secret of this. From the beginning, the raison d'être of Northern Ireland was sectarian. Several Northern Irish sociologists and historians have questioned whether – given its nature and structure – Northern Ireland can be reformed at all.

> The weakening of the links between the state and Orangism/Unionism since direct rule from Westminster was introduced in 1972 has forced enormous changes in cultural and political identity within the Protestant/Unionist/Loyalist community. Just as the increased opportunity to work with and for the state has encouraged changes on the Catholic/Nationalist/Republican side, particularly within the newly emerging Catholic middle-class and within the Catholic church. But sectarianism continues to structure almost every aspect of life within the six counties – if anything, it has intensified since Direct Rule ... The state has intervened to reform some of the more blatant instances of sectarian discrimination. But it has simultaneously vastly increased the capacity of the repressive state apparatus and done nothing to change the sectarian nature of this apparatus (McVeigh, 1995: 631).

From the beginning, the uncertainties of the constitutional position of Northern Ireland forced the Protestants to stay firmly and exclusively united, especially in view of the Irish Free State's (later the Irish Republic's) claims and threats, questioning the legitimacy of the Northern Irish state. To a considerable extent the system was to blame: it was fatal to rely on a political system that could easily be manipulated into something resembling apartheid, rather than on civil rights. Northern Ireland has recently been called 'the graveyard of Britain's unwritten constitution' (Boyle, 1993: 94). Two organizations provided cultural and political identities for the two groups: the Orange Order and the Catholic Church – both institutions very conservative in outlook, and both contributed to the exclusive mythologies of both sides, e.g. the Catholic history of exploitation, sacrifice, emigration, and the nationalist fight for self-determination, with Planter and Gael as oppressor and oppressed. Just as Orangism and unionism stressed the importance of the British connection over the years, and proclaimed loyalty to crown and country, all of which is something of a myth: there was never any great attraction, or similarity of cultures, or love of British lifestyles and values, even if this is what is claimed in their rhetoric, rather the union is/was important as a protection against inclusion in an all-Irish Catholic state. So we may well ask, 'loyalism? loyal to whom/to what?'. Culture can be defined as the whole set of norms, values, attitudes, mores, behaviours, interpretations of the past, and political ambitions for the future. In Northern Ireland, *cultural group* and *national group* are often used interchangeably, just as there is a close connection between religion and culture, since religion constitutes part of, and gives access to, cultural group and political group. We can say that religion is a badge of cultural and political identity. This is seen, for example, from the fact that religious symbols are typically read and understood politically, which is particularly striking when we look at the murals and graffiti of the ghettoes, e.g. the unionist use of the symbols of the crown and the bible; and Northern Irish Protestants clearly associate Catholic religious symbols with the wish for a united Ireland. To get an idea of the degree of cultural separation or integration I chose to look at four parameters, namely *education, employment, cross-community marriages*, and *territoriality/demography*, comparing data from *observations* (*field work*), *interviews*, and *documentary material* during my research in Northern Ireland in 1993 and 1994. The four parameters of course mutually influence and reinforce each other. Marriage and education are clearly controversial issues. Only 1 per cent of children attend integrated schools in spite of more than ten years' hard work on the part of the Integrated Schools Movement. Mixed marriage figures vary slightly, from 2.3 per cent in the 1991 Census to

6 per cent in the 1989, 1991, 1993 and 1994 Northern Irish Social Attitudes Survey (Morgan et al., 1996: 4). This difference can possibly be explained as the difference between religion at birth, and religion at time of marriage. It appears from interviews that couples in mixed marriages may face problems of safety, and have to move away from areas in which they have networks of relationships and family, if those networks were in segregated areas, resulting in social isolation of the couple. The very fact that organizations exist to support and advise couples contemplating marriage 'across the boundary' indicate that it is problematic.However, the territorial aspect proved most significant for identities and attitudes in Northern Ireland. This underlines the importance of field work, in order to gain an idea of popular sentiments and reactions, as bottom-up dialogue in Northern Ireland has been very limited and attitudes from below tend to be disregarded, which, on the one hand, is a sign of arrogance, and, on the other, may be detrimental to any solutions or change.

It is important to distinguish between, firstly, *the Northern Irish problem*, which has existed since the partition of Ireland and the establishment of Northern Ireland in 1922, and which concerns the state's constitutional belonging, political structure and government, and civil rights. And, secondly, *the Northern Irish conflict*, which broke out in 1968 as a result of discrimination against Catholics, and which quickly resulted in armed conflict with paramilitary groups on both sides. Reading certain journalistic accounts from recent years, especially continental ones, one occasionally gets the impression that if only peace were declared, the British army withdrawn, and paramilitary arms decommissioned, then the situation would be solved. This is, of course, far from the case. What remains is the difficult unfinished business of Northern Ireland's political structure and constitutional belonging, where, as already mentioned, attitudes can be very confrontational with very little middle ground. This is where the unfortunate inheritance from a rather hasty and perhaps a little unfair partition of Ireland enters the picture, a partition with very little in the way of hearings, with no plebiscite, which resulted in a polarization of the population from the very beginning, strongly reinforced by the built-in discrimination of the Catholic minority group during the first 50 years of Northern Ireland's existence, and reinforced by the constant, and slightly neurotic, focusing on 'head counts', i.e. 'how many are we', 'how many are they'. This has resulted in attitudes and mentalities which emphasize differences, without respecting them, which confuses myth with history, and which endows members with group identities and strong group loyalties.

This became obvious during the 17-months-long ceasefire. It changed very little, as none of the underlying political problems was tackled, there was no working towards political goals, there weren't even attempts at defining political goals, and the ceasefire was not tied in with negotiations, so when the IRA took up arms again in February 1996, everything was quickly back to square one. Harri Holkeri, the Finnish member of the Mitchell Commission, which published the paper 'Decommissioning the potential for conflict' in January 1996, stressed that 'what is really needed is the decommissioning of mindsets and mentalities in Northern Ireland', and they recommended immediate negotiations which all groups present, in an acknowledgement of all aspirations, however contradictory these might be. Events from the recent marching season also show that deep-rooted attitudes of fear and distrust still characterize large sections of Northern Irish society, and that polarization and majority dominance are still central issues. This is perhaps understandable: nothing has happened to change or challenge people's thought-processes, and the rhetoric of many of the politicians was very confrontational and traditional, and showed up the so-called 'peace process' as hot air. The very fact that the Orange Order and the Apprentice Boys and their loyalist supporters want to march and insist on marching, even when it is seen as confrontation and as triumphalist, indicates a fear of accommodation and that listening to the other side might involve some kind of compromise or sell-out. There is a rationale or a logic of the old 'zero-sum game' or double minority situation here: a Protestant majority acting and behaving as if they were a threatened minority.

Parading is often claimed to be a specific feature of Orange loyalist culture and a parade an expression of Orange culture. The implication of this statement is that parading is not a feature of nationalist parades. But the discrepancy between the number of loyalist and nationalist parade can also be related to the broader political history of Ireland. The imbalance of power in the north has historically been used to constrain nationalist and republican parades, while loyalists have come to regard parading as a key element of their culture and an expression of their inalienable civil rights and liberties. Loyalists expect to be able to march where and when they will in their country: but they regard nationalist parades as a threat to public order. Loyalist parades are inevitably presented as cultural and traditional rather than political, while nationalist, and in particular republican, parades are seen as political and therefore provocative and confrontational. Traditional parades are presented as unproblematic and uncontentious, whereas political parades need to be carefully policed and constrained. The opportunity to demand and to exercise the right to march is thus a symbol of the distribution of political power in Northern Ireland. Tradition is invoked wherever possible, while the language of politics is avoided (Jarman, 1997). So culture has become a significant element in the continuance of the conflict in Northern Ireland, just as culture was a significant element in last century's long campaign for home rule and independence. As Dominic Murray claims, it is not difference itself that causes problems, but rather people's inability – for various reasons – to handle difference. Nor is it the existence of differing cultures that sustains violence, but rather the associations and appendages which accompany their manifestations. An Orange parade provides a good example of this. To the people involved it may be seen as a natural and enjoyable demonstration and celebration of Protestant culture and tradition. However, in a divided society, the enactment of such ritual is less important than how it is perceived. Nationalists may (and do) see such events as examples of Protestant ascendancy, cultural dominance, and as coat-trailing exercises (Murray, 1995). A Protestant march will be seen as an exercise in 'staking out their territory' and 'showing who is boss' by nationalists. So symbols, as manifestations of cultural identity, are very important in Northern Ireland, and divisions are highlighted by marches, which can sometimes take on distinct tribal overtones. As it is the group that is important, as the Northern Irish conflict is a *group* conflict and not an *individual* conflict, the individual is indeed quite acceptable, it is the groups' mutually exclusive interpretations and aspirations that are problematic, we find parallel sets of cultural symbols of myths, heroes, martyrs, songs, marching rituals, banners, and institutions, to the group identities and uphold group prejudices. Group identity (Protestant or Catholic) is salient in Northern Ireland, and focus is on the group in the individual. To return briefly to the issue of territorial segregation in Northern Ireland, the very nature of the separated areas or ghettoes, the way they function and perceive themselves, came as a surprise to me, because it gradually dawned on me that what matters in Northern Ireland is the reality of perception rather than the actual reality of events. So although you either live with 'the other', or are surrounded by 'the other', there are very fixed ideas of what this 'other' consists, what characterizes it and its actions. Representation of 'the other' tends to be stereotypical. In the Protestant areas of Donegall Pass, Tiger's Bay, and the Shankill Road of Belfast, the attitude prevails that the Catholics are getting favourable treatment everywhere, that they are taking over houses, jobs, educational places, etc., in short, that they are taking over or 'winning', however many statistics on higher Catholic unemployment rates one may quote. There is considerable mistrust of the work of the Community Relations Council and the Fair Employment Agency. The population figures of these areas are falling, but this is mainly due to slum clearance and the fact that more well-to-do Protestants move out to the new housing estates on the outskirts of the city. The 'greening' of Queen's University (55 per cent Catholic students today) is not a result of special treatment, but of the fact that young Protestants tend to study at British universities. There is clearly a strong feeling that their state, Ulster, for whose survival they have worked and fought hard and loyally, and in relation to which the Catholic population was regarded as disloyal, is getting 'greener', i.e. more Irish. What used to be understood as their proud and Protestant state and their proud and Protestant industrial city no longer feels this way for the Protestant working class. They interpret their situation as one of loss, and see themselves as surrounded and threatened, or at best disregarded. Many fear change and are uncertain about the future. This is again the problem of 'head counts' and the thinking that one side's gain must entail the other side's loss, because there is felt to be so little common ground, and because regarding 'the other' as the enemy is such a well-internalized response. It is sometimes said jokingly that in Northern Ireland the Catholics have culture and the Protestants have politics, except the Protestants don't really have politics any more; direct rule and successful activities by the many local community groups have seen to that. And on the Catholic side: in spite of some success stories and a much less homogeneous population group today (O'Connor, 1993), there is still strong distrust of the state and a sense of minority status, especially in the Catholic areas of North and West Belfast and some border regions, and a sense of not having benefited much from the changes of recent years. Fear of a Stormont revival in any form is latent, perhaps even strengthened because of Unionist conservatism, and Protestant uncertainty about the future and sense of alienation, not to say identity crisis. It is interesting that in recent years a spate of books has been published analysing and redefining Unionism, so-called New Unionism, Liberal Unionism, and Unionist/Protestant identity (e.g. English and Walker, 1996; Porter, 1996; Cash, 1996). From my interviews and observations in the ghettoes, the significance of yet a further division became clear, namely the old one of class. There is a strong sense in the segregated areas that they have been let down by the middle classes, whom they see as opting out and just making money and leading the good life; that it is the people of the ghettoes who are made to bear the brunt of the conflict and who are economically deprived, and that peace money and special aid rarely trickles down to them. They may have a point. Quite a number of people have profited considerably from the conflict in various ways and were only slightly inconvenienced by it, though they will of course pay lip service to the horrors of terrorism and the embarrassment of punishment beatings. Sectarianism is a 'bad', almost a taboo word, especially in middle-class and intellectual circles, and a certain amount of denial seems to be taking place, or explaining away atrocities as examples of individual psychopathic or irrational pathology. However, sectarianism should not be regarded as a question of isolated evil deeds by paramilitaries, but must rightly be seen in the context of complex social phenomena and old-established structures and mindsets. Perhaps the lessons and messages sent out by the Unionist establishment in the good old days, when it 'played the Orange card', were learnt too well. Even if the two old life-lines to Great Britain and the Irish Republic, respectively, are loosened considerably today, with lack of interest in the North and no wish for a united Ireland on the part of the Republic, where the nationalist project, originating in a premodern pious, romantic, rural Ireland has proved a complete failure and has been largely abandoned by modern Irish politicians in favour of a new Ireland, and the Downing Street Declaration's (1993) statement that the British government has no selfish strategic or economic interest in Northern Ireland, this has not really contributed to an opening up of mentalities or group identities in relation to traditional aspirations and uncertainties.

Harri Holkeri's claim that what needs to be decommissioned is mindsets is perhaps a little facile and begs the question, as culture, economics, and politics are parallel influences in the Northern Irish situation. How does one decommission mindsets anyway? The many well-intentioned initiatives on the part of the Community Relations 'industry' cannot stand alone, and absence of conflict and modification of enemy images and change of attitudes to in-group and out-group are, in themselves, extremely slow processes. This would also involve some kind of understanding by the people of Northern Ireland of how the present creates the past, i.e. an awareness of selectively appropriated and selectively remembered or invented history and mythology, as bases for cultural identities. But what is first and foremost needed, and needed urgently, is a plausible framework to define the future relationship between the two communities, so that people may begin to feel secure enough to let go of the past and the inflexible positions. At the time of writing, it is a question whether the Good Friday Agreement and the poll result of June 1998 can begin to achieve this. It needs strong public support to constitute a real breakthrough and provide the possibilities of long-term peace. It seems that the referendum result of 71 per cent 'yes' and 28 per cent 'no' is a strong indicator of a readiness for change and a willingness to begin to work together. There is understandable international enthusiasm and optimism about this agreement, and, fortunately, similar reactions among the majority of people in Northern Ireland. However, it should be remembered that the quite considerable 'no' may constitute a risk for the successful operation of a future elected Northern Irish assembly. At the time of writing, there is a debate on the different interpretations of the 'no', with Unionists arguing over who speaks for Unionism, echoing the old mentalities. So even if it is a strong 'yes'-vote – it is not clear cut. It would appear that Ian Paisley will not take no for an answer, and he will go down shouting 'no surrender'. There was a debate in the early nineties as to whether the European project could perhaps constitute a framework for peace in Northern Ireland, or help define one; or whether a shared European dimension within a Europe of the regions could help diffuse the situation in Northern Ireland. The questioning of identity, sovereignty, and loss of independence may put the question of self-determination in a new light for the people of both Ireland and Britain. But, on the other hand, the nature of much present-day political debate in Great Britain about Europe and European membership is not very promising. All that can be said is that there is certainly considerable Euro-enthusiams in the North, even if this seems mainly to spring from the economic benefits. So far, the EU has not played a significant role in Northern Ireland, and it is indeed difficult to see any outside actor as Northern Irish problem solver, although increased economic cross-border activity may eventually lead to an erosion of the political significance of the border, and perhaps help redefine it more in the nature of a frontier. So *we* may well define cultural identity as dynamic, as always being in a process of change, but in a Northern Irish context, group identity is the first criterion and a self-protective measure and concept, so as yet, it has been difficult, if not downright impossible, in Northern Ireland to acknowledge that identity is not static, changeable, and open to influence, rather identity is fossilized, a fixed, well-established narrow inclusive construction, shaped around tokenism and symbolism, which you do not question, do not challenge, and rarely joke about, precisely because of the siege mentalities, of perceived threats to culture and identity, and of the cultivation, for political reasons, of difference. So much Northern Irish discourse about culture and identity has been expressed in terms of what you are *not*, just as so much political discourse is expressed in terms of what you do *not* want, what I call the Northern Irish 'negative definitions', such as 'no surrender', 'not an inch', 'Ulster says no', rather than in terms of what you are and what you *do* want. Irish nationalism and unionist nationalism differ in two fundamental respects. It is actually a question whether they are parallel or comparable movements at all. Where the Irish nationalist or republican demand is for the classic 'freedom' and independence, sovereignty and self-determination, and democratic and civil rights, which is internationally understood and a recognized cause to which the world is implicitly sympathetic, unionist nationalism or loyalism is of a different kind and speaks a different language, much less able to command international recognition and sympathy. Unionist nationalism is unique in the sense that it is non-territorial. The last thing they want is independence, but prefer a stronger integration into the UK. This is where the importance of the unity of the crown and the bible comes in. Traditional Unionist Orange order ideology is best understood as an expression of fundamentalist Protestantism: a persecuted, misunderstood, and innocent God-fearing people doing battle against evil, whether republicanism, Catholicism, or mere secularism. This kind of discourse, with its tendency to read back the events in Northern Ireland into a mythical reading of the bible, is incomprehensible or anachronistic to the world at large. Thus the Free Presbyterian Church of Ulster claimed a few days before the referendum that the April agreement has 'hallmarks of devilish craft', and 'is unscriptural, unethical and immoral' (Smylie, 1998).On a much more down-to-earth level it should also be remembered that until recently unionists did not need to justify themselves, to argue their case, or convince the world of their just cause. Northern Ireland was theirs, and they ran it. This inexperience at telling *their* story is perhaps a contributory factor to the 'Ulster says no'-discourse. Whereas Irish nationalism had the world's ear and sympathy, and the famous 'gift of the gab' to put *their* case. If we add to this traditional unionists' fear of a British sellout, their mistrust and alienation perhaps becomes understandable, just as the frequently used 'God save Ulster' took on a different meaning from the time of the Anglo-Irish Agreement of 1985, now that the old friend appeared more like an enemy, and loyalists expressed their loyalty to Britain by being disloyal to her wishes. So to conclude, the new optimistic sense of being Irish, and the openness or healthy indifference about Irish-Irish, British-Irish, Anglo-Irish, or whatever, in the Irish Republic cannot really penetrate into the North, because of the continued uncertain political climate of Northern Ireland. But as already mentioned, the situation may begin to change. The possibilities for change are there: the nature of the debate leading up to the May referendum, the size of the 'yes' and 'no' vote, and the reactions to the referendum results give an indication of where Northern Ireland is moving, and, hopefully, this will justify the initial optimism and so generate its own momentum. What is so significant is that, for the first time, the referendum result cuts across the old divisions, as the 'yes' group comprises almost all nationalists and the majority of unionists. A whole new constellation. Gerry Adams of Sinn Fein and David Trimble of the Unionist Party have managed to redefine their parties' positions and get popular backing for these changes, even if the unionists are divided. But this is perhaps as much a generational thing. The old politicians, such as William Thompson, Robert McCartney and Ian Paisley, with their unforgiving rhetoric and angry refusals to accept the referendum result, and bitter pledges to wreck the new assembly, were clearly given the message that they do not any longer speak for the people they claim to represent. They ought now to withdraw quietly and let a younger generation of politicians carry out the wishes of the large 'yes' majority, which, as already mentioned, cuts across the old division. Politics in Northern Ireland may be about to enter a new stage of a common middle-ground, which may eventually spill over into, and contribute to, changes in attitudes and identities. That is why the elections to the future Assembly in June 1998 were so crucial, and that it is vital that people stick to the 'yes' politicians to make the Assembly workable, so that it may bring about a sense of confidence in a new and, hopefully, stable Northern Ireland. The Northern Irish peace is a fragile peace, and it was clear that many people had given a lot of thought to their response to the peace agreement. It was perhaps a choice between an unknown but different future, and a going back into the all too well-known darkness that had begun no longer to make sense. It was certainly striking that relatives of victims, terrorist prisoners, and exparamilitary politicians campaigned very strongly for a 'yes'. Even if there was much understandable rejoicing after the referendum result, there is clearly also apprehension about the future, about what change will bring, and first and foremost a very realistic sense of all the difficulties still to be faced. Protestant and Catholic will still be salient groups, but difference may become an accepted and unthreatening reality of the North. After all, 'Peace in Northern Ireland has to be built on its divisions, not on a fiction of unity which does not yet exist' (Ascherson, 1998).

References

Adams, G. (1998), *The Irish News*, 24 March.

Ascherson, N. (1998), *The Observer*, 24 May.

Boyle, K. (1993), 'The Irish Question and Human Rights in European Perspectives', in H.O. Skar and B. Lydersen (eds), *Northern Ireland: A Crucial Test for a Europe of Peaceful Regions?*, Norwegian Institute of International Affairs, Oslo.

Cash, J.D. (1996), *Identity, Ideology, and Conflict: The Structuration of Politics in Northern Ireland*, Cambridge University Press, Cambridge.

Darby, J. (1997), *Scorpions in a Bottle: Conflicting Cultures in Northern Ireland*, Minority Rights Group, London.

English, R. and Walker, G. (1996), *Unionism in Modern Ireland: New Perspectives on Politics and Culture*, Gill and Macmillan, Dublin.

Irwin, C. (1998), *The Search for a Settlement: The People's Choice*, Portnight Educational Trust, Belfast.

Jarman, N. (1997), *Material Conflicts: Parades and Visual Displays in Northern Ireland*, Berg, Oxford.

Longley, E. (1990), *From Cathleen to Anorexia – The Breakdown of Irelands*, Attic, Dublin.

Maginnis, K. (1996), *Hearts and Minds: the Future of Northern Ireland*, BBC2, 24 October.

McVeigh, R. (1995), 'Cherishing the Children of the Nation Unequally: Sectarianism in Ireland', in P. Clancy et al. (eds), *Irish Society, Sociological Perspectives*, Institute of Public Administration, Dublin.

Morgan, V. et al. (1996), *Mixed Marriages in Northern Ireland*, Centre for the Study of Conflict, Coleraine.

Murray, D. (1995), 'Culture, Religion and Violence in Northern Ireland', in S. Dunne (ed.), *Facets of the Conflict in Northern Ireland*, Macmillan, London.

O'Connor, F. (1993), *In Search of a State: Catholics in Northern Ireland*, Blackstaff, Belfast.

O'Farrell, J. (1997), 'Reinventing Partition', *Index on Censorship*, No. 6, London.

Porter, N. (1996), *Rethinking Unionism: An Alternative Vision for Northern Ireland*, Blackstaff, Belfast.

Smylie, A. (1998), *The Irish News*, 18 May.

Chapter 9

Ireland and European Police Cooperation

Jason Lane

Introduction

This chapter had originally as its subtitle 'a Case of the Horse behind the Cart?', a metaphor for my thesis that on the ground police cooperation (the cart) was well ahead of the legitimizing political horse (government). The Treaty of Amsterdam and the Agreement for Northern Ireland, if they are ratified, will reinvigorate both the level and nature of policing in Ireland and Europe. The effect this will have for encapsulating 'who we are' as Europeans is profound. Citizenship has traditionally been tied to two precepts, one based on genealogy and the other territoriality, factors that successfully define peaceful and ethnically homogenous societies. Northern Ireland provides an excellent example of the limitations of these factors and the Agreement makes the bold move of removing either as a prerequisite for British or Irish citizenship. Concurrent moves within the Union to maximize our sense of 'Europeanness' will further enhance the 'totality of relationships' between the peoples of these islands and possibly serve as a model for other conflict areas. The horse it would seem, has nearly caught up with the cart.

The Importance of Policing

It might seem strange that a book examining European identity, citizenship and culture should include an examination of police cooperation. Most of the literature surrounding the 'New Europe' has focused on such issues as citizenship, monetary union and the political troika of Council, Court and Parliament. This is certainly not a bad thing, for the impact of these institutions and their policies are fundamental to any understanding of the European Union as we know it. We must know where we have come from to understand where we are and to justify our hopes for the future. Growth of the Union, however, has not been purely economic and political, but has also been an emotional journey for many of the participants. Hopes and aspirations have accompanied applications for membership and while all the member states have a broadly common heritage which is 'European', they are not mutually compatible and interchangeable. The result of this has been a need to create a set of standards which all member states can adhere to and from which have grown the common policies, regulations and directives which govern the Union. Within this framework the necessity of including a chapter on policing should become more understandable. While European law in its pure sense is governed from Brussels and is the predominant preserve of lawyers and the judiciary, it is the police who operate at the level of the individual. Ideally it is the police who should protect our rights of citizenship as it will be the role of the police to prevent fraud and monetary irregularities within a unified monetary system. The police and policing are thus fundamental to the smooth functioning of the European system and in fulfilling this role they provide an important interface between state and citizen.

While the theoretical importance of the police should seem clearer, the role of the police at the supranational level is less so. Police functions are the responsibility of the individual member states and as such, moves to integrate police powers away from national responsibility have been strongly resisted. The reasons for this are simple insofar as the powers of the police to regulate their own and more especially foreign citizens within the national territory are fundamental aspects of state sovereignty. Remove the power of the state to exercise physical control within its own territory and you effectively threaten the survival of the state. To further compound this seemingly intractable problem we are faced with different police systems, not only between states, but within them, together with different legal and procedural systems, funding problems, technological and training differences to name but a few. We are faced therefore, with a European system whose smooth functioning demands greater harmonization of certain policing functions with the intrinsic resistance of the state to do any such thing. Individual states are thus faced with a dilemma. While giving up control of their internal security is unacceptable, it is undeniable that any one state cannot solve the issue of transnational crime on its own. Indeed, it is safe to say that not even the European Union has the resources to effectively tackle such a massive problem. Following the same logic that demanded the four freedoms of movement for implementation of the Single Market, so I would argue that without a concerted effort to establish a uniform and adaptable system for police cooperation the Union will suffer, not only at the hands of the international criminal, but also from a loss of faith by the public.

It is thus not merely a question of national sovereignty, or fiscal economy, but the actual progression of the Union into a more efficient *and accountable* organization which is at stake. It is important to realize that this issue is not one that favours intergovernmentalism over supranationalism or vice versa. Rather it is a necessary development of a European Union that seeks to protect its citizenry, regardless of political or constitutional changes. Of course, political changes will make themselves felt in the future and it is for this reason that any developing system is kept capable of adaptation. While Reiner (1992: 49), has emphasized the police as a 'specialist repository domestically of the state's monopoly of legitimate force', the development of an era where criminality can spread with ease both physically across state boundaries and *via* technological innovations such as the Internet, begs the question should or even can police operate solely within their own jurisdiction? That having been said, it would be foolish indeed to imagine that the 'police' or those agencies concerned with the well-being of the state have ever limited themselves strictly to their own national boundaries. However, the broad notion that police activity should be limited purely to their own national territory only benefits the criminal.

The majority of agreements concerning police cooperation in Europe are thus bilateral agreements concerning non-institutionalized cooperation against terrorism and related offences. This is in the main due to government's wish to keep a firm grip on security related issues and also because compared to far-reaching agreements, they are far easier to negotiate, being area specific. Thus domestic opponents of 'intervention' in internal affairs, who are the protagonists of the absolutely sovereign nation state, are bypassed, and public ideological discussions avoided. Movement in this arena of theoretical high politics has therefore been tedious and slow, yet difficulty in providing for treaty recognition of the issue has not prevented a multitude of cooperative ventures developing, of which one in particular, that between the United Kingdom and the Republic of Ireland provides an important example. While the case of Ireland is in many facets unique, its provides a broad conception of some central concerns, namely what has driven development of police cooperation, and what effect might this have for European identity and citizenship?

Types of Police

The system of policing in Ireland, with the Royal Ulster Constabulary (RUC) in Northern Ireland and *An Garda Síochána* in the Republic of Ireland reflects both the political settlement of 1922 and the legacy of the pre-partition force, the Royal Irish Constabulary (RIC). Both forces have maintained many of the traditions of the RIC and to a certain extent have a great deal in common because of this. They are however, fundamentally different police forces designed initially to fulfil different roles. While there are many different types of police organization in existence, they broadly fall into four main styles, namely the European, English, colonial and (post) socialist. The European, or Continental system grew out of the centralized states that emerged in the eighteenth century, notably in France and Prussia. Within this system the policeman was expected to aid and protect the state, rather than the citizen. Initially recruited from former soldiers, police in this form were a highly disciplined armed body whose modern counterparts, the *Gendarmerie* remain a part of the military structure. The English system, in contrast attempted to separate the powers of the police from the function of government and reflected the deep misgivings of English parliamentarians of providing any government with an organization which could be used to undermine the rights of the individual citizen. The English therefore evolved the local watch and the common law rights and duties of the citizen into the modern constable, the so-called 'citizen in uniform'.

The colonial system was devised essentially by the British for use in the Empire. Policemen were armed paramilitary style and expected to use confrontational tactics against the native peoples they policed. The police hierarchy was more military in its style of rank and privilege reflecting the ethnic difference between officer and other ranks. The colonial police officer was however a vital cog in the machinery of government, being foremost an administrator and official with policing duties in the modern sense of preventing crime having a secondary importance. Lastly, the socialist system created a police organization designed to promote and protect the interests of the ruling party and the state. Armed not only with physical weapons, but with a bureaucracy that tolerated human rights abuses, policing was more a matter of controlling the population according to inflexible ideology than it was concerned with providing the public with general security and safety. While these explanations of the four policing styles are somewhat perfunctory, they do serve to characterize some of the main differences between the four groups and illustrates the problem that the European Union faces with incompatible police styles.

Police Development in Ireland

The integration of the different police bodies in Ireland into a centrally organized Irish Constabulary was accomplished by Drummond's Act of

1822. While Dublin city kept its own Metropolitan Police, the rest of Ireland was to be policed as a single unit, administered by an Inspector-General from a specially created depot situated in Dublin's Phoenix Park. The Irish Constabulary, subsequently the Royal Irish Constabulary after 1867, has often been referred to as a colonial police operating in a territory that was more British colony than integral part of the British state. This is not strictly true, however, for the RIC was in fact a hybrid, representing the best (from the government's perspective) of both the colonial and English systems. The RIC thus operated in the main in a similar fashion to the English police, utilizing the common law powers of the constable and keeping the peace, often armed only with a baton. In times of outrage, however, the paramilitary structure of the Constabulary provided the government with a reliable and disciplined body of armed men capable of putting down insurrection and lessening the requirement for military intervention that would have placed the legitimacy of the British government in question. The fact, however, that it was a body of police, rather than a military force was particularly evident by its inability to restrain the organized onslaught of violence orchestrated by the IRA. After the Anglo-Irish Treaty of 1921 the RIC was disbanded, but both successor forces inherited to a great extent the same bureaucracy and style, albeit with different results.

The RUC was on formation a mirror image of its RIC parent. It had the same uniform, rank structure, bureaucracy and often personnel. Here, however, the resemblance ended, for while the RIC had been a predominantly Roman Catholic force with strong prohibition against involvement in politics, the RUC was recruited in the main from those Protestants in Northern Ireland whose interests lay in dominating all the structures of government and thereby preventing further loss to that incurred by partition. The Northern police, therefore, were hardly in a position to deny the ideological baggage which they brought with them from the Anglo-Irish War and yet, as will be seen, their relations with the newly formed *Garda* were not antagonistic. The *Garda*, for their part, recruited almost totally from chosen members of the former IRA flying columns that had done so much during the independence struggle. Politically therefore, they could not have come from a more contrasted group to their RUC equivalents. Faced with limited resources and a police network that had been all but smashed by the IRA, the *Garda* had little choice but to utilize the remaining bureaucracy and equipment that the RIC bequeathed them. Although the uniform changed from rifle green to blue, the *Garda* soon acquired a reputation for bureaucratic stubbornness that any RIC Inspector-General would have been proud of, and the sole change to the RIC Code governing the force was to substitute the word 'guard' for 'constable'.

Early Cross-border Cooperation

The early history of these two police forces, established during a time of conflict and great uncertainty would tend one to suppose that they would have been at best antipathetic towards one another, if not down right hostile and yet this does not appear to be the case. Relations soon became regularized as Mr Hegarty[1] (*Garda Síochána* 1923–64) explained:

> There'd be fellas might be wanted here and they'd go into Northern Ireland and they'd [the RUC] hand them back to you.
> So how would relations have been between the Guards and the RUC?
> Very friendly. Not 'very' friendly, but it's as well … As far as duty was concerned they were very friendly … and they were very dependent on that line.

It would seem, therefore, that even in times of political unrest a common understanding can be reached between unlikely partners. It is often said that police have a tendency to cooperate through a common bond brought about by the job and there does seem to be some evidence of this as a general rule. In this instance, however, such an explanation offers nothing for neither force at that time was operating in a peaceful environment and both were lynchpins of their respective political master's efforts in state building. As previously mentioned, the police are the most obvious manifestation of state power and are at the forefront of any attempt to establish a sense of legitimacy for a government or nation. This was recognized by the IRA during the Anglo-Irish War when they concentrated their attacks on members of the RIC and then by the Free State government when it became vital to send out newly sworn *Garda* to the countryside to legitimate the new government. Likewise the government of Northern Ireland made it plain to the British government that control of the RUC had be given over to them if they were to cement their control over their territory.[2] Both police organizations were fundamental to their respective government's efforts to create a new identity for their jurisdictions and while circumstances have long since changed it should not be forgotten that both governments were threatened by large numbers of rebels threatening to overthrow them. This fundamental point has been the principal reason for the joint police relationship enduring as long as it has. While citizens of the Irish Republic are now totally reconciled both to their own identity and to their form of government, in 1922 this was not so. The legacy of the ensuing Irish Civil War has been a powerful one and successive Irish governments, even those stemming from the republican tradition, have remained aware of their potential vulnerability to subversion from within the state. The rivalries in Northern Ireland are naturally better known and being based on ethnic as well as political division have proved the longer lasting. The situation in Northern Ireland at partition, however, was in many ways more peaceful than in the South. The majority, if not all of the IRA volunteers, left the North to fight for one of the southern factions in the Civil War and this period of relative calm allowed the Stormont regime the time it needed to fully establish its administration. The sense of vulnerability felt by the Unionist administration was also similar to that felt in the South, with the added threat of possible irredentism always at the back of their minds. Within this whole scenario the basis for cross-border cooperation was simple, both jurisdictions and their police services faced a common threat from a common enemy and following the principal that 'my enemy's enemy is my friend' they were able to put strong political differences to one side.

Public Rivalry: Private Contact

While armed struggle against the Anglo-Irish Treaty had all but ended by 1924, the Free State government was faced with a formidable group within its territory that denied its legitimacy and right to govern. The *Garda* were at the forefront of the government's attempts to pacify and control these anti-treaty republicans and relations between the Guards and this section of the population were very poor. The formation of the *Fianna Fáil* party and their subsequent election in 1932 placed the new government in a dilemma. While many of their supporters clamoured for the disbandment of the *Garda* and the establishment of a new force of Irish Republican Police, this would have only reversed the sense of alienation that needed to be removed if a truly united nation was to be built. For that reason de Valera chose to keep the basic structure and name of the *Garda,* but totally reformed and restructured the Special Branch, filling it with untrained but politically loyal men 'selected mainly for their skill and expertise with the gun ...'.[3] While this shake-up had a negative impact on both morale and efficiency at the time, it was an extremely important move to make in establishing the legitimacy of the *Garda*, a point noted by Sir Robert Mark (1977: 35), then Commissioner of the London Metropolitan Police:

> I believe that the police system of each and every country must reflect the society it serves. Each society determines the numbers, the organisation, the powers and the accountability of its police force or police forces.

The relative inability of the RUC to fulfil this criteria, while not their failure insofar as it reflected the political dissatisfaction with Northern Ireland's political status, did not lead to an end to their relationship with the *Garda*. Cooperation between the two forces continued, low-key and unofficially sanctioned on a day to day basis. The public pronouncement of a republican agenda by the Irish Government, leading to the 1937 Constitution, Articles 2 and 3, and culminating in the Republic of Ireland (1948) Act did, however, restrict the possibility of enacting legislation which might publicly legitimate cross-border contact. The establishment of the Republic was particularly significant not only insofar as it completed the separation from Britain begun in 1922, but vitally that it legally created a different citizenship. Prior to the Act, Irish citizens could be considered British subjects, but henceforth they acquired a separate status, albeit within the peculiarities of the Common Travel Area. The effect of this on policing was trivial if any, but it did have consequences in Northern Ireland. The right of Irish citizenship to all people born in the island of Ireland or of Irish decent was incorporated into the 1937 Irish Constitution, however, to claim that citizenship a person had to have the signature of a state official or notary public attesting to this right.

The trouble occurred for people in Northern Ireland who wished to take up this right getting a policeman to sign the form. As one RUC officer explained:

> This fella came up to me at the station and asked me to sign this form for his Irish passport, but I couldn't, even though I'd known the fella for years. I couldn't put my signature in my official capacity as a policeman to a document of a foreign government that doesn't recognize this state.

This difficulty shouldn't be interpreted as bloody-mindedness on the part of the RUC officer concerned, but reflected the legal weight, or in this case the lack of it, that his signature would confer. Games of legal fiction and political interference over questions deemed of higher importance, in this case the issue of partition, are often used by government for short-term political advantage in the knowledge that private discussions are unlikely to be affected. Thus while the Irish Government must have been well aware of the repercussions in Northern Ireland and Great Britain that would occur as a consequence of the passage of the Republic of Ireland (1948) Act relations had sufficiently recovered by 1954 that the British Ambassador could report[4] Dublin's acceptance:

> that the Chiefs of Police in Eire and Northern Ireland should re-establish secret
> but effective contact and interchange of information … I said that I was sure
> that this would be welcome to the Police in Northern Ireland, and that they
> would be as anxious to keep the contact secret as the Eire Police would be.

Relations between the two police forces have always been directly influenced by the necessity of not exciting political extremists on either side of the border, for whom open official police cooperation would have reinforced their own coloured perceptions that the 26-county state was a lackey of the British, or that Ulster was about to be delivered into the hands of Irish republicans. This relationship, though good in times of political calm, could not hope to survive periods of hostility where allegiance to one's state and government (and worries of job security) proved greater than the individual ad hoc relationships that might have occurred.

Joining the EEC; Patching up the Differences

The outbreak of widespread politically inspired violence in Northern Ireland during 1968–69 destroyed the delicate network of relations that the *Garda* and RUC had developed. All contact dropped off as the Irish Government debated direct intervention and the British procrastinated between offering greater support to Stormont or proroguing the assembly. Restoration of cross-border links began in 1973 after both governments had recognized the need for a common approach. The ensuing Sunningdale Agreement, although a political failure, encouraged both the RUG and *Garda* to reinvigorate their relationship which was further solidified in September 1974 by the meeting at Baldonnel Airfield, Dublin of the RUG Chief Constable Jamie Flanagan and Patrick Malone, the Commissioner of *An Garda Síochána*. The date is not an incidental one, for the accession of the United Kingdom and the Republic of Ireland to the European Communities was particularly significant. Although politically independent, the Republic of Ireland was still tied economically to Great Britain. Trade was overwhelmingly dependent upon the United Kingdom and the southern pound remained sensitive to the fortunes of sterling. The balance of prestige and influence was therefore particularly one-sided and while efforts had been made to lessen this dependence, it could not have offered the possibilities that came with membership of the European Economic Community (EEC). It is safe to say that 25 years of Irish membership of the EEC has had more impact upon Irish society than any other historical period save perhaps the Great Famine. The massive development programmes have changed the country from an essentially agrarian society to one with a dynamic manufacturing base and a thriving middle class within an economy that more than eclipses that of Northern Ireland. This has done more to change the relationship with the United Kingdom than any intergovernmental agreement could have achieved. The sense of inferiority once prevalent has been replaced with one of self-confidence that has allowed the Republic to face the British as a partner and equal, rather than stereotype poor relation.

Common membership of the European Communities thus had two main effects on bolstering police cooperation. The first was particular to the political sensitivity of the Irish case and involved providing a vehicle of legitimization within which Anglo-Irish relations could improve and become less captive to political (mis)fortune. The ability to hold discreet bilateral meetings during Community sessions allowed participants from both jurisdictions to avoid the unwelcome attention such meetings would have provoked back home. The importance of these private sessions and the opportunities they gave for British and Irish civil servants and politicians to interact together should not be underestimated. Secondly, the decision to press ahead with the project of European integration demanded a police response and this coincided with a large increase in international crime, particularly hijacking, kidnapping and terrorism. The 1970s were significant in that the decade saw evidence not only of growing terrorist sophistication, but of increasing terrorist cooperation and governments became particularly aware of their vulnerability to groups previously operating outside of their territory. Perhaps the worst example of this was the ability of the PLO to murder Israeli athletes during the 1972 Munich Olympics. These and other atrocities persuaded governments of the need to coordinate their intelligence and develop common strategies against international terrorist organizations. The role of Interpol in providing up to date intelligence and information on terrorist suspects had been shown to be wholly inadequate, as politically motivated crime had been specifically exempted from its remit (Article 3, ICPO) when the organization was re-established after the Second World War. To counter this threat to their common security, CELAT, the European Committee on Anti-Terrorism was established and other groups dealing with drugs (CELAD), money laundering (GAFI), fraud and illegal immigration (UCLAF) soon followed. National membership of all of these groups had important consequences for police cooperation in Ireland. Thus officers investigating political subversion are able to place demands for information on all these intergovernmental groups within the context of a single operation against domestic terror groups. Fitzpatrick (1993: 43) summed this up stating that:

there is no doubt that further investigation would reveal an overlapping relationship between the actual crimes and criminals engaged in each of these group areas ... There is a case then for the collation and expedient exchange of relevant information and practical co-operation between all groups.

Perhaps the most important of these groups, however, was TREVI, an organization designed for information exchange on security matters of mutual interest. Benyon (1994: 60) points out that it does not appear to have been a spur to the side of further integrationary processes between its members, insofar as legislative or constitutional change is concerned. Yet, just as the contacts between British and Irish representatives to the European Union have helped to build a new working relationship between them:

there is also evidence to suggest that on an extremely informal level cooperation is enhanced through the mere fact of TREVI meetings and discussions which bring together representatives from different police forces. Through the development of personal relationships co-operation is in fact enhanced even though it is not provided for formally.

Benyon's research thus complements the structure of RUC-*Garda* cooperation initially outlined and sees it writ large on the European stage. The existence of these groups, therefore, whatever the political motivations of the member governments and the restrictions which they place upon them, will have the effect of boosting contact between police officers and as a direct consequence provide an impetus, whether intended or not, for further development. This has certainly proved to be the case in Ireland, where both political and police cooperation have gone hand in hand. Perhaps one of the most important early developments in Ireland to come out of this renewed contact and political vigour were the joint-consultative committees (JCC), designed to examine methods of closer coordination of border security operations and exchange of intelligence. Meeting quarterly from November 1974 until October 1982, the JCC agreed:

1) the extension of existing and secure radio links between RUC and *Garda* border stations;
2) the installation of secure portable radios in patrol vehicles on both sides of the border;
3) the installation of secure speech equipment for telephones;
4) secure telex equipment between special branch units of the RUC and *Garda* similar to that used by Interpol;

5) a uniform system for marking and identifying detonators;
6) research into methods making the extraction from fertilizer of ammonium nitrate, a chemical used in bomb making, more difficult;
7) information on suspicious cars owned or likely to be used by terrorists. The exchange of daily stolen car lists and selective stops and searches at border checkpoints when required.[5]

Although the JCC improved the links between the RUC and the *Garda*, it did not go far enough in coordinating the anti-terrorist response of both governments, which reflected the difficulties of the Irish, both in constitutional and practical terms. Willingness of the police to move in this area thus had to wait for political assent, partially realized in the Anglo-Irish Agreement, signed at Hillsborough Castle, County Down on 15 November 1985. Put very succinctly, it established an Intergovernmental Conference to facilitate regular meetings of Ministers, civil servants, and police and security personnel. Of specific interest is Article 2, which deals with political, legal and security matters, together with cross-border cooperation and Article 9, which states:

> The Conference shall set in hand a programme of work to be undertaken by the Chief Constable of the RUC and the Commissioner of the *Garda Síochána* and, where appropriate, groups of officials in such areas as threat assessments, exchange of information, liaison structures, technical co-operation, training of personnel, and operational resources.

The organized protests by unionists at the signing of the Agreement offered the RUC an immediate test of resolve and was vital to the success of the new relationship. Their ability to pass this test[6] was vital to restoring the confidence of the Irish government and while it has had its problems, the Agreement has proven to be a vital platform for further cooperation.

European Initiatives

While it is questionable that the European Union had any direct impact upon the negotiations leading up to and since the Anglo-Irish Agreement, the significance of their common membership was noted by both states in the Agreement's preamble.[7] The zero-sum relationship of the past, when perceived British gain was Irish loss, has been changed into one allowing integrative agreements, the so-called 'win-win agreements' that reconcile both parties' interests to their mutual benefit. Thus, the United Kingdom receives the increased security and political support necessary for anti-terrorist activities, while the Republic has its claim to represent the interests and aspirations of the nationalist minority formally acknowledged. The key factor in this equation is trust. When this is lacking practical cooperation and conciliation is bound to suffer. The continued evolution of the European Union must be recognized to have played a significant part in providing this level of trust. By being part of a social-political project as revolutionary as that at present taking place in the Union, past differences are being moderated in intensity or negotiated out of existence. It is particularly significant for Ireland that the 15 member states are committed to a 'frontier-free Europe' and the concomitant increase in police cooperation needed to achieve this throughout Europe will also cause the Irish border to fade in intensity.

As has been mentioned, the need to establish cooperative policing as a precursor for the attainment of the Single Market and Common External Frontier has been accepted by all member states. What they have so far failed to agree, however, is what 'cooperation' actually means. The member states appear to be divided into two camps, those that favour increasing harmonization of policing within Union competence and those who prefer to keep cooperation at the intergovernmental level. Prior to the Treaty of Amsterdam, police cooperation had moved in two directions. The first major development was the 1985 Schengen Convention (augmented in 1990 by a second) that aimed to provide a common set of procedures for mutual security as a response to the anticipated abolition of frontier controls. Membership of Schengen, although not at that time legally part of the Union structure, included all Member States with the exception of the United Kingdom, Ireland and Denmark. The second development, that of the European Police Office (Europol), although supranational, does not presuppose harmonization as a prerequisite basis for its intelligence gathering. Indeed, as Dorn (1993: 31) points out, 'there is a sense in which police cooperation ... positively thrives in a "non-harmonised" legal environment'.

The Treaty of Amsterdam has revitalized the question of policing and, by inclusion of the Schengen *Acquis* has ended the previous dual-system and the danger of multi-speed integration. Although the new treaty has greatly simplified aspects of the Third Pillar, transferring much to direct Community competence the resulting document does not provide clear and binding procedures for all member states. As den Boer (1997: 8) points out:

> flexibility re-enters the stage through the backdoor by means of opt-in and
> optout protocols, temporal clauses, and even flexible conditions for the

ratification of Third Pillar conventions ... The results achieved ... will give lawyers and implementing officials many sleepless nights.

It seems, therefore, that even after Amsterdam, we are to be faced with a two or three tier system of police cooperation that will be dominated by the Council.

The New Third Pillar: Changes and Initiatives for Police Cooperation

The new Title VI in the Amsterdam Treaty calls for the establishment of an 'area of freedom, security and justice', and:

> measures in the field of police and judicial co-operation in criminal matters aimed at a higher level of security by preventing and combating crime within the Union in accordance with the provisions of the TEU.

There are two questions that should be asked at this point. Firstly how exactly do we reconcile state security with citizens freedom and justice within a system that is not directly publicly accountable and transparent. Secondly and perhaps more worrying, how can we instil western democratic policing ethos into central and eastern European states now preparing to join the Union in the next wave of enlargement. The concern over these issues has been at least partially addressed within the new Treaty and a greater role of scrutiny has been given to the European Parliament through Article K. 11. Thus the Parliament must be consulted by the Council before any new legal position is adopted, with the exception of common positions. The role of the European Court of Justice has not fared so well, being given in Article K.7 the ability to give preliminary rulings on decisions and conventions, yet being specifically excluded from any competence concerning operations by the police or other law-enforcement agencies. This will remain a matter for national courts and the European Court of Human Rights.

Movement in sustainable cooperation has also been implemented by the police and other competent authorities, most usefully in the field of technical harmonization. This will provide both the easiest path to greater efficiency and to political agreement, as it need not affect member governments rights over their own jurisdiction. Greater ease of information exchange and more importantly, data collation does, however, pose serious problems with regard to civil liberties. It is therefore essential that this problem receive immediate attention. It should be tackled on two fronts. Firstly, a common code of practice must be agreed about what information is held for storage and retrieval. Associated with this must be guarantees concerning individual rights to privacy. Secondly, both the European institutions and the member state governments need to provide information to the public concerning the system, its operation and their rights. This must be an active policy, otherwise the information will not get through. This is amply illustrated by the low level of knowledge which the public have about the police and while information is not restricted, neither is it openly offered. In this way the introduction of common codes of practice could be seen as strengthening civil liberties, rather than weakening them.

Another justification for better management of police resources on the part of the IGC concerns duplication and associated waste. Europol, for example, is responsible on a Union-wide basis for information exchange concerning drugs and money laundering, illegal immigration, illicit trafficking in radio active and nuclear materials and illicit vehicle trafficking. However, external agencies, such as Her Majesty's Customs and Excise (HMCE) in the UK, also investigate these matters and provide the greater number of Drug Liaison Officers (DLOs) worldwide, as well as in Europe. Linked to this is the fact that many international crimes are inter-related, drugs and terrorism being perhaps the best example. There does not seem, however to be much liaison between these agencies and the TREVI-inspired Police Working Group on Terrorism, or the Counter-Terrorism Liaison Officers. This matter is not unknown to the police themselves. In a recent report[8] the British Association of Chief Police Officers (ACPO) noted that Interpol, Europol and the DLOs are undertaking a very similar role and found little evidence of their coordination, which they recommended to review. On the other hand, it is useful that Europol does have HMCE input which gives it a particular advantage over Interpol with regard to the intelligence on offer.

While long-term harmonization of legal practices still appears to be some way off, it is important to mention in the course of this debate. Again, there is a long and short-term perspective to be taken. While wholesale harmonization is unrealistic at present, it should not prove insurmountable to adopt a common criminal code with regard to future 'European' offences, that against the Community budget being a good example. Further development might be the case of computer crime, or crime against the environment. What ought to be avoided, however, is the situation where law is not regularly updated in all member states. When this occurs, crime that is permissible in one state defeats the possibility of international cooperation against it. This desire for greater coordination of legal practice is not to be confused with the call for a European Juridical Space. The differences between common law states and civil law states are such that it would require a revolutionary progression of the entire justice system, that is, police, law and courts, that does not presently seem realistic. The alternative of European law sits well with both systems, as the precedent for EU law to dominate over national law is long established. The rights of the EU institutions are strongest with regard to Directives and Regulations designed to safeguard the Internal Market. It is certainly possible that a case could be made for harmonization of future law along those lines. This would have two main beneficial effects. In the first part, it would begin the process of harmonization which must inevitably create greater efficiency, whilst its second and equally compelling result would be the application of general human rights provisions which are incorporated in EU law.

While there remains concern over transparency and accountability within the Third Pillar, it is much more worrying in the states of Central and Eastern Europe now preparing for membership. As King (1997: 1) points out:

> Whilst these states are all to varying degrees subject to processes of transformation and democratization, such processes may not be amounting to thorough revolutionary change, but rather passing over certain systems of establishment power.

The slow pace of police cooperation has been difficult enough to accomplish between forces strong in democratic tradition without contemplating the inclusion of forces which still either seek to justify undemocratic measures as a response to unprecedented public order problems or whose members remain closely associated with the previous regime and thus restrain the growth of popular legitimacy. While these questions remain unresolved there should be no question of providing these forces with unrestricted access to EU police databases, nor of giving them full member status within the Europol/Schengen frameworks. This might seem to be a drastic and even draconian measure, especially when one considers the implications which it has for the EU external frontiers and the workings of the internal market. Aid in the form of training, both operational and psychological must be given and eastern governments required to follow through police reform as a statutory provision of EU membership. There really can be no half measures if we intend to build our police relationships upon the basis of public consent. The alternative is to adopt a two-tier approach to police cooperation, with states not conforming to democratic standards not being accorded full status. This will have two effects.

Firstly, it will undermine public confidence and reinforce the concerns of those already fearful that greater police cooperation is a threat to civil liberties. Secondly, it will ridicule the idea of a common external frontier, as an inner frontier would have to remain as a defence against 'irregularities' arising from the unreformed police. Accountability and legitimacy are, therefore, the basic building blocks for producing a European system of police cooperation. Using Baldwin's (1987) five original criteria, it is forcefully brought home that development on a pan-European front is not only necessary, but vital to legitimate police contact. These criteria assess the extent to which institutions and practices are authorized by a legislative mandate, that institutions are liable to democratic account, that a 'due process' exists giving individuals rights under a system of rules and procedures, that there is a degree of expertise which is related to performance and finally a reference to overall institutional effectiveness in reaching objectives. Neither Europol nor Schengen meet these criteria in full as they stand, let alone the police systems of the former socialist states. There is thus a wide gap to fill.

Conclusions

The timing of the Multiparty Agreement in Northern Ireland and the Treaty of Amsterdam, allow a more positive ending than the original paper this chapter is based on. While it could have been argued in the past that individual states were solely responsible for their own internal security as defined by their territorial boundaries, the creation of the Single Market and the right to free movement has firmly eliminated that already weak argument. Police cooperation, handled properly, offers benefits for both Europhiles and Europhobes. Those favouring the purely economic advantages of the Union should be swayed by the need to reduce criminality and thus boost efficiency in the Single Market, while for those favouring greater structural integration the need for police cooperation must be seen as a bare minimum and precursor of some kind of fully functional European Police organization. Thus, it is possible to move forward confidently neither with a sense of structural fatalism, nor naïve separatism.[9] As Fitzpatrick (1993), points out:

> The overall pattern is one of formal and informal police co-operation in response to common security problems. If the results are controversial the politicians can disown them, but if they are positive, then the informal police arrangements are welcomed and even ... institutionalised by ... politicians who then go on to encourage the police to even greater efforts. The Anglo-Irish

Agreement, as it related to policing, is one example of politicians adopting, as their own, existing police practices and then giving them a more formal and structured framework.

The importance of consolidating the process of cooperation between the RUC and the *Garda* and of reconciling the two communities in Ireland thus remain irrevocably linked. There cannot, therefore, be a mutual standard of justice and jurisprudence unless there is an agreed identity within which it can operate, however delineated in actual practice. It is thus not only government or the state which determines identity, but a complex interplay of social forces, both national and transnational, within which the police play a crucial role. Justice, the courts and the policing of the system must be felt by the population to be their own, rather than belonging to another. It is for this reason that the development of policing within the European Union has tended to be driven by state and substate forces, rather than at the behest of the Union itself. The police have increasingly become aware of the importance of harmonization within the EU, not only for the selfish purpose of making their own job easier, but for the very real virtue of making the implementation of a Single Market and a frontier-free Europe a reality. It is for this reason that they have lobbied their governments to negotiate political agreements which mirror and legitimate the private agreements which they have been steadily building up between themselves. While the future of police cooperation is good, and although optimistic for the possibility of further developments, it is important to realize that an agreed formal treaty is not the end. States can and do fail to carry them out, situations can change and legislation need updating and with an issue as relevant to all sectors of European society as is policing, this cannot just be left to chance. There is thus a need for some kind of independent authority to supervise implementation of any treaty. If that could be structured around the existing Union institutions, so much the better, but answers to these sort of questions await further political dialogue on the part of the member states.

Notes

1 Interview with author, 2 November 1995.
2 See CAB 23/22, PRO, London.
3 Summing up of Mr Justice Hanna on the choice of men for the *Garda* Special Branch (Broy Harriers) after their killing of a youth at Marshes Cattle Yard, Cork in 1934. In Brady (1974: 222).

4   Conversation between Swinton with Cosgrave, 4 November 1954. In DO/121/219, PRO, London.
5   Fitzpatrick, 1993: 62.
6   Garret Fitzgerald (1991: 574) noted after the loyalist demonstrations that the RUC displayed 'by their firmness their capacity for even-handed action and the extent to which under the leadership of John Hermon the force had become non-political …'. Fitzgerald (1991).
7   The Government of Ireland and the Government of the United Kingdom: Wishing to develop the unique relationship between their peoples and the close cooperation between their countries as friendly neighbours and as partners in the European Community.
8   ACPO, 1996: 40.
9   Walker (1994: 23) uses these terms to describe respectively the idea that police arrangements cannot be concluded until the final shape of the Union is known or when ideas are evaluated without regard to possible political resistance.

References

ACPO (1996), *International, National, Inter-force Crime: A Study Commissioned by the Association of Chief Police Officers*, Final Report, February 1996, Part III.
Baldwin, R. (1987), 'Why Police Accountability?', *British Journal of Criminology*, Vol. 32, pp. 97–105.
Brady, C. (1974), *Guardians of the Peace*, Gill and Macmillan, Dublin.
Dorn, N. (1993), 'Subsidiarity, Police Co-operation and Drug Enforcement: Some Structures of Policy-making in the EC', *European Journal on Criminal Policy and Research*, Vol. 1, pp. 30–47.
Fitzgerald, G. (1991), *All in a Life*, Gill and Macmillan, Dublin.
Fitzpatrick, B. (1993), 'The Implications of the European Treaties on Policing in Ireland', unpublished MA Thesis, University of Ulster.
King, M. (1998), 'Policing Change in Eastern and Central Europe: Some Contemporary Concerns', *Innovation*, Vol. 11, No. 3.
Reiner, R. (1992), '*Fin de siècle* Blues: The Police Face the Millennium', *Political Quarterly*, pp. 62–74.
Walker, N. (1994), 'European Integration and European Policing: A Complex Relationship', in M. Anderson and M. den Boer (eds), *Policing Across National Boundaries*, Pinter, London, pp. 23–49.

Chapter 10

Eastern and Western Europe: Towards a New European Identity?

Edward Moxon-Browne

The collapse of communist regimes in eastern Europe and their subsequent gradual transition towards market economics and political pluralism, has created a new insecurity in both parts of the European continent. The familiar landmarks of the Cold War have been replaced by new problems: ethnic unrest; mass migration; high unemployment; and political volatility. Multilateral organizations and agreements, rooted in, and rationalized by, a bipolar world now find themselves challenged by the search for a new *raison d'être* and the prospect of another EU enlargement. Against this background of shifting political signposts, the concept of a pan-European identity has acquired a new urgency and a new relevance. The politics of exclusion which once emphasized the distinctiveness of the European Union (EU) is now being replaced by the politics of inclusion whereby boundaries are being transformed into bridgeheads across which a flow of people, goods, capital and ideas is blurring the differences between the two parts of Europe. Will it be possible to create a new European political identity that transcends the old east-west divide? Will it be possible to merge concepts of liberal democracy that have hitherto been largely monopolized by western Europe with the political experiences, equally valid, of the former Soviet satellites? At a time when the European continent is coming to terms with the dissolution of its ideological divisions, it seems appropriate, if not highly desirable, to explore the political dimensions of European identity. The EU acts inevitably as a catalyst for the formation of a European political identity both among its own member states and, by different methods, in eastern Europe. The EU is being forced to reflect not simply on its institutional response to a flood of new members but also to ponder deeply the 'core' values that lie at the heart of its own existence. Basic political concepts like 'sovereignty' 'state' and 'citizen' are being debated in eastern and western Europe. Coming from very different directions and with no certainty of similar outcomes, debates on the efficacy and legitimacy of political institutions in both parts of Europe are being driven along by the need to tackle effectively the social effects of economic failure. So, beneath the search for more responsive institutional procedures to accommodate a more heterogeneous group of member states, the EU is simultaneously engaged in a more profound discourse at the deeper level of political values. This debate, unlike the one surrounding the reform of the EU institutions, actively engages the attention of east Europeans. Their own immediate political inheritance has taught them that there is no 'quick fix' for either political stability or economic prosperity; and even their discourse focuses on the same issues of sovereignty and society that preoccupy citizens in the EU – albeit for different reasons. In eastern Europe, democratic institutions remain fragile. The 'pull' of the EU as an attractive vehicle for the journey towards economic and political consolidation may be illusory in two senses: membership may not be the magic medicine that is often imagined and, secondly, membership may, in any case, be long delayed. Any discussion of political identity in a European context also needs to take account of the security dimension. The concept of 'European security' has obviously undergone fundamental change since the end of the Cold War and now needs to transcend the traditional emphasis on the purely military aspects. The concept of 'societal security' (Waever, 1996:102–32) goes beyond the restricted military focus and considers economic, demographic and cultural factors as well as matters of human rights. The withdrawal of the Soviet military presence from eastern Europe left behind a vacuum whose consequences are difficult to predict. However, the way in which the vacuum is filled is directly linked to the matter of a common political identity since the civic duty to defend one's own society presupposes a shared sense of identity. The notion of a 'pluralistic security community' seems appropriate here. Karl Deutsch (1957) characterized such a community as a group of contiguous countries that are sufficiently interdependent not to fear attack from one another and therefore able to abandon all defensive preparations with respect to each other. Such a concept is relevant in Europe today at a time when the former opponents of, and justification for, NATO are now associated with it in the Partnership for Peace agreement as part of a new emergent European security architecture. The zone of mutual trust in Europe has been steadily extended since 1989 and although this zone may not be exactly coterminous with the emergence of a common European political identity, there is an underlying dynamic that links the two, and makes them mutually reinforcing. The Common Foreign and Security Policy (CFSP) of the EU is an attempt to respond to the collapse of bipolarity in Europe; and as the CFSP extends its umbrella to embrace new member states in eastern Europe, two questions will need to be answered: against what sort of aggression is a European security policy intended to respond; and will the EU be prepared to defend one of its members against such an aggression? The roles of the 'nation' and the 'state' are also crucial components of an emerging European identity; and here we may detect differences of emphasis between east and west. In the member states of the EU political identity can be expressed through state structures that take their national and ethnic composition largely for granted. Well-established democratic processes, well lubricated mechanisms for allocating scarce resources among salient groups in society, all contribute to a civic harmony on which the state builds and through which its legitimacy is consolidated. In eastern Europe on the other hand in the wake of authoritarian state structures there is a new revival of citizen attachment to ethnic and nationalist loyalties which results in state structures being challenged; and their legitimacy being called into question. The discourse in eastern and western Europe is equally preoccupied with the concepts of 'nation' and 'state' but the sources of concern are almost diametrically opposed, and the conclusions reached inevitably different.

An authentically European political identity, however, may provide a resolution of these divergences. For east European societies, a political identity offers the citizen an opportunity to identify with institutions and policy processes at the European level and thus circumvent the state structures he or she deeply distrusts. At the same time, east European elites can reinforce their own legitimacy by participating in decision-making processes that involve mutually beneficial cooperation with ruling elites from other European states. In western Europe, the shortcomings of national state structures are compensated for by transnational policy-making processes at the European level. Indeed, the dynamo of the integration process may be exactly the need of national elites to promote their own legitimacy by achieving overtly national objectives in decision-making arenas well 'beyond the nation state'.

The task of defining a European political identity is not easy but cannot be postponed indefinitely. The term 'identity' forms an essential part of intellectual discourse in many disciplines in the humanities and the social sciences. In psychology, for example, we are concerned with identity of the individual, the traits that make that person unique. In anthropology, identity relates to ethnic, tribal, and national characteristics that distinguish those societies from other analogous societies. A useful metaphor that may be borrowed from anthropology is that of 'contour lines' of identity that encircle 'core' areas. According to this analogy, a sense of political identity would not be constrained within a neat watertight compartment but would shade almost imperceptibly towards other communities with divergent or even opposing identities. Instead of clear cut lines of demarcation between political communities, we would therefore have 'grey areas' where identity is vague, ambiguous, ill-defined or volatile. In this context, societies possessing a common political identity have a clear idea of who they are and what constitutes 'us' and 'them'. It is these parameters that define the borders of a nascent political community. The existence of grey areas separating distinct political identities is especially pertinent in any discussion of European political identity since Belarus and the Ukraine, for example, currently constitute exactly such a grey area between Russia which is normally excluded from a discussion of an emergent European identity and countries like Poland, Hungary, Bulgaria and Romania, which are normally included.

Having cleared away some of the semantic undergrowth it is possible to offer a working definition of the term 'European political identity': the assumption throughout this chapter is that Europeans share a common political identity inasmuch as they accept among themselves a redistribution of resources and an equitable pattern of rights and duties that can be upheld by common institutions responsible for the authoritative allocation of values. Although this is a fairly stringent formulation to apply even to the EU, let alone a pan-European context, it nevertheless provides a yardstick against which progress towards a common European political identity might be measured.

Any kind of identity is reinforced by the existence of contrasting or opposite identities that provide a definitional frame of reference. My identity as a man is reinforced (even defined) by the existence of women; my identity as a Briton is sharpened by the existence of Frenchmen or Irishmen; the identity of the blind is contrasted with those who can see; the identities of the sad, the mad and the bad are reinforced by the happy, the sane and the good. So it is with Europeans. European identity, with all its internal schisms and fuzzy boundaries, is reinforced by the existence of two powerful 'others' – one in the east and one in the west.

Despite the oft-repeated assertion that American values and culture have invaded Europe, it is possible to argue that the United States still provides a powerful other against which European political identity can be defined. Beneath a rather superficial layer of 'cultural colonialism' epitomized perhaps by EuroDisney and a heavy diet of TV soap operas, a specific European political identity remains intact. In a general sense, one might see American politics as emphasizing self-help, individual rights, and idealism while seeing European politics as emphasizing social responsibility, duties to society, and realism. Contrasting histories produce contrasting political assumptions: American history is a record of almost unchallenged expansion and unfettered economic success won by a people whose unity (at least since the Civil War) was never in doubt. European history is replete with conflict, territorial challenges, and failures to unite except under forced conquest. In Europe, the great debates of left and right, nation and state, individual and society, run deep in politics and are strongly ideological in tone. In Europe, moreover, government has regulated society to a degree unthinkable in the United States. In the latter, the authoritative structures of government have been kept at arms length: the great political debates have been less ideological and more pragmatic, not so much speculative as problem solving. That quintessential European creation the welfare state combines such a degree of state intervention, social responsibility, fiscal imposition and redistributed wealth that an import of these practices into the American political system is almost impossible to imagine. This remains true despite current evidence for 'transatlantic convergence' based on proposals to set up a public heath care system in the United States while Europeans are generally dismantling theirs; the resistance to both projects, respectively, merely proving the point.

Since the dissolution of the Soviet Union, Russia is crystallizing as another powerful 'other', especially as east and central European countries are courted as partners by the West in both economic and security spheres. As Russia appears to turn in on itself in its effort to redefine its own national identity, it is perceived wrongly perhaps by the west as distracting itself from western Europe. There are plenty of historical precedents on which suspicion and fear of Russia can thrive in the West: the despotism of the tsars; and the Stalinist legacy. The absence of an all encompassing ideology results in Russian society having lost its sense of direction and purpose. One Russian writer speaks of a 'mental orphanage' in which the Russian citizen is trapped; and the problems of adaptation to new realities are compounded by the fact that people who were once told what to think are now forced to think for themselves. The complex ethnic composition of the Russian federation, not to mention the sheer size of the country, make either a purely European or a purely Asiatic identity for the new Russia highly problematic. The failure of the economy to provide Russian citizens with an adequate standard of living has bred apathy, mistrust, and alienation from the political system itself. The seductive lure of the 'Communist' label in Russian party politics reflects a pessimism, and a polarization, that may not augur well, for the short-term future at least.

Between these two powerful 'others' how confidently can we speak of a European political identity that encompasses east and west? Even within the EU, there exist important differences regarding political values; and it is therefore difficult to speak of a homogeneous political identity across the 15 member states. To begin with, the borders of neither the EU, nor western Europe more generally, are sharply enough defined to suggest a sense of identity that is sufficiently distinct from its immediate external environment. Moreover, it is clear that much greater affinities of political identity exist among groups of countries within Europe than exist across the Union as a whole. For example it can be argued that a stronger sense of political community exists among the Scandinavian social democracies, and the Mediterranean countries, respectively, than between those two regional groupings. The degree of clientelism nepotism and corruption that is tolerated in some southern European systems, while not in northern ones, poses the question whether common fundamental assumptions about the operations of parliamentary democracy in all parts of western Europe can really be made. We can, perhaps, answer in the affirmative because although the actual workings of the parliamentary systems are different between northern and southern Europe, there is a sense in which 'southern' politicians emulate their northern neighbours: there is a grudging respect (sometimes misplaced) for both British and Scandinavian democratic processes and an acknowledgement at least that this is how things ought to be done: and yet this respect is not reciprocated by the northern democracies. This implies that there is a 'gold standard' for political behaviour and one that is universally recognized even in systems where the currency of political conduct has become rather debased. Democratic politics in east and central Europe do not approximate to either the 'northern' or the 'southern' model although one can make comparisons between the recent authoritarian legacies of Spain or Portugal on the one hand and the more recent emergence from communist authoritarianism on the other. Leaving aside the important contrasts between right-wing and left-wing one party states, there is a sense in which the role of the citizen in any fledgling democracy is faced with similar challenges of transition of civic passivity to expectations of choice, influence and participation in the newly established democratic regime. The prospects for this transition are influenced by the ambient economic conditions, previous experience of democratic rule, the entirely fortuitous qualities of political leadership, and the salient cleavages in society on which the party system comes to be based.

In assessing whether a common European political culture is likely to develop in both parts of Europe, we need to look more closely at the differences that exist at all levels of society. There are four important contrasts that seem to lie at the heart of the east-west divide. First, west European political systems have been able to evolve gradually in a way that has allowed significant electoral cleavages (rural-urban; catholic-protestant; linguistic, ethnic) to be moderated by compromises and cross-cutting fissures. In eastern Europe, strong cleavages on which party systems can be based result from a basically unstructured political society in which political formations coalesce around the most visible societal divisions. Second, a certain disillusionment with political parties can be discerned in both western and eastern Europe suggesting a superficial, not to say negative, basis for convergence. In fact apathy towards political parties in eastern Europe stems, rather ominously, from a feeling of anomie which, if exacerbated by a serious conjuncture of adverse economic indicators, could lead to an outright rejection of the party system itself. In the west, apathy towards parties indicates, paradoxically perhaps, a certain level of satisfaction in the sense that electorates expect little more than they already get from parties, and there are other ways in which the voter can express disenchantment and bring pressures to bear for change.

Thirdly, the left-right axis as the reliable tool for comparative analysis of western political parties is less relevant to parties in eastern Europe despite the nomenclature of parties that suggest analogous ideological attachments. In particular, the emergence of what might be termed 'chauvino-communism' renders the orthodox left-right classification rather problematic. The eventual outcomes of such differences remain difficult to predict but could clearly lead to contrasts between western political systems where parties chase the 'middle ground' and eastern systems where high levels of electoral volatility, deeper cleavages of ethnicity and nationalism, and a wider spectrum of parties, could produce more polarized party systems with few familiar landmarks to provide stability or continuity. Fourthly, the emergence of parliamentary systems led by directly elected presidents may in the long run prove unable to produce the stability required to achieve a successful transition to market economics. Political pluralism has been encouraged by generous proportional representation systems of election in reaction to the monolithic party structures of the communist epoch; and even though these systems are lent some stability by popularly elected presidents, there is a danger of pitched battles or, simply, stalemates developing between parliaments and presidents, given the powers of the latter to intervene in matters of government formation. It may be that these constitutions are suitable for transitional democracies while the honeymoon period of multiparty politics can be enjoyed to the full, but for the serious consolidation of democratic and free market systems in the long term, constitutions that place a higher premium on stability and continuity, and less on the need to represent the entire kaleidoscope of political opinion, may need to be deployed, or developed from those currently in existence.

Analysis of opinion surveys carried out by Professor Rose (1994) at the University of Strathclyde enables us to gauge the fragility of attachment to liberal democratic institutions in east and central Europe. The most pervasive legacy of communism appears to be widespread distrust of political, social and economic institutions. The mean level of support for institutions in civil society is (in ten east and central European countries) as follows: president 43 per cent; parliament 20 per cent; parties 13 per cent; the military 47 per cent; the courts 33 per cent; the police 31 per cent; government 26 per cent; and civil servants 25 per cent. It is perhaps significant that the two institutions that command the highest support are the president and the military (but even these are below 50 per cent) since both reflect a preference for order over democratic participation and a certain nostalgia for the *ancien regime.* An outright return to communist rule is rejected everywhere in east and central Europe (the highest levels of support for communism are in Belarus and the Ukraine). Despite present difficulties, political and economic, there is substantial optimism for the future. When asked to evaluate the present regime there is mean support of 53 per cent throughout the region, but 73 per cent giving support to what they believe will be the regime in five years time. Only in Belarus and the Ukraine is there more support for the old communist regime than the anticipated regime in five years' time. As most east European households have experienced declining living standards, there is little general support for the present economic systems but massive support for the command economy of the past combined (a little ironically perhaps) with strong support for anticipated economic systems in five years time. All in all, economic conditions do not seem to distort political attitudes: a lack of freedom rather than a lack of money seems to have been the principal cause of disaffection from the former communist societies. Even if there is a certain nostalgia for the economic and social security of the communist epoch, it is not sufficient to make people want to return to that era. Although expectations of higher living standards in the future will copperfasten commitment to the new political regimes, that commitment has already been secured despite economic hardship, and despite a lack of faith in political parties, parliaments and politicians. This implies a growing attachment to the liberal democratic systems qua systems, even if there is a little scepticism about the way they are working right now.

At the outset we hypothesized that the EU would act as a catalyst for the development of a European political identity in both western and eastern Europe. A political identity implies the acceptance on the part of society of mutually exchanged civic rights and duties, an aspiration or reality of being governed by common institutions, and the willingness to see resources (tangible and intangible) redistributed among members of that society. Clearly, the extent of a common political identity will be limited by the extent of the cultural identity that lies behind it since the 'we-feelings' inherent in a common cultural identity are a necessary but not sufficient condition for the existence of a common political identity. The EU acts as a catalyst for the evolution of a European political identity within itself by providing a new centre of legitimacy beyond the state. Following the important insights of the neofunctionalists, we can posit the transfer of political allegiances to new centres of authority as a result of elite-driven bargains that produce more satisfactory outcomes for the citizen than was possible in the previous national under transnational control, and providing that the integrated outcome is more beneficial than the sum of the original independent state actions, there will be a shift in power and, later, loyalty to the new higher level. This political authority, once it has demonstrated its efficacy at the supranational level, acquires the quality of legitimacy. The recent attempts by the EU, via the mechanisms of the Maastricht Treaty, to codify notions of citizenship and supranational decision-making, are the formal recognition of informal processes that have blended nation state sovereignty with the pooled sovereignty of the EU institutions.

If it is true that the EU acts as a catalyst for creating a political identity within the EU it also does, in a different way, in relation to eastern Europe. The various economic agreements linking the EU with other European states are posited on the same logic that propels the evolving emergence of a 'political community' in western Europe. Just as the EC used the granting and suspension of trade concessions to cajole Spain and Greece towards democratic political processes in the 1970s so today the Commission is a powerful actor in stimulating and protecting the nascent democratic reforms in east and central Europe. Sometimes this process is quite overt. In 1990, when the Commission outlined the desiderata of the Europe Agreements it specifically mentioned 'political and economic reform and allowing the development of close relations, which reflect *shared values*' (my emphasis); and later referred to a '*shared sense of European identity*' (my emphasis). In its relations with east and central Europe, the EU is operating on the same assumptions that guided EC policy with regard to the Mediterranean enlargement in 1986, and indeed lay at the heart of the Rome Treaty itself: namely that economic integration provides a suitable bedrock on which political integration and a developing sense of political identity can be based. Whether these assumptions can be readily applied to east and central Europe is a central question. On the one hand, if the integration process is elite-driven, the position of elites in some east and central European countries is precarious. On the other hand, there are powerful arguments, for that very reason, for elites to transfer some legitimacy to transnational political actors. The limits of this process lie not so much in eastern Europe as in Brussels where the borders of Europe's political identity may in fact be determined on economic criteria and 'Euro-compatible' legal and financial adaptations. Finally, if the future of global politics is being determined not so much by ideology as by civilizations – in other words cultural blocs – then the limits of European political identity may be shifting eastwards to a point where Russia constitutes the crucial slavic 'other' against which Europe's own identity will come to coalesce. Huntington has argued that these major fault lines in global politics will be these 'clashes of civilization' and in this sense the world, and Europe with it, are returning to more traditional sources of identity as possible causes of future conflict.

Note

An earlier version of this chapter appears in *Contemporary Politics*, Vol. 3, No. 1, pp. 27–34.

References

Deutsch, K. et al. (1957), *Political Community and the North Atlantic Area*, Princeton University Press, Princeton.
Rose, R. and Haerpfer, C. (1994), *New Democracies Barometer III: Learning from What is Happening*, University of Strathclyde, Glasgow.
Waever, O. (1996), 'European Security Identities', *Journal of Common Market Studies*, Vol. 34, No. 1, pp. 102–32.